RESEARCH IN
THE SOCIAL SCIENTIFIC
STUDY OF RELIGION

Volume 11

Research in the Social Scientific Study of Religion

Joanne Marie Greer and David O. Moberg, Series Editors

Volume 1: 1989
 edited by Monty L. Lynn and David O. Moberg

Volume 2: 1990
 edited by Monty L. Lynn and David O. Moberg

Volume 3: 1991
 edited by Monty L. Lynn and David O. Moberg

Volume 4: 1992
 edited by Monty L. Lynn and David O. Moberg

Volume 5: 1993
 edited by Monty L. Lynn and David O. Moberg

Volume 6: 1994
 edited by Monty L. Lynn and David O. Moberg

Volume 7: 1996
 edited by Joanne Marie Greer, David O. Moberg, and Monty L. Lynn

Volume 8: 1997
 edited by Joanne Marie Greer and David O. Moberg

Volume 9: 1998
 edited by Joanne Marie Greer and David O. Moberg

Volume 10: 1999
 edited by Joanne Marie Greer and David O. Moberg

RESEARCH IN
THE SOCIAL SCIENTIFIC
STUDY OF RELIGION

Edited by JOANNE MARIE GREER
Loyola College in Maryland

DAVID O. MOBERG
Marquette University

VOLUME 11

JAI PRESS INC.
Stamford, Connecticut

ISBN: 0-7623-0656-4
ISSN: 1046-8064

Manufactured in the United States of America

CONTENTS

PREFACE

This eleventh volume in the series, *Research in the Social Scientific Study of Religion,* is exemplary of the editors' desire to span a variety of the social sciences with the primary focus on religion. Contributions from students of religion in a variety of institutional settings enhance this volume. Several papers in this volume continue our policy of providing ample space for longer contributions to the social scientific study of religion. As an annual, we can edit and publish contributions of substantial length and depth, offering a scope not possible in a quarterly journal.

This exciting collection of papers opens with Founding Editor *David O. Moberg*'s salute to the millennium, as he asks *What Most Needs the Attention of Religion Researchers in the Twenty-first Century?* A revision and expansion of an earlier oral presentation on "Passing the Torch" to a new generation of researchers, this paper reflects Moberg's more than 50 years of experience in religious research, from 1947 to the present.

Next the reader will find three related papers on religious change. *Carlo Prandi* offers a reflective view of *The Reciprocal Relationship of Syncretism and Fundamentalism from the Early History of Religion to Modernity.* A related paper explores a concrete manifestation of these two processes in Africa; *Cornel du Toit* discusses *Issues in the Reconstruction of African Theology: African Hermeneutics as Key to Understanding the Dynamics of African Theology.* Yet another perspective on religious change in response to historical events is found in *Religious Minorities during Russia's Transition from Atheism to Secularism* by *Alexander Agadjanian*.

Next we see a grouping of three papers on psychometrics in religious research. *Judith V. Kehe* reports *An Empirical Assessment of the Wagner-Modified Houts Questionnaire: A Spiritual Gifts Inventory*. *Leslie J. Francis* and *Stephen H. Louden* report the development and validation of a new mysticism measure in *The Francis–Louden Mystical Orientation Scale (MOS): A study among Roman Catholic Priests*. Finally, the issue of what religious measures add over and above personality measures is addressed in *An Evaluation of the Incremental Validity of the Spiritual Experience Index-Revised*, by *Richard J. Csarny, Ralph Piedmont, William J. Sneck, S. J.*, and *Sharon E. Cheston*.

Pui-Yan Lam and *Thomas Rotolo* examine a different aspect of the interrelationship of religious and nonreligious variables in their empirical study *Re-Examining the Relationship Between Religiosity and Life Satisfaction*. In his paper, *Moral Boundaries in Christian Discourse on Popular Music, Andreas Häger* focuses on the process by which religious institutions react to secular stimuli such as "rock" music.

Finally, four papers look at various aspects of the organizational structure of religious institutions and movements. *Leslie J. Francis* and *Christopher J. F. Rutledge* explore the question *Are Rural Clergy in the Church of England under Greater Stress? William Smith* surveys the aging cohort of *Contemporary Irish Priests in America* for their recollections of their American ministries and their mixed identifications as Irishmen and as Americans.

Amy Schindler and *Jennifer Carroll Lena* apply a process model to the study of *Promise Keepers in Perspective: Organizational Characteristics of a Men's Movement*. The volume concludes with Part II of *Julia Day Howell* and *Peter L. Nelson*'s research on *Demographic Change and Secularization in an Asian New Religious Movement: The Brahma Kumaris in the Western World*.

We hope that our readers will enjoy and be stimulated by this delightful assortment of contributions to the study of religion. As usual, the volume reflects the work of anonymous referees in addition to that of the authors and editors. We offer them our heartfelt thanks for their painstaking efforts to improve the manuscripts. We offer special thanks to those faithful reviewers who, year after year, are willing to go through several cycles of revision in helping a junior colleague make a start in the world of research publications. This process offers us as editors the special joy of nurturing the next generation of researchers on religion. We encourage "ABD" students and new Ph.D. graduates to send us manuscripts if they are in search of a publishing mentor.

Both of us receive support, as editors, from our respective academic institutions, Loyola College in Maryland, and Marquette University. We are grateful for this support, and especially for the assistance of Rosemary Cook, our graduate editorial assistant.

As editors, we are always eager to receive good manuscripts for consideration. All submissions that are judged relevant to our primary focus of attention are refereed. The current final acceptance rate for submitted manuscripts is approximately 50 percent.

We particularly seek a diversity of contributions, which cross over academic disciplinary lines, or take unusual perspectives in the analysis of subjects that are relevant to the social scientific investigation of religion. Strictly descriptive historical studies are outside our domain unless they also integrate social or behavioral science perspectives. In addition, we recognize that the social scientific study of religion is not done only by academics. We encourage contributions from research staffs of various religious organizations and denominations. We also encourage contributions from the humanities, and from human services professions, theological school faculties, and the research of graduate students.

Prospective authors may communicate with either coeditor: Dr. David Moberg, 7120 Dove Court, Milwaukee, WI 53223-2766; DOMOBERG@JUNO.COM; or Dr. Joanne Greer, Graduate Programs in Pastoral Counseling, Loyola College in Maryland, 7135 Minstrel Way, Suite 302, Columbia, Maryland, 21045-5255, FAX 410-617-7644; phone 410-617-7609 or 301-949-9357.

Submission of manuscripts as e-mail attachments is acceptable, and can be directed to JGREER@LOYOLA.EDU. Submissions should follow one of the traditional style formats. In addition, please note the following: Endnotes should be kept to a minimum, and should be incorporated into the main text when possible.

All accepted papers require a PC-formatted 3.5" computer disk containing the entire text in BOTH of the following PC formats: (1) ASCII text; (2) Wordperfect (any version). We prefer not to process disks in Microsoft Word. We cannot process disks in Macintosh format. It is not necessary to mail a hard copy of the entire text with your disk, but hard copies of all tables and figures must be enclosed.

Joanne Marie Greer
David O. Moberg

WHAT MOST NEEDS THE ATTENTION OF RELIGION RESEARCHERS IN THE TWENTY-FIRST CENTURY?

David O. Moberg

ABSTRACT

Religion was central to early sociology, yet many mid-twentieth century sociologists thought studying it was a waste of time. Seven challenges for attention in the social sciences of religion are summarized: renewed attention to the metasociological foundations of research, building upon past findings, caution in the use of modern technology, awareness of subtle limitations and biases woven into methodology, sociocultural values that link or separate religion and society, differentiating between spirituality and religion, and monitoring and evaluating other topics and trends.

Methodological issues include confusing statistical with social significance, using secondary data, emic and etic orientations, the "ecumenical methodology" of triangulation, reification, faulty sampling of variables, and researcher biases. Needed research should address the decline of institutional ecumenism, post-denominational evangelicalism, and fundamentalists as a new minority group. Work on these and on public relations issues can return religious research and theory to the place of prominence it deserves in the social sciences.

Research in the Social Scientific Study of Religion, Volume 11, pages 1-21.
ISBN: 0-7623-0656-4

IS THERE STILL NEED FOR RELIGION RESEARCH?

As I began my career in the sociology of religion, I was informed that it was an obsolete field of investigation. When I was seeking a thesis topic on religion for my M. A. degree in sociology in 1947–1948, a prominent professor told me that no more research on religion was needed. He supported his opinion by reference to the character studies of Hartshorne and May (1928), which allegedly proved that the religious education of Protestants, Catholics, and Jews was ineffective in preventing cheating and promoting honesty among adolescents (an oversimplified conclusion from their somewhat limited data). It is likely that he also believed the dogma that was fervently expressed in *The Twilight of Christianity* by Barnes (1929), whose card-stacking arguments against "dogmatic theism and supernaturalism" insisted that "orthodox religion and Devout Modernism" are both harmful to human progress and that Christianity was in its final stages of demise, soon to be completely replaced by education and science.

Despite the general disdain for religion among most of my professors, I eventually discovered that it had been a prominent subject among early sociological theorists, although usually with notable revisionist motivations. A century earlier Auguste Comte (1798–1857), "the father of sociology," had argued that the ecclesiastical establishment should be replaced by a "Religion of Humanity." Patterned after the Catholic hierarchy, its priesthood of sociologists would eventually produce "the true religion," a system of Sociocracy, as the final evolutionary development emerging out of traditional religions (Arbouse-Bastide 1966). Social Darwinist Herbert Spencer (1820–1903) likewise believed that religion was destined to be outgrown by the evolutionary progress of humanity, and Emile Durkheim (1855–1917) claimed that worship of the Deity was actually the veneration of a collective representation, society itself. Max Weber (1864–1920) developed the "ideal type" methodology of his interpretive sociology mainly through the analysis of various religions' relationships to economic systems.

Thus, with reference to religion, the first century of sociology's historical heritage generally was one of macrosociological philosophizing and theorizing that reflected, at best, a prophetic type of opposition to entrenched ecclesiastical establishments and faiths. Yet, because order and meaning were recognized as central to society, the "founding fathers of sociology" could not ignore religion. Instead, they addressed it in different ways and with different sets of assumptions (Turner 1991, p. xi). Their recommendations for change tended to center around an implicit or sometimes explicit elimination and replacement of existing religious institutions more than around using the social sciences to sustain and modify them, as if the only way to improve them was to replace them. Goldsmith (1989, p. 387) attributes this "long-held antipathy toward religion in general and conservative Christianity in particular by the mainstream of American social scientists" in large part to their theological illiteracy (see also Donahue 1989). Yet even Barnes (1929, pp. 426–427) conceded that "a secularized social religion like

Unitarian Humanism or advanced Christian Socialism may be of great value in the future in organizing group sentiment in support of decent and just causes" and that "to retain the term religion may have certain pragmatic value in forwarding the transition from the old to the new secular regime."

Especially during the last half of the twentieth century, developments in both society and the social sciences have disproved the ill-grounded predictions of the demise of traditional religions. Christianity and the other world religions still are very much alive. Except for the increasing concentration of Jews in Israel, they are now more widely distributed over the face of the globe and far less concentrated in specific geographic regions than a century ago, although they all reflect internal changes from the ebb and flow of denomination-type groups within specific nations. Hundreds of new religious groups also have emerged on the modern scene.

Theorists have concluded that religion has been central to a great deal of social theory (Turner 1991) and that humanity is "homo religiosus" because "religion is the vision by which people, and peoples, live" (Towler 1974, p. vii). Heddendorf's (1990) metasociological study in the sociology of knowledge has demonstrated that "hidden threads" from the Christian Scriptures are woven into a great deal of social thought and sociological theory. Meanwhile, the study of religion became a well established subject in sociology, anthropology, psychology, political science, epidemiology, nursing, and many other fields of investigation during the latter third of the twentieth century. With few exceptions, that research has shown that religious beliefs and practices are highly significant human variables. As in all areas of scientific investigation, "the more we know that we know, the more we know we don't know." The subjects related to religion that social scientists recognize as deserving attention in research and theory are continually increasing, not diminishing.

NEEDED RESEARCH

Despite various hurdles and the lack of courses of study in the sociology of religion in two universities, my own academic career included research on religion for both graduate degrees (Moberg 1949, 1951). Then or soon afterwards, I began to record interesting topics that merited new or additional research, both to provide students with suggestions for their choices of projects in the broad range of courses that I taught (initially as the sole sociology instructor of a liberal arts college major) and to stimulate my own thoughts whenever I might need research ideas. Those messy files grew, and grew, and grew. Even without consulting any of them in my initial work on this paper, I quickly developed a list of thirty categories of important subjects deserving research, all of which seemed to "most need attention in the next century." That troubled me greatly, for presenting each in the scope of even as little as one or two paragraphs would make a far too lengthy presentation. Every social scientist of religion could similarly develop a long list. Perhaps "what is needed most" is relative, for what's most needed by each researcher must be realistically delimited in terms of each person's background, specialized abilities, social contexts, resources, interests, and opportunities. As each works on his or her own perceptions of what is most needed within the delimiting context of that which it is pragmatically possible to do, the social sciences of religion will continue their remarkable surge forward.

Therefore, rather than listing a series of specific topics, I have categorized some foundational needs under seven major headings that apply to all researchers, whatever our differences may be. Experiences of research, reading, listening, observing, study, and reflection have all contributed to the thoughts I'll share, but most of the sources are deeply hidden in my subconscious mind, with only some in my consciousness or semi-consciousness. My intent is to call to attention some of the basic ways to strengthen the foundations of our future work as social and behavioral science researchers of religion, not to summarize a "state of the art" with its thousands of significant contributions already made to research and theory.

Continually Renew Attention to the Metasociological Foundations of All Research

All too often the philosophical underpinnings of social science research are only implicit and unexamined, in spite of the Doctor of Philosophy degrees most of us hold. As a result, unwarranted and unrecognized reductionisms, determinisms, implicit theologies, erroneous logics, and value biases easily distort our work. Sometimes these flaws also contribute to subtle forms of intolerance and to supports for censorship within or outside our disciplines, even while we claim to be objective and impartial.

Many questions can help us to identify the underlying values that influence our research, consultation, and teaching. Are we aware of the unexpressed postulates, presuppositions, and assumptions that undergird our own work? How fully do we realize the extent to which our personal ideologies and religious (including antireligious) convictions influence such things as our choice of topics to investigate, the variables we examine for each, the research methodologies and techniques we choose to use, and our selective interpretations of findings, our conclusions, and our applications to life in contemporary society? Do we perhaps condemn the censorship efforts of the sociopolitical and religious right, while we simultaneously support censorship efforts of the left that aim to eliminate all vestiges of traditional religion from the public square, (or the other way around)? In support of liberty, do we defend cultural and religious minorities on the right while helping to repress those on the left (or vice versa)? Does our alleged openness, tolerance, and political correctness in fact incorporate a hidden but harsh intolerance of those whom we judge to be intolerant? Are those findings that we report as much a product of biases, opinions, preferences, and ungrounded attributions as they are of impartial observations? Do we conscientiously try to discover both the negative and positive results of the religious variables we study?

Are we aware that all values are linked with at least implicit religion, and that all "theories about math and physics, sociology and economics, art and ethics, politics and law can never be religiously neutral ... [and] are all regulated by some religious belief" (Clouser 1991, p. 3)? Has our attempt to carry out research in tune with the rampant individualism of current Western culture supported a system of moral and ethical relativism that threatens to undermine the social value consensus and thus eventually to destroy our academic disciplines and society itself (see Garrison 1988, pp. 77–78)? Does the subjectivism of post-modernism and the individualistic selfism of our hedonistic society, including many versions of self-esteem, ultimately militate against the goals of all of the social sciences? Are naturalistic and materialistic determinisms essential normative principles for all scientific work, as logical positivists insist, or are they only delimiting concepts that indicate the boundaries of observations that may properly be labeled as "scientific"?

Reductionisms and determinisms have often dominated social and psychological theories of religion (for a balanced evaluation of determinisms see Myers 1978, pp. 201–266). Do we cling to the hidden assumption that eventually everything people label as "supernatural" can be explained away by genetic, physico-chemical, sociosychological, or other mechanisms? Or do we, like many of the sixteenth to eighteenth century physical and biological scientists (Hooykaas 1972), leave room in our thinking for the possibility that there is a Supreme Being of the entire universe who is so far above and beyond us that we can never fully understand that Creator's ways and works?

Whether we realize it or not, our implicit theologies do inform much of our research on religion. Historically the theologically liberal Social Gospel, of which "Christian Sociology" was a part at the beginning of the twentieth century, was a significant foundation for the development of American sociology because of their mutual focus upon social welfare, poverty, and other social problems (see Shore 1987). Many early American sociologists were clergymen or "preachers' kids" who tried to use sociology to solve the problems of society (see Swatos 1984). Even today, theological liberalism is often associated with much of the United States' political correctness, moral relativism, and "value free" motifs focused on denying the particularistic claims of Christianity in an antiempirical assumption of religious universalism that claims every religion is equally valid and wholesome for humanity. Meanwhile, from the other pole, theological conservatives tend to hold that most religions, although different from each other, are equally deceptive and harmful in terms of ultimate salvation. Researchers who subscribe to either position will incorporate that position into their work.

To summarize, in order to be true to reality about ourselves as finite human beings, as well as about our complex social world, we need to renew our attention to "the sociology of sociology" (see Friedrichs 1970), as well as to the history, theologies, philosophy, and other grounds upon which our own personal approaches to the social sciences rest (Griffioen and Verhoogt 1990).

Always Build upon Past Findings

This may seem like a truism, but it is easy to overlook when we are in the grip of creativity, making what seem on surface to be completely original contributions. Even the most original of human products has a background and precedents. Therefore we need to discover and share how our work is continuing an earlier legacy, accomplishing much the same goals as in the past, but building more systematically upon it and recognizing the value, not only the mistakes, of both old and recent contributions to our own achievements. Far too often, once a study is completed and published, it is either accepted as if definitive or else filed and forgotten. What a contrast to the care that is taken in pharmacological research to confirm the results of new medications!

Replications of past work are important, despite the academy's pressures against their publication, as if those that do not overturn previous results are insignificant because they only confirm past findings and reveal "nothing new." Replications and pseudoreplications of past work, especially with the help of sharper conceptualization and niceties of distinction, are building blocks in the foundation of valid generalizations about religion. From them serendipitous surprises often emerge. When hypotheses are not supported, and when findings are inconsistent with our theories or other expectations and suggest modifications of conclusions rather than blanket rejection or support, we should report such negative evidence, too.

The more things change, the more they remain the same with respect to the basic features of humanity (including religion; see Greeley 1989), in sharp contrast to the material trappings and technological equipment that we continually invent and modify. The communalities of everyday spiritual experiences and of conventional religious agencies and practices deserve continual attention, even though those that seem new, unique, or "oddball" catch the researcher's curiosity and attention more quickly and may entice us into the trap of devoting most of our attention to the titillation of that which is exotic, in the mode of popular journalism.

Social science, especially sociology, has a tendency to focus more upon latent problems, dysfunctions, deficiencies, and other negative phenomena than upon that which is manifest, functional, and "normal." There indeed is a "crying need" for debunking, but we should also devote some research attention to documenting wholesome consequences and obvious benefits of conventional religions for individuals, families, small groups, social organizations, institutions, and society at large. They, and not only new religious movements (NRMs) and imports from the East, deserve major attention.

Use Modern Information Technology Carefully

The electronic and communications revolution has produced tremendous benefits. Computers have brought not only word processing that eliminates the need to physically erase errors and retype entire sections of papers for only relatively minor changes, but also the benefits of once unimaginable statistical calculations. We now have e-mail, which promotes quick and relatively easy interchange of communications around the entire globe, and the boon and bane of the Internet with its vast streams and reservoirs of commingled good information and sloppy misinformation. These developments make the need to develop, practice, and teach the basic information, methodological skills, philosophical understandings, and linguistic appreciations that are necessary to recognize and control GIGO (garbage in, garbage out) more important than ever before.

ADRIS Newsletter (Association for the Development of Religious Information Systems), now on the Internet at <http://members.home.com/dodds>, is one of the tools that can strengthen our research. Its purpose is to promote organizational cooperation, reduce unnecessary program duplication, and share applicable data and tasks. Each quarterly issue contributes to networking and cooperation by articles on significant technologies, websites related to religion, inexpensive technological resources, databases, software upgrades, product developments, organizational profiles, and many other helpful resources on religion. Its *International Directory of Religious Information Systems* (Moberg, 1971a) stimulated global cooperation across professional, disciplinary, religious, denominational, and other boundaries. Editor Dodds (1995) has already identified thousands of entries for the revision under preparation.

The American Religion Data Archive (ARDA, on the Internet at <www.arda.tm>) under development by sociologist Roger Finke at Purdue University, is another promising development that will greatly increase the use of existing survey data files for secondary analysis. Additional data archives that include religion are located at several other research centers.

The data banks facilitated by computers and other developments that go far beyond the dreams of earlier generations have stimulated research based upon secondary analysis. Yet the proper uses of data are always limited by whatever were the original methods used, so caution is advisable. Unless the strengths and weaknesses of survey data, including public opinion polls, are clearly recognized, we can easily be led into erroneous conclusions about the place and role of religion in contemporary and past society. As we reanalyze data bank variables, we must become more conscious than ever of basic questions: Whence came the data? Were any errors introduced by overt or hidden assumptions, poor methodologies, or wording that was inappropriate for the subjects? Are the 40 percent to 60 percent returns typical of recent survey research so genuinely representative of their populations that they provide an adequate basis for practical applications of the findings? Remember GIGO—garbage in is still garbage out, no matter how sophisticated and beautiful its garb of statistical measures.

Become More Fully Aware of Additional Biases and
Limitations That Can Subtly Distort Our Research

The rapid growth in sophistication of statistical technology, exemplified by the easy availability of SPSS, SYSTAT, and other PC computer packages, has brought a growing confidence in *statistical significance* that tempts us to think superficially that it is the same as *social significance*. In fact, the mere use of large data bases can by itself alone make minute differences that are pragmatically unimportant seem consequential for social life as well as for mathematics. As Deutscher (1998) reminds us, an emphasis on measurement techniques all too easily interferes with understanding how well social programs actually accomplish their stated goals.

The debunking motif of sociology often reveals significant hidden structures of organizational life and consequences of social behavior, but it also tends to reduce all religious phenomena to other social or psychological variables. Sometimes that is appropriate, but usually religious data should be investigated as *sui generis* phenomena that have an existence in their own right. One result of reductionistic debunking is that much research tends to examine religion as only a dependent variable—simply an effect of other causes—rather than as also an independent variable that is a root cause of much social data.

Far too many social scientists have shifted their loyalties exclusively to either qualitative or quantitative research methods without acknowledging the complementary strengths and weaknesses of each approach. The benefits of both methods need renewed attention in our research on religion, for each can help to balance, complement, and correct the disadvantages and faults of the other.

Especially in evaluation research, as in functionalism and the study of topics like "spiritual well-being" and "wholistic health," we all tend to impose our own values upon the groups we study. When the subjects of our investigations consider conducive to wellness an indicator that our own value-based opinion rejects, we are tempted to apply only our own evaluative criteria, whether in the analysis of case studies or the construction of survey instruments and scales for empirical measurement. That *etic* approach of imposing the values of outsiders upon the people or culture under investigation contrasts sharply with the *emic* methodology of appreciating and applying the values of whatever group we are studying so that we will not arbitrarily impose inappropriate judgments upon them. The *emics and etics* concepts were first published by linguist Kenneth F. Pike in 1954 (Headland et al. 1990). Now widely used in anthropology, they have only slowly entered sociology and the other social sciences, perhaps more through the works of Denzin (1989) than any other one person.

The *emic* perspective does not require the exclusion of our own criteria, but rather it insists that we be fully aware of what we are doing when our accounts, descriptions, and analyses are expressed in concepts, ideologies, and categories that we as outsiders to a subculture regard as appropriate and meaningful, especially if we ignore or denigrate the ideologies and concepts that indigenous members of the group under investigation regard as meaningful and appropriate. The *emic* approach of respecting the subjects' perspectives and values helps to fulfill our duty to protect other cultures against ourselves (Dascal 1991, p. 294). Surely we must find room to adapt, develop, and compare both *emic* and *etic* perspectives in our investigations of religion and spirituality.

Utilizing both an *emic* and *etic* approach in a research project is one aspect of "triangulation," the process of applying more than one ideology, theory, conceptual frame of reference, disciplinary orientation, methodology, analytical approach, or measuring instrument in research (Denzin 1989, pp. 234–247). Each perspective adds to the possibility of viewing every object of study as a multifaceted reality, for each perspective calls attention to important aspects that otherwise might be ignored.

In research on religion, triangulation can be viewed as an "ecumenical methodology" in which inter- or nondisciplinary study is analogous to the ecumenical movements of interdenominational and interfaith cooperation in religion. The need for triangulation is becoming all the more important in American society as the number and range of both prominent and minor, even exotic, religious groups increase. Bridging the boundaries created by the exclusiveness of each does not disallow the inclusive viewpoint of the overarching themes of religion. Both particularism and universalism have a place (see Krausz 1991).

The fascination with NRMs in research during recent decades may have contributed to paying too little attention to the nuances of, and the subtle and gross variations among and within, established religious groups and movements. In the interest of innovation and of respect for religious liberty, some religion scholars have tended to lean over backwards to honor the beneficial aspects of innovative and exotic NRMs with little or no mention of their negative aspects while, at the same time, treating established faiths in an opposite manner, by minimizing their positive contributions and emphasizing the mistakes, inconsistencies, stuck-in-the-rut orientations, hypocrisies, foibles, and failures found within them. (To what extent not mere curiosity about new developments, but personal biases against traditional Judeo-Christian values lie behind that prejudice, whether from the researcher's rejecting a childhood religion or other sources, is itself a topic for research.) Obviously, we ought to respect the wholesome functions of both spiritual innovations and religious traditions, including the role the latter often play as a "balance wheel" that stabilizes society, instead of viewing "the old time religion" as if it is the only impediment to human well-being and progress.

Research can tempt us to treat sociological and psychological scales or other scientific and philosophical concepts as reified constructs that trap us in ontological reductionism, as if the reality they represent is "nothing but" whatever is "measured" by the instrument (see especially MacKay 1974, pp. 36–47). Objectified concepts do sharpen our observation of selected realities, but focusing attention exclusively upon the measures may divert attention from other realities that may be even more important. Our operational definitions, scales, and survey instruments are primarily a product of sampling that uses but a few among dozens or hundreds of variables that could have been included among the relevant indicators. The faulty sampling of such variables in the study of religion is an even greater source of discrepancies between our findings and the realities of the topics we study than is the faulty sampling of persons and groups.

Researcher biases are especially strong in regard to religion and spirituality. Our personal lives tend to be caught up in our work whenever we do research on religion. Statements like "The respondents in this study gave no evidence that religion and spirituality were relevant to their lives" might often have the hidden meaning, "We did not attempt to discover such evidence. By focusing the subjects' attention only on other topics, we made them ignore religion and spirituality. They told us only what we asked them to say." Prejudgments of researchers thus indirectly determine the topics excluded, as well as those included, in research findings.

Personal biases are evident not only in the affirmation or rejection of various forms of religiosity and spirituality, but also in what may casually seem to be "objective" choices of topics to investigate, theoretical orientation, conceptual definitions, methodology, interpretation of findings, recommendations for further research, policy implications, and much more. It is possible that current Western religious research methods are so oriented to the Christian values, whether rightly or wrongly interpreted, that once dominated Western societies, that they are biased against the study of values that emerge from other religious and ideological schools of thought. As Turner (1991, pp. 5–6) says,

> Comparative sociology of religion is hazardous, both epistemologically and methodologically. Our understanding of 'other religions' is not achieved naively…, but through the mediation of traditional perspectives or discourses that shape and control the ways in which we encounter and account for other cultures and belief systems.

Study Religion in Relation to Sociocultural Values

Contemporary analysts of "the spirit of our age" call attention to the social and psychological impact of philosophical undercurrents of sociobiological determinism, reductionism, existentialism, postmodernism, and scientific rationalism as the measure of all things. For example, Colson (1989, pp. 107–108) goes so far as to say that ours is

> …a new dark age. Having elevated the individual as the measure of all things, modern men and women are guided solely by their own dark passions; they have nothing above themselves to

respect or obey, no principles to live or die for. The reigning god of relativism and the rampant egoism it fosters coarsen character, destroy any notion of community, weaken civility, promote intolerance, and threaten the disintegration of those very institutions necessary to the survival and success of ordered liberty.

Some social critics trace the widespread sense of loneliness, *anomie*, depression, and lack of self-worth to acceptance of evolutionary theories of accidental human descent from earlier forms of animal life, in contrast to the implications of faith in a uniquely human creation by Almighty God.

As social researchers, we should give high priority to identifying and evaluating the outcomes for wholistic well-being of the strongly entrenched American individualism, including the cultural values of selfism, greed, and "gimme because you owe it to me" that are poorly disguised components of self-actualization theories. In distinct contrast are, for example, the biblical ideals of servanthood, concern for the community, stewardship, and the spirit of self-giving that is exemplified in the New Testament by Jesus Christ, the servant (Matthew 20:25–28). Yet it is appropriate to research the issue of whether major differences in daily life and in community integration indeed do result from those alternative worldviews, or if the Christian verbiage about them is empty jargon. Studies of altruism are but the beginning of such work. The United States culture wars (Hunter 1991) associated with these and other contrasting worldviews extend far beyond the oversimplified versions of conservatism and liberalism.

Social science has contributed to the widespread deterministic view in Western society that all dysfunctionally deviant and criminal acts are a consequence of forces outside the actor, whether in the form of parental rearing, defective schools, the mass media, peers, use of alcohol or drugs, and so forth, rather than a product of his or her own volition. Perhaps distorted versions of both Calvinistic predestination and sociological determinism have contributed to removing personal accountability under doctrinaire assumptions or beliefs that people have little or no choice in their decision making, and hence are not responsible for their actions. Is it possible to discover whether the popular and increasingly legalized departure from personal responsibility has occurred, at least in part, because many religious groups have shifted their ethical and moral norms from *what ought to be* to a culturally "relevant" form of "majority rule" that bases moral values upon *what is*?

Concepts of sin, guilt, and forgiveness are changing, perhaps most of all in the domain of norms related to sexual behavior, but few social scientists have given them attention (Lyman 1989 is one exception). Perhaps most fascinating for researchers is the ways in which societal values on many norms have been inverted in recent decades. *De jure* moral codes, religious "commandments," and proverbial wisdom have been replaced with a *de facto* libertarianism, which holds that, since many people will not conform, we should change the rules to fit the behavior. This means that much of what previously was labeled as sinful nonconformity, lawbreaking, or deviance is now openly and legally permitted or even subtly encouraged.

There are many examples of such value transformations, all deserving both an *emic* and an *etic* approach in our descriptive and evaluative research. Let us again look at the convenient example of America. In contrast to past centuries, American society at large no longer advocates sexual abstinence outside of marriage, in part because so many people would not conform; instead it distributes free condoms in many high schools and other youth groups. Homosexual behavior once was almost universally considered sinful, and it remains a crime on the books of some jurisdictions, but now in many communities the real "sin" is homophobia. (Yet, why religious conservatives play up sinfulness in homosexuality while they ignore other biblical sins like gluttony, gossip, and greed is yet another research puzzle.) Nonmarital cohabitation by Hollywood stars and other folk heroes is paraded as if it is a virtue, and that even when it results in childbirth. To bear babies out of wedlock and rear them as single, self-supporting, middle-class parents is heralded as a heroic venture rather than an imprudent act. Deliberately killing an unborn infant was considered murder until abortion was legalized; now the pro-lifers who still believe in that traditional view are often treated with contempt by the academy as well as American opinion-makers. Parental discipline by spanking children, once nearly universal, is being redefined as a criminal act.

These and other inversions of traditional American values, fueled by the movies and popular culture (Medved 1992), arose partly in reaction to the inhumane extremism of some people and groups at the center of "the old moral regime." But now merely to question publicly the wisdom of the revised folkways and mores is considered a mark of backwardness at best, and of utter indecency or even a "crime" at worst. As columnist Laura Schlessinger (1998) wrote recently,

> [Ours is] a unique society in which those who do bad things are shown compassion and understanding, and those who point out the badness and expect consequences and justice are called judgmental and mean. ... [T]his attitude is so pervasive because it provides a huge gray area in which no one has to assume any responsibility for their actions, and they are immune from annoying judgment.

Other examples of changing folkways and mores are easily identified. Early in the twentieth century cigarettes were called "coffin nails." Later the anti-tobacco "crusaders" were labeled negatively as repressive "puritans," yet now, under the impact of medical research, the tide again has turned. Watching to see if there will be similar shifts under the impact of research on such topics as the long-term consequences of sexual intercourse outside of marriage, of telling lies about it, or of other violations of the Judeo-Christian Decalogue, would be an interesting undertaking. And might honest research reveal that the Religious Right has a sociologically warranted position in some of its efforts to return the Ten Commandments to the heart of public morality, even though many other Christians believe its stance is not theologically warranted?

The core values of American society and its legal system, with their respect for autonomy, freedom, self-determination, and justice for everyone, were derived from Christianity, or at least were justified by it. We need systematic research, not only journalistic and essayist opinion pieces, about what is happening to these and other religiously based foundational values as America becomes increasingly pluralistic religiously and as the insistence upon religious neutrality in the public square is legally and pragmatically strengthened (e.g., see Carter 1993). Is there any solid research evidence for the gloomy view that society itself could collapse as the consensus about moral and ethical values that are cornerstones of democratic society are eroded and destroyed? Is a new value consensus about significant core values emerging in American society? If so, can this new value consensus reinforce social solidarity, strengthen the integration of society, and promote the well-being of all citizens? To what extent do the various religious groups support or clash with society's current norms?

Extend Our Research on Spirituality

Religion and spirituality are intrinsically interrelated, but the distinctions between them all too often have been ignored, even in the social sciences of religion. In the future it is especially important to differentiate them from each other in our research. *Religion* pertains not only to conventional organizational forms of religious beliefs and practices, but also to any implicit or pseudoreligions, ideologies, and philosophies that sometimes displace them. It includes public and private modes of worship, explicit and implicit religiosities, and religious organizations like the denominations, sects, cults, and NRMs that seem ever more numerous and diverse. When traditional religions are rejected or repressed, whether by rebellious individuals or an oppressive society, substitutes pop up in new garb and sometimes strange forms.

Many people in the human service professions are discovering along with psychologist Allen E. Bergin that:

> the human spirit, under God, is vital to understanding personality and therapeutic change. If we omit such spiritual realities from our account of human behavior, it won't matter much what else we keep in, because we will have omitted the most fundamental aspect of human nature (Richards and Bergin 1997, p. xi; see also Hart 1994).

The reawakening of interest in the human soul among scientists from many disciplines reflects the current upsurge of interest in things that are both spiritual and material (Brown, Murphy, and Malony1998). While the human spirit remains empirically unobservable, a large number of humanistic, historical, and experiential evidences support the conviction that it is ontologically "real" (Moberg, 1967). The Bible likewise implies that the universality of religion among human cultures results from the Creator's having "set eternity in the hearts of men" (Ecclesiastes 3:11, NIV), again making the spirit the very core of human nature. If we accept that as indeed the case, then spirituality is the reason for being that is behind and beneath all religions, and their ultimate or central goal is, or at least ought to be, enhancing the spiritual well-being of all people and especially of their constituents.

Many religious and ideological persuasions besides Christianity similarly incorporate spirituality into their worldviews and interpretations of human nature (see Richards and Bergin 1997, pp. 49–74), although the ways they express this vary widely. "Islam, at its core, makes no distinction between the spiritual and the temporal" (Moughrabi 1995, p. 72). Buddhism has a diversity of doctrines and variability of forms, but at least in India its "ultimate goal of nonpossession was to gain spiritual liberation from the slavery of materials" (Hong 1995, p. 116). Hinduism likewise "consists of a rich tapestry of belief and practice spanning five millennia and myriad cultures, ethnic groups, and languages" (Puhakka 1995, p. 122). Its quest for liberty and transcendence generously affirms "human beings' unlimited capacity for spiritual perfection and realization of ultimate truths" (pp. 124–125). The very words *spiritual* and *spirituality* have become prominent in New Age religious parlance, as well as in specialties like humanistic psychology, holistic health, and alternative therapies in medicine.

Accordingly there are far more operational and implicit definitions of spirituality than is true of the central concepts of most relatively new subjects for scholarly and scientific investigation. Because the human spirit is invisible, we can study it only indirectly through observing its empirical indicators or reflections. (The same is true, of course, of alienation, *anomie,* depression, intelligence, motivation, and many other behavioral science concepts.) If it indeed is the essence or the very core of everything human, we as humans can never fully succeed in attempts to step outside our humanity to inspect it "objectively" or from a distance. Yet, because it pervades all of life, its indicators can be seen and interpreted from the diverse vantage points of countless experiential, ideological, religious, observational, conceptual, methodological, and theoretical perspectives. When studied in a frame of reference that is too constricted, focused on but a few aspects of its all-pervading supraempirical reality, the narrow reductionistic definitions typically are incongruent with other narrow definitions that focus upon different aspects. No wonder so much confusion is evident in studies of spirituality!

The results of the section on Spiritual Well-Being of the 1971 White House Conference on Aging (Moberg 1971b) have shaped the course of much social and behavioral science research on spirituality, as well as of interfaith dialog and cooperation through agencies like NICA (National Interfaith Coalition on Aging), for three decades. By 1974 NICA found it necessary to construct a working definition for its research, "Spiritual well-being is the affirmation of life in a relationship with God, self, community and environment that nurtures and celebrates wholeness" (Thorson and Cook, 1980, p. xiii). However, it became increasingly clear that the criteria used to evaluate spiritual wellness and illness in its member organizations were very diverse because each had its own, usually implicit, operational definition of every concept included in the allegedly common definition.

The vexatious relativism of diverse ultimate authorities has led to basically incompatible operational definitions of spiritual health and illness even among those who use nearly identical verbal definitions. Those definitions are of several types:

1. Some have been derived from Judeo-Christian Scripture passages that proclaim *what ought to be*,
2. others from scientific observations that make descriptions of *what is* primary,
3. some are from *hedonistic ideologies* that aim to enhance subjective sensations of human pleasures or happiness,
4. some from secular humanism that lifts up one or another version of *self-esteem and self-actualization*, and
5. a few can be traced to various types of *mysticism* (see Moody 1995).

Zinnbauer and colleagues (1997) found that some of the diversity results from differences about beliefs in God. Whether those beliefs are pantheistic, theistic, deistic, agnostic, or atheistic makes a difference in people's definitions of *religiousness* and *spirituality*, as well as in their self-descriptions based upon those concepts. The entire Spring 1997 issue of *Aging & Spirituality*, the newsletter of the American Society on Aging's Forum on Religion, Spirituality, and Aging, was devoted to the topic of defining spiritual well-being, but without reaching any definitive agreement (Ellor 1997).

The social components and implications of spirituality are far more underdeveloped in research and theory than those that are more individualistic and psychological. Far too often the research and theory have reduced spirituality to such variables as institutional membership, religious group participation, ethical behavior per se (in contrast to ethics as a consequence or outgrowth of spiritual commitments), meditative privatism, private prayer, feeling good (emotions, ecstasy, trance behavior, self-actualization, and the like), or other narrow indicators and slippery terms.

After considerable study, it is now my measured opinion that we will not be able to establish clear and genuinely universal criteria for honest evaluations of spiritual wellness and illness that apply to people in every religious and cultural context until after extensive research has compared the specific components and outcomes of a broad range of religious faiths and practices, initially using the value-based criteria for spiritual health of each group itself. Only after comparing such particularistic studies can we determine whether there are any universally applicable indicators by which to evaluate spiritual well-being for all humanity (Moberg 1997a; 1997b).

Despite these limitations, social, psychological, nursing, and epidemiological research is increasingly revealing the generally wholesome effects of spiritual orientations and ministries upon physical and mental health (Koenig 1994, 1997; Pargament, Van Haitsma, and Ensing 1995), although much of the research is still young and needs considerable elaboration (Levin and Tobin 1995; Moberg 1995). Yet pastoral services, chaplaincies, and other formalized caregiving to nurture spirituality still are marginalized in the caring and health professions, partly because of a dearth of empirical assessments to demonstrate their monetary contributions to economic profit and loss ledgers of health care delivery corporations.

Social research can complement and test the findings of other studies on the results of individuals, communities, social institutions (including the economy and government), and society at large. We need to learn which forms of spiritual awakening, nurture, and development are usually beneficial to wholistic well-being, which tend to be harmful or destructive, and the circumstances and manner in which these consequences occur. Intensive research on the consequences of various theories, schools, and "paths" of spirituality similarly can reveal the concomitants and results of each and compare their relative desirability in terms of their own (*emic*) and cultural or other (*etic*) value systems. Inevitably questions will arise about whether we can judge them fairly by their "fruits" because each imposes different spiritual baggage upon its adherents and to some extent promises different outcomes. Even after we have agreed upon the basic evaluative criteria to use (if we ever do), we still will need to discover which indicators of each criterion are amenable to and appropriate for evaluative measurement.

Monitor Other Topics and Trends That Deserve Research Attention

There is no end to the specific subjects that are worthy of evaluative research and theoretical attention. For example, among the significant tidal waves of change sweeping Christianity globally is displacement of the ecumenism that emphasized formal cooperation or sometimes even mergers of "mainline" religious bodies by looser "evangelical" forms of grass roots fellowships consisting of parachurch organizations, denominations, and other cooperative ventures based upon the belief that all institutional actions and structures are secondary to personal faith in Jesus Christ as the highest value and hence the foundation for cooperation (see Moberg, 1987b). Obvious evidences of this trend include the struggles for more than a quarter-century by COCU (the Consultation on Church Union, which initially was in quest of a "Church of Christ Uniting") and the radical decline of local, national, and global councils of churches over the past half century, alongside the sharp rise of evangelicalism with its almost countless non-denominational megachurches, denomination-transcending evangelistic crusades, congregations without denominational names, women's and men's movements, missionary associations, world relief agencies, and other ministries.

We need research on why Christian, Jewish, and Islamic orthodoxy are usually left outside the doors of respect in the academic and mass media framework of political correctness in contrast to and in spite of popular membership trends. And have fundamentalists, including the "Religious Right," which sacralizes many political, social, and economic perspectives that most social scientists abhor, become a new minority that needs protection from the religious and civic discrimination that they often face? At the other extreme, the religious and atheistic "left" receives considerable moral support from our academic and judicial systems, but many of its members feel that politicians and the conservatively dominated mass media give it a beating (see Berkman 1999).

The cost–benefit analyses that are so central to rational choice theories of religion need in-depth analytical and empirical data on all of the functional and dysfunctional contributions and consequences of each of the alternative choices of religion that are on the lengthy menu of spiritual options offered the members of various societies. For example, sociohistorical studies can explore whether religion remains a part of the social capital at the base of all democratic societies, even when overlooked by many people within that society. And what of the influence of the Almighty Dollar as the reigning god; what becomes of a core of spirituality that is not directly reducible to dollar values and sometimes contradicts them? While many consequences of religion and spirituality are related indirectly to economic losses and gains, most of them go far beyond that domain. Monitoring the conditions, trends, and results of the numerous types of religion and spirituality in contemporary society can be a distinct service to lay and professional leaders in society, the religious sector, and scholarship in many disciplines besides our own.

Countless other topics in the ever-changing web of religion and society deserve our continuing and renewed attention. They include newly emerging and old syncretisms of religious faith and practice, the impact of popular entertainment on worship, pragmatic and spiritual consequences of different styles of worship, religious hypocrisy (see Moberg 1987a), the conquest of much religious thought and practice by popular psychologies, the role of humor in religion as both a reflection of the dilemmas, hypocrisies, and ironies of everyday life and as a tool used by persons and groups for coping with them, and dozens of other topics each reader can identify. Obviously, every suggestion deserves its own background study, which ideally begins with an interdisciplinary search for related previous work.

CONCLUSIONS

In the early history of sociology, religion was recognized to be so important and central a component of society that new religious or pseudoreligious alternatives were advocated by the social theorists who believed that the dominant religious faiths were incurably deficient. The growth of sociology and emergence of its dozens of subspecializations gradually relegated the study of religion to its own relatively independent specialty alone. By the mid-twentieth century, religion had been almost completely removed from its previous prominence in general socio-logical analyses, and parallel shifts pushing religion out seem to have occurred in the other social sciences. Yet recent research has gradually revealed that in fact religion, and especially spirituality, permeates all areas of personal and social life, including politics at home and abroad. Demonstrating the significance of spiritu-ality through research and theory may bring the study of religion back from the fringes of the social sciences to their mainstream.

The social sciences of religion also face a pragmatic issue: how can we make the scientific study of religion more marketable in a society of powerful pressure groups that attack any research that carries even as little as a possibility of threat-ening their vested interests (see Hunt 1998)? This question has at least four dimensions:

1. What can we do to entice more students at all levels of education to major or minor in our disciplines and thus to understand religion and spirituality better and become prepared to join our research professions?
2. How can we convince more foundations, legislatures, denominational and parachurch agencies, corporations, and other funding agencies to support our educational programs and research projects?
3. In the area of sociological practice, how can we better "sell" our consulta-tion, evaluation methods, and research services as tools available to serve the cause of authentic spirituality and wholesome religion?
4. And is it possible to do all this honestly, without "selling out" and merely becoming pawns whose work is oriented only toward one-sided support of economic and theological vested interests and power structures?

There has been much progress. Besides developments within the social sci-ences per se, biblical studies and social theology are benefitting greatly from the use of anthropological and sociological concepts and perspectives to illuminate Scripture passages and demonstrate their applicability in modern society. Denom-inational and congregational studies are enriching the ministries of many religious bodies. Social science analyses are contributing to hermeneutics by clarifying the ways in which the doctrines of various faiths, sects, and denominations have been influenced by attention to their original and subsequent cultural contexts. Many other aspects of theology and religious studies deserve the stimulation potentially available through the social sciences of religion.

Much of what I am suggesting is, in effect, an admonition that, while we eagerly try to be innovative, original, and on the growing edge of religious stud-ies, we must always remember the basic foundations and the limitations, as well as the strengths and assets, of the tools of our trade. If we slip up on these, we might hypocritically disseminate ungrounded opinions or even gross falsehoods as if they are "solid facts," while simultaneously treating the truths of important ontological realities as if they were false.

In some Judeo-Christian circles there is a saying that "The future is as bright as the promises of God." Religion research will have a bright future in the twenty-first century if we grasp wisely the verdant opportunities before us and build upon the remarkable progress that was made during the last half of the twentieth century.

ACKNOWLEDGMENT

This paper is an elaboration of a presentation in a session on "Passing the Torch" in the annual meeting of the Association for the Sociology of Religion in San Francisco, August 22, 1998, that was organized by its president, James R. Kelly. Its revision has benefitted from the critiques of three anonymous referees, for whose suggestions I am thankful.

REFERENCES

Arbouse-Bastide, P. 1966. "August Comte et la Sociologie Religieuse." *Archives de Sociologie des Religions* 22: 3–57.

Barnes, H. E. 1929. *The Twilight of Christianity*. New York: Vanguard Press.

Berkman, D. 1999 (July 22). "Religious Rodneys: Why Do Atheists Get No Respect from Politicians and the Media?" *Shepherd Express Metro*, p. 18.

Brown, W. S., N. Murphy, and H. N. Malony (Eds.). 1998. *Whatever Happened to the Soul? Scientific and Theological Portraits of Human Nature*. Minneapolis, MN: Fortress Press.

Carter, S. 1993. *The Culture of Disbelief. How American Law and Politics Trivialize Religious Devotion*. New York: Basic Books.

Clouser, R. A. 1991. *The Myth of Religious Neutrality*. Notre Dame, IN: University of Notre Dame Press.

Colson, C., with E. Santilli Vaughn. 1989. *Against the Night: Living in the New Dark Ages*. Ann Arbor, MI: Servant Publications.

Dascal, M. 1991. "The Ecology of Cultural Space." Pp. 279-295 in *Cultural Relativism and Philosophy*, edited by M. Dascal. Leiden, Netherlands: E. J. Brill.

Denzin, N. K. 1989. *The Research Act*. Englewood Cliffs, NJ: Prentice-Hall.

Deutscher, I. 1998. *Making a Difference: The Practice of Sociology*. New Brunswick, NJ: Transaction Publishers.

Dodds, E. W. (Ed.). 1995 et seq. *ADRIS Newsletter,* Vol 22, P. 0. Box 210735, Nashville, TN 37221-0735.

Donahue, M. J. 1989. "Disregarding Theology in the Psychology of Religion: Some Examples." *Journal of Psychology and Theology* 17: 329–335.

Ellor, J. W. (Ed.). 1997. "Spiritual Well-Being Defined." *Aging & Spirituality* 9(1): 1–2.

Friedrichs, R. W. 1970. *A Sociology of Sociology*. New York: Free Press.

Garrison, C. E. 1988. *Two Different Worlds: Christian Absolutes and the Relativism of Social Science*. Newark, DE: University of Delaware Press.

Goldsmith, W. M. 1989. "Through a Glass Darkly, but Face to Face: Comments on Psychology and Theology Eyeing One Another." *Journal of Psychology and Theology* 17: 385–393.

Greeley, A. M. 1989. *Religious Change in America*. Cambridge, MA: Harvard University Press.

Griffioen, S., and J. Verhoogt (Eds.). 1990. *Norm and Context in the Social Sciences*. Lanham, MD: University Press of America.

Hart, T. 1994. *Hidden Spring: The Spiritual Dimension of Therapy*. New York: Paulist Press.

Hartshorne, H. and M. A. May. 1928. *Studies in the Nature of Character: I. Studies in Deceit*. New York: Macmillan.

Headland, T. N., et al. 1990. *Emics and Etics: The Insider/Outsider Debate. Frontiers of Anthropology*, Vol. 7. Newbury Park, CA: Sage Publications.

Heddendorf, R. 1990. *Hidden Threads: Social Thought for Christians*. Richardson, TX: Probe Books.

Hong, G.-Y. 1995. "Buddhism and Religious Experience." Pp. 87–121 in *Handbook of Religious Experience*, edited by R. W. Hood. Birmingham, AL: Religious Education Press.

Hooykaas, R. 1972. *Religion and the Rise of Modern Science*. Grand Rapids, MI: Eerdmans.

Hunt, M. 1998. The New Know-Nothings: The Political Foes of the Scientific Study of Human *Nature*. New Brunswick, NJ: Transaction Publishers.

Hunter, J. D. 1991. *Culture Wars: The Struggle to Define America*. New York: Basic Books.

Koenig, H. G. 1994. *Aging and God: Spiritual Pathways to Mental Health in Midlife and Later Years*. New York: Haworth Pastoral Press.

_____. 1997. *Is Religion Good for Your Health? The Effects of Religion on Physical and Mental Health*. New York: Haworth Pastoral Press.

Krausz, M. 1991. "Crossing Cultures: Two Universalisms and Two Relativisms." Pp. 233–241 in *Cultural Relativism and Philosophy*, edited by M. Dascal. Leiden, Netherlands: E. J. Brill.

Levin, J. S., and S. S. Tobin. 1995. "Religion and Psychological Well-Being." Pp. 30–46 in *Aging, Spirituality, and Religion: A Handbook* edited by M. A. Kimble, S. H. McFadden, J. W. Ellor, and J. J. Seeber. Minneapolis, MN: Fortress Press.

Lyman, S. M. 1989. *The Seven Deadly Sins: Society and Evil*, rev. ed. Dix Hills, NY: General Hall.

MacKay, D. M. 1974. *The Clock Work Image: A Christian Perspective on Science*. Downers Grove, IL: InterVarsity Press.

Medved, M. 1992. *Hollywood vs. America: Popular Culture and the War on Traditional Values*. New York: Harper Collins.

Moberg, D. O. 1949. *Religious Instruction in State Institutions of Higher Education*. M. A. thesis (Sociology), University of Washington.

_____. 1951. *Religion and Personal Adjustment in Old Age*. Ph. D. dissertation (Sociology), University of Minnesota.

_____. 1967. "The Encounter of Scientific and Religious Values Pertinent to Man's Spiritual Nature." *Sociological Analysis* 28: 22–33.

_____. (Ed.). 1971a. *International Directory of Religious Information Systems*. Milwaukee, WI: Marquette University.

_____. (Ed.). 1971b. *Spiritual Well-Being: Background and Issues*. Washington, DC: White House Conference on Aging.

_____. 1987a. "Holy Masquerade: Hypocrisy in Religion." *Review of Religious Research* 29: 3–24.

_____. 1987b. "The Paradox of Modern Evangelical Christianity: The United States and Sweden." Pp. 47–99 in *Comparative Social Research: Vol. 10, Religion and Belief Systems*, edited by R. F. Tomasson. Greenwich, CT: JAI Press.

_____. 1995. "Applications of Research Methods." Pp. 541–557 in *Aging, Spirituality, and Religion: A Handbook*, edited by M. A. Kimble, S. H. McFadden, J. W. Ellor, and J. J. Seeber. Minneapolis, MN: Fortress Press.

_____. 1997a. "Spiritual Well-Being Defined: A Response." *Aging & Spirituality* 9(1): 8.

_____. 1997b. "Tensions Between Universalism and Particularism in Research on Spiritual Well-Being." Paper presented at the joint annual meeting of the Illinois and Wisconsin Sociological Associations, Rockford, IL, October 31.

Moody, H. R. 1995. "Mysticism." Pp. 87–101 in *Aging, Spirituality, and Religion: A Handbook*, edited by M. A. Kimble, S. H. McFadden, J. W. Ellor, and J. J. Seeber. Minneapolis, MN: Fortress Press.

Moughrabi, F. 1995. "Islam and Religious Experience." Pp. 72–86 in *Handbook of Religious Experience*, edited by R. W. Hood. Birmingham, AL: Religious Education Press.

Myers, D. G. 1978. *The Human Puzzle: Psychological Research and Christian Belief.* New York: Harper & Row.

Pargament, K. I., K. S. Van Haitsma, and D. S. Ensing. 1995. "Religion and Coping." Pp. 47–67 in *Aging, Spirituality, and Religion: A Handbook* edited by M. A. Kimble, S. H. McFadden, J. W. Ellor, and J. J. Seeber. Minneapolis, MN: Fortress Press.

Puhakka, K. 1995. "Hinduism and Religious Experience." Pp. 122–143 in *Handbook of Religious Experience*, edited by R. W. Hood. Birmingham, AL: Religious Education Press.

Richards, P. S., and A. E. Bergin. 1997. *A Spiritual Strategy for Counseling and Psychotherapy.* Washington, DC: American Psychological Association.

Schlessinger, L. 1998. "Daughter Has No Respect for Two-timing Dad." *Milwaukee Journal Sentinel,* June 10, p. 1F.

Shore, M. 1987. *The Science of Social Redemption: McGill, the Chicago School, and the Origins of Social Research in Canada.* Toronto, Canada: University of Toronto Press.

Swatos, W. H. Jr. 1984. *Faith of the Fathers: Science, Religion, and Reform in the Development of Early American Sociology.* Bristol, IN: Wyndham Hall Press.

Thorson, J. A., and T. C. Cook (Eds.). 1980. *Spiritual Well-Being of the Elderly.* Springfield, IL: Charles C Thomas.

Towler, R. 1974. *Homo Religiosus: Sociological Problems in the Study of Religion.* New York: St. Martin's Press.

Turner, B. S. 1991. *Religion and Social Theory,* 2nd edition. London: Sage Publications.

Zinnbauer, B. J., K. I. Pargament, B. Cole, M. S. Rye, E. M. Butter, T. G. Belavich, K. M. Hipp, A. B. Scott, and J. L. Kadad. 1997. "Religion and Spirituality: Unfuzzying the Fuzzy." *Journal for the Scientific Study of Religion* 36: 549–564.

THE RECIPROCAL RELATIONSHIP OF SYNCRETISM AND FUNDAMENTALISM FROM THE EARLY HISTORY OF RELIGION TO MODERNITY

Carlo Prandi

ABSTRACT

The history of religions from early ages to modernity presents two phenomena in a dynamic tension. On the one hand, the phenomenon of *syncretism* results from the mutual encounters of different religions and their competing struggles for dominance. As indigenous religions continue on in history, they carry along a partial absorption of a religion of the Book. The phenomenon of absorption continues to show an ongoing development in postcolonial history. The phenomenon of *fundamentalism* may be seen as a complementary phenomenon to that of syncretism. Fundamentalism in general opposes imposition of religious ideas from outside. Fundamentalisms react to meeting a new religion by a stiffening of observance of the letter of the law. Today fundamentalisms focus their attention on a strong reaction against incorporating modernity and its ideologies into the core belief system.

Research in the Social Scientific Study of Religion, Volume 11, pages 23-35.
ISBN: 0-7623-0656-4

The history of religions from early ages to modernity presents two phenomena in a dynamic tension. On the one hand, the phenomenon of syncretism results from the mutual encounters of different religions and their competing struggles for dominance. In cases where the religions of the Book have been stronger, they have imposed at least a part of their message and of their symbol system on the indigenous or ethnic religions. Thus, as these indigenous religions continue on in history, they carry along a partial absorption of a religion of the Book. This phenomenon of imposition from without is typical of the colonial age. But the phenomenon of absorption shows an ongoing development in postcolonial history, as is seen today, for example, in the indigenous and ethnic religions of Central and Southern America.

The phenomenon of fundamentalism may be seen as a complementary phenomenon to that of syncretism. Fundamentalism in general opposes any imposition of religious ideas from outside. Fundamentalisms react to meeting a new religion by a stiffening of observance of the letter of the law. In the past ages there were varied ways in which fundamentalism manifested itself, but today fundamentalism focuses its attention on a strong reaction against incorporating modernity and its ideologies into the core belief system.

PROBLEMS OF METHOD

The history of the civilizations, as Arnold Toynbee has reminded us, is also the history of their increase or decrease to the limit condition of extinction. Therefore it includes an ongoing sequence of encounters, amalgamations, conquests, and assimilations. Such a course of history was both the cause and the result of culture-to-culture encounters which were sometimes harsh, even catastrophic, to the indigenous religions, as in the case of pre-Colombian societies which were completely enveloped by the Spanish *Conquistadores*. From a religious perspective, these encounters produced new cultural artifacts in both cultures. These new artifacts were characterized by possessing a bicultural simultaneity, a set of forms and figures functional for the process of intersection between the two cultures.

Within such complex dynamics, one sees clearly the birth of religious realities which, on the one hand, participate in two (or more) different traditions via a process of interplay, but on the other hand don't identify *tout court* with either. These new religious realities have been named *syncretisms*.

It is useful to review the etymology of "*syncretism.*" In its earliest use, the term indicated the temporary union of the Cretan peoples in order to resist to their common enemy. During the Protestant Reformation the same word indicated either an alliance between Reformed tradition and Humanists, or between Lutherans, Calvinists, and Roman Catholics. Later, philosophical trends composed from interplay of different ideological and/or religious elements were also termed *syncretisms*. In the present, *syncretism* is above all a religious term, and it ordinarily points to a cultural process in those countries discovered or conquered by European states. These conquests exerted a deep influence of acculturation and/or deculturation. The conquered, according to M. de Certeau, had history written upon their own persons (de Certeau 1977, p. XV).

I am going to propose here some reflections both on more relevant features of religious syncretism, and on reactive tendencies in the opposite direction: a shrinking from every religious interaction. These latter movements are sometimes termed "*integralisms*" and sometimes termed "*fundamentalisms.*" This latter term is the more common usage in the Western culture, but the term is offensive to the Islamic world.

History of religion knows very well the integralisms of the past, but modernity is proposing new ones. These integralisms balance themselves between tradition and modernity, so they pose a problem of synchrony within a diachrony.

First of all synchrony means comparison. According to Pettazzoni: "In methodological terms, we have to decide whether the comparison is much more than a mechanical recording of similarities and differences, or if there can be a comparison which, passing over the descriptive and classifying approach, could stimulate thought, by pushing forward to find new relationships and a deepening of the historical conscience" (Pettazzoni 1968, p. 108; author translation from the Italian). Clearly, sociohistorical knowledge has to be based on comparisons.

Pettazzoni's theories turn out to be important for the sociologist who works from a historical perspective, especially when he or she ventures, as V. Turner says, into the "Forest of Symbols" in which religious traditions are entangled. Unavoidably, studies of the histories of various religions present to us well defined and distinct religious systems, each with traits of unreplicated specificity which historians defend as a principle. But when religious historiography is opened to influence of the social sciences, the stress shifts toward the affinities, the borrowings, the intersections which affect various religious traditions over the period of their historical development. Social scientists often discover within different religions comparable structures. Attention to these overlapping traits seems useful to comprehend the particular dynamics of religion as a general phenomenon (according to P. Bourdieu).

It is necessary to distinguish between the *process* of religious search and the *object* of religious search (as R. Otto's [1923] thesis that *the sacred* is a category *a priori*). I do not speak here about phenomenology aiming to define the essence of religion, for example, in the manner of M. Eliade or Van der Leeuw, and leading to theology. There is no doubt that there is one function of a religious phenomenology which is not involved in the object of the search per se. I speak of the ongoing process of the construction, with a strong historical sensibility, of ideal-typic forms which are present. In all the different religious traditions, at least to some degree, such ideal-typic forms are seen: myth, ritual, sacrifice, mysticism, holy kingliness, and so on. In their myriad dimensions these ideal-type forms are characterized by a higher level of generality in comparison with their concrete manifestation within any specific case. They are "ideal types" because *ideal-typus*, by the relations to which it points, allows us to understand that which often is inexplicable in its singularity. (The use of *ideal types* sometimes called *constructed* or *pure* types, pervades Weber's significant theoretical work on religion and other subjects. It is derived from the German adjective *ideal*, referring to an *idea* that is drawn out to its most precise conception for analytical purposes. The reference in every case is not to a moral evaluation of qualities that we necessarily ought to idealize or emulate but to distinct, often logically contrasting, concepts or alternative categories.–Eds.)

The approach I am proposing here is the historical phenomenology of George Widengren, which aims to give "a synthetic description of the various religious phenomena, so that it becomes a systematic complement to the history of religions. The history of religions makes an historical analysis, whereas the phenomenology of religion gives us the systematic synthesis" (Widengren 1984, p. 63; author translation from the Swedish). In fact the Swedish scholar opts for the *relative autonomy of religion*. One does not find in the analytical procedure of Widengren any particular philosophical assumption, either of the hermeneutical type, or on the contrary, linked to the theories of the *erklären*. Widengren avoids the classical hypothesis of the phenomenologists (e.g., Otto 1923) who refer to Scheiermacher. According to this latter group, to quote Paul Ricoeur, "we have to believe in order to understand." Widengren chooses an option which tends to protect the relative autonomy of the religious dimension: "Religion," the Swedish author writes, "is not something which can be explained through historical development, but a fact based on a particular relation with existence which depends on a power dominating the human destiny. . . . A distinctive feature of religion is not the belief in some phenomenon permeated with power in the worship of spirits, but, above all, the faith in the divinity." (Widengren 1984, p. 86; author translation from the Swedish).

It is a substantive definition which, on one hand preserves the specific religious dimension. On the other hand, this definition can push deep inside history, working as a selection criterion within the huge accumulation of material that the Swedish historian takes into examination. In Widengren's work, if on the one hand the autonomy of the religious life is confirmed, at least in the sense of the impossibility of dating back to a reliable historical *prius*, on the other hand, the phenomenon is based on an extraordinary historical knowledge.

Also relevant to this discussion is the expansive sociolinguistical enterprise of G. Dumézil (1955) that encompassed all the vast territory of the Indo-European cultures. Within this context, the French scholar actualized his celebrated trifunctional model, whose fit to the area examined has sometimes been criticized. In this context, Dumézil speaks of the "bi-uni-vocal" correspondences between social world and divine world. In *Jupiter, Mars, Quirinus*, Dumézil wrote that if on the one hand "the myth remains the superior religious phenomenon which gives efficacy and meaning to the others," on the other hand "the modern comparative mythology is not possible unless it incorporates at all the different levels all the phenomena relating to the myths, that is the whole sociology" (Dumézil 1955, p. 8; author translation.)

In this way Dumézil regained, and this is substantially the meaning of his research, the underpinnings of society as a place not of the determination, but of the ideation/construction of the religious dynamics, and of their diffusion and interaction in an analytical view.

THE ADVENTURES OF RELIGIOUS SYNCRETISM

The preceding outlines the history of the ancient religious traditions to stress that syncretism is not a novelty of our time. During the last centuries religious syncretisms followed great cultural transformations produced by European penetration in the colonial countries of the so-called Third World. In general we can say that religious syncretisms were caused by the horizontal mobility pushing peoples, or their armies and missionaries, out of their countries, with a consequent overlapping of cultures. These collective movements present different characteristics and they developed at different paces. For example, between 2500 and 1500 B.C. Aryan peoples occupied the valley of the Indian river, imposing themselves on the Dravidian societies: this produced the Hindu civilization and its book, *The Veda*. During the early Middle Ages, Berber, Islamic, and Norman invasions also deeply influenced preexisting societies and cultures around the Mediterranean Sea. Sometimes military conquests produced the devastation (or annihilation—as in the case of the *Conquistadores* in South America) of the autochthonous religious traditions. But the ancient culture does not die altogether—transformation is very complex. So deculturation and enculturation follow, accompanying the crisis of the preexisting religious institutions and traditions, and the birth of the syncretisms.

P. Duviols, in the preface of his volume *La lutte contre les religions autochtones dans le Pérou colonial*, explaining the program of his research, gives a synopsis of the background of the missionary strategy in those territories:

> The effort of the Church and of the Spanish Monarchy to abolish the autochthonous religions and establish Catholicism among the indigenous masses has been [as he writes] the essential factor in the cultural transformation of societies which composed the ancient *Tawantin-suyu*, and the extirpation of idolatry produced great problems, both material and spiritual, during colonization. This process caused, in great part, the merging of the two civilizations on contact (Duviols 1971, p, 15).

Our theory is that generally ethnic religions (i.e., those without a founder or Book) are more permeable to syncretisms. The absence of a Book as a coercive reference point facilitates the emergence of forms of cultural deviation of which African religions present the clearest examples. This statement does not imply that absence of a Book leads the ethnic religions to simplistic surrenders—syncretistic reorganization often produces a new religious frame, the novelty of which is at first not totally realized or clear.

Religious syncretisms are often functional to the physical and cultural survival of a society. The ancient religious (and magic) traditions keep their roots in the collective mind; on the other hand the religious (generally Christian) exogenous pressure undergoes a kind of "genetic manipulation" shaped by the sociocultural surround and its specific needs.

The African continent is a typical laboratory of syncretism because of the multiplicity of solutions produced by the various meetings of the local cultures with the ministries of various Christian missionaries. These ministries were accompanied by the influx of Western culture (technology, arms, medicine, economics, and so on). While there is a massive institutionalized presence of Christianity (both Catholic and Protestant), the churches and clergy are more and more autochthonous. In recent years, research has been ongoing, even if not altogether profitable, on a possible "African Theology." There is also a notable presence of prophetisms and new pre-and postcolonial religious movements. Also, one must not underestimate the diffusion of the so called "Independent Churches." The span of African syncretisms is therefore vast and various.

An African intellectual of Western education, E. Bolaji Idowu (1968), clearly expresses the conflict between the two worlds, often revealed within a syncretic religious figure, when he wrote that

> at the birth of the independent Churches (prophetic, Pentecostal and so on) we can see the revival of the ancient cults. They are a reaction against African Church connected with Europe and against its spiritual and liturgic aridity. African people ask to practice the cult like African Christian people. They do not accept to be converted into European people before practicing the cult. These movements try to complete what is lacking in European Christian preaching; they ask Christianity to satisfy spiritually and emotionally the needs of the African people. Therefore prophetism is for them a good replacement of the ancient divination (Boaji Idowu 1968, pp. 434–435).

Roger Bastide, with reference to the Afro-American syncretisms, has emphasized the persistence of ancient tribal beliefs among the black people of Central and South America. They worship in a mythical–ritual universe which appropriates Christianity and its intermediate figures (the Virgin Mary, the saints, the angels). This French anthropologist, examining the different syncretisms developed in the vast cultural expanse found from the Antilles to Argentina, has been able to identify some constants in the processes of religious interaction. However, the prescriptive character of Bastide's "constants" might be challenged in different contexts (in time and space). This is particularly true when he states that:

> Institutionally, syncretism is much stronger when we pass from the 'preserved' religions to the 'alive' religions, because the life of an organism, both social and biological, consists of assimilating what comes from the outside. [Moreover], according to what G. Gurvitch has defined as 'la sociologie en profondeur,' the syncretic forms vary their nature when from the

> morphological level we pass to the institutional level (with the system of correspondences
> between the African gods and the Catholic saints) and from the institutional level to the level
> of the facts of the collective consciousness (Bastide 1970, p. 177; author translation).

The references both to "preserved" religions and to the "alive" religions indicate the cultural dynamisms induced by their differing traditions. These, in fact,
impose themselves with more or less flexibility according to their localized or
universal natures. Catholicism has lent/imposed its intermediate figures to the
American religions of African origin. It is an uneven relation. The exchange, on
one hand has revealed the capability of a tradition based on the Book to remold
itself, at least in part. But this process has taken place on the substratum of a
preexisting ethnic scene. Thus, in this transfer Catholicism perhaps faces the
extinction of its universality and its consequent reduction to a syncretic cult.
This may be the inevitable cost that every universal religion has to pay when it
imposes itself on a specific cultural context and it also pushes to be involved in
the local paradigm, the original tradition. Bastide raises the same point in his
essay on the African cultures of the New World, despite the fact that his focus
does not correspond to the above:

> This universal religion has local shapes, according to the ethnic groups and to the races: these
> variations are not fundamental and a religion can always be 'translated' into another, by mak-
> ing each African divinity correspond to a saint or to the Virgin Mary. When the faithful iden-
> tify *Shango*, for example, with St. Jerome, it is not appropriate to talk about superstition or
> logical absurdity. In a strict coherent system they occupy the same intermediate position in a
> net of connections and they carry out the same functions: control the powers of the fire and
> directing lightening only towards the wicked. (Bastide 1970, p. 179).

Bastide is not attracted by the ethnic–universal relationship as a theoretical
problem. His interest focuses on those particular forms of religious interaction
which date back to the preservation of threatened cultural or physical identities. In
his remarkable research, the French anthropologist has traced the history of Afro-
American syncretisms from the colonial age when the slaves had to hide their
native cults in front of their masters. When they were obliged to take part in the
Catholic ceremonies, during the liturgy they danced invoking the African divinities which they saw behind the statues of the saints. The God of the whites was far
too distant (like the supreme tribal beings). They needed some intermediate figures and the Catholic saints could perfectly accomplish this task: they were redefined for the black and became the *orisha* and the *vudun*. Bastide explains that the
one religion was "translated" into the other by making every divinity of the original African tradition correspond to a particular saint or to the Virgin Mary. The
specialities of the merged figures were the same—control of the fire, launching of
lightning against the wicked, and, above all, help of the faithful in case of disease.
This phenomenon is still going on with different manifestations to adapt to the

effects of industrialization and urbanization, so that, Bastide concludes, "the Afro-American cultures are far from being dead."

A remarkable manifestation of syncretic development is represented by the phenomenon of the Messianisms and Prophetisms, which have been in decrease for a few years, in the excolonial societies of Africa and Oceania. These societies are still burdened to some extent with the functional control and the economic exploitation of the West, as well as their own never ending interethnic conflicts. These movements played an important political role, especially in Africa, in the last period of the colonial age but, currently, where they are not already extinguished, they have reduced their activity within a strictly religious context. They offer a type of cult which is more satisfactory for emotional relief and daily needs—the prophetic element occupies the place which was previously occupied by ancient divination. In former times, the prophet was asked to take the initiative to save his people from the foreign oppression; today his task is to cure the diseases with prayers and holy water. During the colonial age, the Messianic movements had their revolutionary aspect in the recovery of old traditions concurrent with having freed the country from the white. If on one hand they looked at the missionary church as the inspiring model on which they could shape the future society, on the other hand they were pressed by nostalgia for the *status quo ante*. In the case of Congo, the political program of Messianic movements which developed there aimed to reestablish the prestigious kingdoms of the past. Their doctrine took its inspiration from the Bible and the desired form of government was a theocracy ruled by a political–religious hierarchy. The founder prophets, such as S. Kimbangu, strained to give vigor to the indigenous power, relying on the forces of a sacred nationalism.

After independence there was a slow and inevitable decline of the old messianic tension—the ancient kingdoms of Congo were forgotten and, in their place, appeared, with urgency, all the daily problems, in particular poverty and disease, of nations now abandoned to their own efforts toward progress. The Independent Churches, which were already present in the colonial age, increased remarkably. Their main goal was, and still is, to obtain healing of the faithful by resorting to confession, to prayers, and rituals of different kinds, especially those connected with water.

Recent research verifies that in the case of the Water Carriers of Ghana, the majority of the followers do not affiliate themselves because of their faith, but only to get healing from sickness or to get success in business. Water Carriers often hold membership in different religious confessions; for them the religious side is less important than the curative function of the "Water's Church."

Various elements characterize the syncretism present among African Independent Churches. The leader is often a prophet receiving revelations from his spirit–guide and communicating them to the believers[1]. Two complementary dimensions are present: on the one hand, the emotional style of the cult with ecstasy and the phenomena of possession, and on the other hand, the cult of the Christian God with faith as salvation (from illness). The Christian cult is in tension with the magic and ritual of the local collective cult.

The specific marker of the syncretistic churches is the mixture not only of new ideas with elements coming from ancient animistic beliefs, but of tales from Old and New Testament about a Savior whose function was once political, but now is turned to daily and personal life.

In summary, syncretistic phenomena are produced by the meeting of two religious traditions, the first of which is universal and based on the Book. The syncretism revolves around the Messiah who will come to bring salvation. The second religious tradition is of an ethnic kind and racked by eternal problems of illness and daily risks. In the historical passage from before to after political independence, the figure of Messiah is central. Modernity disrupts old traditions, and produces a new religious marketplace whose central trait, even in the ongoing presence both of Christian preaching and ethnic cults, is syncretism, evolving from a battle between religious traditions with differing potentials of penetration.

SYNCRETISM AND RELIGIOUS RADICALISM

Syncretism is not found only in societies which have undergone Western colonialization. In the West itself there are similar phenomena in the diffusion of sects and "groups of the sect type" (J. Séguy) of different kinds. These groups appear to be typical products of modernity. Sometimes these groups and the traditional churches live side-by-side. In the West one also observes forms of syncretism in which movements of Eastern or Protestant origin are joined to Catholicism (Yoga and Catholicism, Pentecostalism and Catholicism, and so on). From this point of view the religious market presents many choices and possibilities.

But in the present time, a phenomenon which is totally opposite to the syncretism, almost its shadow-self, is also active side-by-side with syncretism. It is the phenomenal growth of radicalism or, to use a current term (born in the first decades of this century in the Protestant churches in the United States), *fundamentalism*. But clearly, it is not the case that the *concept* of fundamentalism was born in the first decades of twentieth century in the United States. Fundamentalism flowered in the United States at that time, as a negative answer to the systematic marginalization of the sacred produced by advancing of modernity or by the heavy demand of the latter to reach those linguistic compromises which J. Séguy has termed "metamorphosis of religion." (Hervieu-Léger 1996, pp. 103–118). Fundamentalism as a concept existed both before and after its upsurge in the United States.

Fundamentalism considered across cultures and throughout history, consists of attitudes, expressed by religious groups such as the extreme wing of Islam, which radically oppose every inter-religious contact or influence. Fundamentalist religious groups in pluralistic political settings consider indigenous religious traditions—even, in extreme case, their own (see Algeria and Afghanistan)—as enemies. The phenomenon seen in radical Islam today is not a new one—radicalism or fundamentalism is a social style which is typical and cyclic in the history of religions of the Book. Such movements represent a defensive answer to the perception of a siege, both real or imagined, where the conflict divides the Book, or the different and contrasting interpretations of the Book itself. Fundamentalist movements start from the accepted principle: "Outside the Book there is no salvation!" In these situations the group held in opposition, the majority compared to the minority, the external world compared to the insiders and so on, is considered as the incarnation of evil or the devil. Therefore it is a religious act to limit or abolish that which is opposed.

We can look back through 20 centuries of history and find fundamentalism. The culture, the mentality, the ideology of the Pharisee and the Scribe during the Roman occupation in Palestine, are paradigmatic of fundamentalism. Flavius Joseph in *The Judaic War* (II, 8, 2 etc.) refers to the presence of groups and sects, in Palestine under the pressure of Hellenism after Macedonian conquest, which opposed the religious policy of the Seleucidae and of the Asmoneae sovereigns. Among these, the Pharisee (the "separated") distinguished themselves for rigorous fidelity to the Law. "For the Pharisee," H. Ringgren (1987, p. 383) writes, "the fundamental element is the interpretation and the rigorous observance of the Law, and the separation from the 'sinners' (that is the non-Jewish and the Jewish who do not practice). What distinguishes Pharisaism is the scrupulous observance of the prescriptions."

The Pharisees considered themselves the real Israel and defended the Law as the most precious inheritance that Jahvéh gave to his people. They observed the prescriptions of the Law (the sacred times, the ritual purification, the tithe) with the most scrupulous accuracy. They presented their casuistric explanations of the Law as if they were obligatory and they thought that God had foreseen in the Law every future reality: the resurrection of the dead, for instance. The foreign occupation of Palestine had menaced the cultural and religious identity of the people of Israel and had reinforced the radical components who translated the Law into strict ideology.

We can therefore put forward the assumption that we find fundamentalism when a religious tradition is translated into a group of postulates which are to be accepted absolutely, without interpretative mediation. The examples are manifold. For example, it could be argued that Protestantism per se, by reducing the tradition to the *Sola Scriptura*, is a type of fundamentalism.

It is worth considering the crisis which fell on the Russian Orthodox Church during the seventeenth century from the movement called *Raskol*. This movement exploded because of a new revision of the liturgic books by the Moscow Patriarchy (after a century had passed since the failure of a previous try). The reforms addressed matters such as the number of fingers to use in making the sign of the cross, or the number of alleluias to sing during the religious ceremonies, or the itinerary of the procession, or the right to be allowed to wear a long beard or not. These church events took place in the context of initiatives toward modernization of the state in Western terms. These initiatives also reached the Church; they had also touched on some liturgic traditions and found supporters in the hierarchy, presenting a newly emerging risk of occidentalization and the loss of the Ortho- dox tradition. *Raskol* was inflexible in supporting the thesis that the reform was due the Anti-Christ and it represented the last apostasy—mankind was close to the end of the world. This feeling permeated the whole religious thought of the Old- Believers and all of the different factions loyal to *Raskol*. Fundamentalism can then take, in its extreme forms, an apocalyptic hue.

SOME CONCLUSIONS

The analysis presented in this paper proposes that the distinctive aspects of two sets of phenomena so different as the syncretisms and the fundamentalisms, nev- ertheless incorporate a profound mutual tension which shares, at least in part, the same origins and motivations. When a religious tradition passes from a system of monoculture to a pluralistic system, the passage does not happen without suffer- ing or without social consequences. The social choice of syncretism versus funda- mentalism is dependent on the historical, theological, and anthropological condi- tions associated with the cultural incursion. Concretely, an example is the cultural incursion of moving from separateness to the more or less compulsory living side- by-side with strangers.

We can state, in general, that in the developments of syncretic type the process occurs without a voluntary engagement by at least one of the traditions which came together. Instead, we might find the corporate will of one society overpow- ering another society. Syncretisms imply local, national, and ethnic traditions coming in contact with religions of the Book whose power of penetration depends on the Book itself. The contact starts a universal tension situated on an institutional base composed of professionals in charge of the diffusion of the Message. The Book arrives in concert with the objective conditions of power which support the religions of the Book (the monotheisms). This has been the historical and cultural situation in the mission countries where the preaching of the Message was based on the dynamics of the colonial expansion (and on its bureaucratic apparatus).

One manifestation of this process is seen in those countries in Central and South America where there were already ethnic traditions which met yet other traditions brought by the slaves imported from Africa, but where the religious and political hegemony continued, since the time of the conquest, in the hands of the Catholic whites and their descendants.

As a result the slaves and their descendants have been obliged to adapt them- selves to a Christian environment. In order to preserve their prior religion, they had to put some Catholic masks on the faces of their divinities. They gave to their *Orix* some names of saints, but behind those masks, is the *Orix* who is still worshiped (Bastide 1971, p. 267). The syncretism has been facilitated by strong inequalities between the levels of theological complexity of the component traditions. The resulting amalgamated theology reflects the situation of the marginalized in the course of assimilation. It also expresses a mysterious alchemy of reinterpretation of the Catholic values into pagan values or of pagan values into Christian. In contrast, reflections such as Bastide's cannot be valid about the Christian presence in India where, despite the centuries-old British colonial domination, the syncretisms happened as completely marginal phenomena, while the possibilities of meeting between Christianity and Hinduism have been the interest mainly of a small elite of intellectuals, such as M. Gandhi, Aurobindo, or R. Pannikar.

Religious fundamentalism, as a refusal of any and every dialogue with other religions and an aim at conflict even unto violence, comes from the conviction of holding exclusive truth which was literally written in the Book. In general fundamentalism flowers when a group feels its cultural, religious, and territorial identity threatened. It represents one of the possible results of the clash between a future imagined full of dangers (not written, but sometimes announced in a symbolic or cryptic way by the Book) and the past which would be guaranteed once for all by faithfulness to the letter of the Book.

If there is not a Book, fundamentalisms are infrequent. Here reside the deep, and not only religious, roots of the conflict between Arabian and Jewish people in the Middle East. The Books of each serve as a symbolic bully pulpit either for defending the rights of existence of the "besieged" state of Israel, or the rights of the Koranic traditions against "besieging" modernity.

In Western societies there is a Christian nebula of new movements —Neo-Catechumenals, Charismatics, Pentecostals, and so on, and non-Christian movements, such as Jehovah's Witnesses, which, beyond their differences, present a centripetal and fundamentalistic ideology everywhere showing the same pattern of discourse: *We are the center; our knowledge is privileged. Salvation comes only from our Revelation and Book.*

Weberian disenchantment was once interpreted as the necessary path of history and the ideological source of modernity. But it left without answer the central question of meaning, now raised on the one hand by religious realities whose structure is, so to speak, "esperantist," and on the other hand by movements aiming to put history on the obligatory track of Tradition as testified to and fixed by a revealed Book.

Fundamentalisms aim to transform the world into a field of battle (sometimes gory—see Algeria) between opposite views of truth. They claim to be the keepers of an absolute knowledge, and stand against every form of religious dialogue and cultural pluralism; to a certain degree, they do not like modern democracy.

Fundamentalisms—or "radicalisms" as some scholars think they should be called (Guolo 1994) can be found in past civilizations, but they also appear to be one of the defining religious aspects of modernity. Paradoxically, they also seem to be one of the antimodern results of modernity. We can say that fundamentalisms are, so to speak, the *boomerangs* of modernity.

NOTE

1. E. Cerulli in *I Water Carriers nove anni dopo* (*Religioni e civiltà*, vol. I, 1972, Dedalo, Bari, p. 69–124) observes that in the African Independent Churches every eschatological tension has disappeared. Despite the claim that prophet Harris received his inspiration directly from the Holy Spirit, his innovations occurred almost always in the traditional and African sense. In other words the birth and the affirmation of the African Independent Churches has marked a process of "ethnicization" of the Christian message under the pressure of the more or less successful tries to make the ancestral religion live again.

REFERENCES

Bastide, R. 1967. *Les Ameriques noires* (*The Black Americas*). Paris: Payot. (Ital. transl. 1970. *Le Americhe nere*. Firenze: Sansoni).

Bastide, R. 1970. *Le prochain et le lointain* (*The Neighbour and the Far*). Paris: Éditions Cujas. (Ital. transl. 1971. *Noi e gli altri*. Milano: Jaca Book).

Boaji Idowu, E. 1968. "The predicament of the Church in Africa," in Baëta, C. G. (ed.), *Christianity in tropical Africa*. Oxford.

de Certeau, M. 1975. *L'écriture de l'histoire* (*The writing of the History*). Paris: Payot. (Ital. transl. 1977. *La scrittura della storia*. Roma: Il Pensiero Scientifico).

Dumézil, G. 1955. *Jupiter, Mars, Quirinus*. Paris: Gallimard (Ital. transl. 1955. *Jupiter, Mars, Quirinus*. Torino: Einaudi).

Duviols, P. 1971. *La lutte contre les religions authoctones dans le Pérou colonial. L'extirpation de l'idolatrie entre 1532 et 1660* (*The struggle against the autochthonous religions in the colonial Peru. The extirpation of the idolatry since 1532 until 1660*). Lima: Institut d'Études Andines.

Guolo, R. 1994. *Il partito di Dio. L'Islam radicale contro l'Occidente* (*The party of God.The radical Islam against the Western countries*). Milano: Guerini & Associati.

Hervieu-Léger, D. 1993 *La religion pour mémoire* (*Religion and memory*). Paris: Éditions du Cerf. (Ital. transl. 1996. *Religione e memoria*. Bologna: Il Mulino).

Otto, R. 1923. *The Idea of the Holy*. Oxford: Oxford University Press.

Pettazzoni, R. 1968. "Il metodo comparativo. (The comparative method). In *Religione e società* (*Religion and Society*) pp. 99–113. Bologna: Ponte Nuovo.

Ringgren, H. 1963. *Israelitsche Religion* (*Jewish Religion*). Stuggart: Verlag W. Kohlammer. (Ital. transl. 1987. *Israele. I padri, l'epoca dei re, il giudaismo*. Milano: Jaca Book).

Widengren, G. 1969. *Religionsphänomenologie* (*Phenomenology of Religion*). Berlin: Walter de Gruyter & C. (Ital. transl. 1984. *Fenomenologia della religione*. Bologna: EDB).

ISSUES IN THE RECONSTRUCTION OF AFRICAN THEOLOGY

AFRICAN HERMENEUTICS AS KEY TO UNDERSTANDING THE DYNAMICS OF AFRICAN THEOLOGY

Cornel du Toit

ABSTRACT

This paper reflects on the process of reformulating African religion in a postcolonial and postmissionary environment with special reference to the postapartheid context in South Africa. Special attention is given to hermeneutic problems in this regard. The distinctive nature of African theology (taking the oral tradition into account) is indicated. African theology is seen as the contextual formulation of African religious experience by taking both African traditional religion and Christianity as sources, and without simply reverting to indigenization, eclecticism, or syncretism. African theologians have today become more confident about what one might call African Christianity. This means following a hermeneutic demanded by the African text, which is much broader than a certain phase in Western Biblical hermeneutics. African hermeneutics is a contextual hermeneutics, aware of the

Research in the Social Scientific Study of Religion, Volume 11, pages 37-64.
ISBN: 0-7623-0656-4

legacy of colonialism, the history of African oppression and exploitation, but determined to recover African identity and formulate a theology which takes cognizance
of African culture and African traditional religions. It is proposed that African symbolism must replace the cultural presuppositions of Western Christianity, namely
logos and *ratio*. The God of missionary preaching was a distant God, foreign to the
history of the colonized peoples. Exploited and oppressed, they found it difficult to
identify this God with the God of Exodus. The primary role of the Bible, and especially the Old Testament, is seen in African religious movements as supporting the
reaction and revolt of African Christians. A Western kind of individualism, typical
of modernism, is foreign to African people who hold a hermeneutic of potential or
initial trust because of shared beliefs, practices, conventions, and traditions. African
hermeneutics comes naturally in the sense that most aspects of African life are integrated into a harmonious unity. The African Initiated Churches (AICs) can be seen
as accomplishing the task of bridging Western mainline traditions and the world of
African traditional religion. Against the broader background of third world hermeneutics, black hermeneutics, liberation hermeneutics, and the distinctive hermeneutics of African theology are examined. *Third world hermeneutics* stresses the
contextual nature of hermeneutics in third world countries where theologians cannot ignore the poverty, exploitation, illiteracy, and suffering of their people. The
essay concludes with the conflicts of opinion between the so-called old-guard and
newer theologians.

INTRODUCTION

Questions abound when one takes up the topic of African hermeneutics. What is
African theology? (What is Africa?) Is it possible to speak of theology at all if one
lacks an established theology, as is the case with the African Initiated Churches
(AICs) or African traditional religions (ATRs)? What is the nature of an African
theological self-understanding? These questions contribute to African hermeneutics. This paper will concentrate on the phenomenon of African hermeneutics as a
key to understanding the present dynamics of African theology.

The three important religions in Africa are Islam, Christianity, and the African
traditional religions. These religions could again be subdivided into a multiplicity
of groups and traditions. One could also consider the theologies of Afro-Americans and the liberation theologies from the third world, since their hermeneutics
have exerted an important influence on African hermeneutics. One could also try
to give a formal description of the history and theologies of different African religions, which would not necessarily be responsive to the issue of hermeneutics.
One might also try to find common hermeneutic themes like colonialism, oppression, and poverty, with which to describe these religions. These may all be very
important hermeneutic keys, as consideration of the question of poverty, for
example, shows. Perceptions of God, religious experience, self-esteem,
world-view, and the like are all vitally influenced by one's basic living conditions.

It would seem sacrilegious to expect uncritical adoption of a Western hermeneutic consciousness by peoples lacking the basic means of existence.

Looking within the African Christian tradition one has to reckon with different cultures. There are the histories of the so-called mission churches and the establishment of black "main-line" churches. Or one could concentrate on those churches that have enculturated Christianity and given it a specific African identity (like the African Initiated Churches). However, one has to bear in mind the influence the African traditional religions have exerted on AICs, and their continuing importance for African theologians writing from a postcolonial perspective.

Hermeneutics is the science of interpretation and gets its name from the Greek myth of Hermes, the winged messenger of Mount Olympus, whose job it was to interpret (Greek: *hermeneuein*) the sayings of the Oracle at Delphi. But how are African "oracles" interpreted and by whom? How are African messages conveyed and received by the African people? The voices of the ancestors, mediating the will of the gods, have been muffled for many years, overwhelmed by the many voices of missionaries proclaiming the one and only way to the one and only truth. Until recently this missionary truth was accepted in Africa, with all the delights and burdens it brought. After many years of servitude and struggle, however, this yoke has been lifted and Africa is taking stock of its gods. The single truth proclaimed in Africa divides into many different church denominations and traditions, each claiming to have the correct interpretation, the best hermeneutics, the best messengers of God. One can imagine Africa's current scepticism about the claims of Western hermeneutics.

From the very beginning in Africa the Christian fundamentalist hermeneutic tradition was inclined to find a single spiritual truth within a particular Biblical passage. We do know, however, that most texts allow for numerous interpretations, and that to accept one single truth is almost invariably a sad reduction of reality. Western biblical hermeneutics cannot be understood apart from its preoccupation with the book of the Bible, seen as the final revealed truth of God. Anyone claiming to represent the one and only interpretation of this truth could also, on this higher biblical authority, expect acceptance of his or her interpretation. But this situation has changed with current developments in hermeneutics and with our new insights into the nature of understanding.

When one reads present-day African theologies it soon becomes clear that African hermeneutics is of a very specific kind and includes the African world-view and culture, its histories, and religions. African hermeneutics considers the Bible and African traditional religions as sources of equal importance. In the past little serious attention was given by African theologians to the problem of Biblical hermeneutics. Fasholé–Luke (quoted in Parratt 1983, p. 91) indicates that historically the missionary penetration of much of Africa was done by male Europeans with a fundamentalist view of the Bible, and until fairly recently this heritage has tended to circumscribe biblical studies on the African continent.

Even in the Western world hermeneutics has shown truth to be open, dynamic, and subject to reinterpretation and recontextualization. The so-called hermeneutical circle shows the interpretative process as an involvement in examining a certain text or event through a systematic investigation of the general and the particular, the results of which, in turn, are related to what is already known by the interpreter. This process continues in a circle, moving from one subprocess to another, until the interpreter is convinced of a satisfactory interpretation. But the process is never-ending. Understanding, the interpretation of texts, and the search for truth are continuing and open-ended processes. This implies that any final meaning keeps evading us. Our existence remains a mystery. We keep on trying to explain this mystery to which the multiplicity of texts and interpretations bear proof. No final hermeneutical method is possible. The dream of developing an ontology hermeneutics is not only impossible but contradicts the open-endedness of human nature (Ricoeur 1974, p. 23).

But what is the case in Africa? What is the relationship between African and Western hermeneutics, if one can speak of such a relationship at all? Do Africa and the West meet perhaps in the same way as the premodern and postmodern meet? Thornton (1996, pp. 144–145) considers the South Africa condition is more postmodern than it is postcolonial. In contemporary South Africa there are literally no names, no vocabulary, to discuss major aspects and parts of its political situation. There is no agreement on what are the boundaries of "black" or "white." No one knows whether to refer to "tribes," "ethnic groups," "language groups," "peoples," or "races."

Parratt (1983, p. 92) urges African theologians to take the problem of a genuine biblical hermeneutics seriously, as a preparatory stage of African theology, and argues that a good deal that passes under the name of African theology is inadequate because it lacks a solid foundation in biblical exegesis. This does not mean that African scholars should simply quote European scholars as authorities. He enthusiastically quotes D. N. Wambudta, who stresses the need for African theologians to return to the original biblical languages, but who warns against interpreting the Bible too easily in the light of African religions, rather than according to its own canons (Parratt 1983, p. 92).

The demand to give up dependency on European authorities has led to a counterreaction by many African theologians who concentrate exclusively on African religions as their source, and discard the Bible altogether. African theologians have today become more confident about what Maluleke (1996, p. 4) calls African Christianity. This means following a hermeneutic demanded by the African text, which is much broader than a certain phase in Western Biblical hermeneutics. Parratt displays an insensitivity to the nature of African culture and the hermeneutics he proposes is still solidly embedded in the Western world-view, culture and literary theory, epistemology, view on the nature of truth, and so on, which in turn have all changed since the time Parratt wrote his article.

The time has passed in which Western hermeneutics/theology is normative. Furthermore, in many instances the Western theologians are looking at African religiosity with renewed interest. It is not a duplication of Western Christianity, it has a deep spiritual strength, it operates within an oral culture, it is free from Western metaphysical constraints, and it renders important critiques on Western culture, science, and technology. It offers an alternative to Western forms of doing theology, succeeding in relating in interesting ways traditional religious ideas to those ideas brought into Africa. Faith in the West has lost its innocence and is seen as an ever-interpreting faith seeking a second naiveté (Thiselton 1992, p. 348). Although Africa is critical of Western interests in its affairs, it can offer Westerners this religious innocence which is still intact in African communities. Individualism, which is typical of modernism, is foreign to the African peoples, who hold a hermeneutics of potential or initial trust because of shared beliefs, practices, conventions, and traditions.

Hermeneutics is neither a Western nor a scholarly prerogative. All people practice hermeneutics since they communicate every day and are challenged to understand correctly, to relate conflicting ideas and to re-express their ideas when initially misunderstood. People practice hermeneutics when listening to the radio, when reading a paper, when talking politics, or when participating in gossip! This hermeneutical activity can be cultivated to become an art, enabling us to understand and speak more carefully. Although hermeneutics may be studied by a minister of religion or a theologian, the process actually belongs to the community. In African context, hermeneutics is the *indaba* of the community. It means listening to the sage and asking him or her critical questions. It means challenging the system that we may have become accustomed to—especially if we find it oppressive or outdated. It means re-listening to the stories of our fathers in order to explain difficult present-day problems, and telling our own stories in the present. We relate to stories since they embody our understanding of ourselves, our fears, and hopes. Through stories, as through texts, we reinterpret and renew our existence. Existential issues have always been very much part of African self-understanding and hermeneutics.

Although people see and interpret things differently, there are always good reasons why they understand as they do. Hermeneutics helps us to understand why people differ in their understandings. It shows the power strategies people use to get their point accepted. It also helps us to come to agreement. The task of hermeneutics is not to undermine creative and individual approaches to understanding (and so create a one-dimensional way of seeing things), but to make us aware of our specific *culture of understanding,* of possible logical mistakes in the process of interpreting, and of possible power strategies underlying our style of interpretation. It also helps us to understand ourselves and others and to recognize the influence of culture, religion, preunderstanding, and many other factors codetermining the dynamic understanding process.

Hermeneutics concerns our *world-view*—that is, the way we try to find meaning in our lives and world. It concerns our understanding of God and humans, our relationship with the past and the ancestors, and how these affect us today. It concerns our present difficulties in our families and communities, our suffering ,and hardships. It also concerns our understanding of the future and how we will act to influence it. Hermeneutics concerns the language we speak, how we express ourselves, and understand the expression of others (communication); it concerns our customs and belief systems, and how they influence our views, and other aspects of our lives.

THIRD WORLD HERMENEUTICS AS BLACK, LIBERATION, AND AFRICAN HERMENEUTICS

To place African hermeneutics one must remember the wider context of so-called *third world hermeneutics* within which it has developed. The term *third world hermeneutics* stresses the specific context of hermeneutics in the third world countries. Theologians in third world countries could not ignore the poverty, exploitation, illiteracy, and suffering of the people of these countries. For them, theological hermeneutics meant first and foremost to understand and interpret the situation in which they found themselves. To read a text is to read life through the lens of the text. The hermeneutical process moves from life to text and from text to life. In this bidirectional movement texts question our lives, and our existential experiences are also brought against the text. We not only understand and interpret ourselves and our world in a certain manner, we are also affected and changed by the texts we allow into our lives. This is especially the case in third world hermeneutics.

Third world hermeneutics implies that there is also a first—and perhaps a second—*world hermeneutics*, from which it differs. Third world countries have often found the gods and the guns, the texts, and the truths of the oppressors to be quite intimidating and difficult to disagree with. *Third world hermeneutics* alleges that to understand a text, text and reader must meet on the same level. Texts want to convince, inspire, teach, change, and influence the reader. In communicating with another I also want to convince, influence and the like. I cannot, however, meet a text like another person. Texts tend to have the last say—as they are written and therefore fixed. But my dialogue with the text becomes but another text. Therefore, the world of texts is actually not fixed and autonomous but open. This becomes clear in the inter-text (the influence of other texts in a specific text) in which texts are always in communication with each other.

When text and reader meet each other as free entities, without the purpose of each simply overpowering the other, then free discourse, critical questioning, and creative interaction become possible. *Third world hermeneutics* refuses to meet any text like a victim approaching its oppressor. It is a hermeneutic which challenges and reinterprets the text. The text is to serve life. *Third world herme-neutics* recognizes that texts are brought to us by text-bearers and that these text-bearers often structure the text-receiver relationship through the way they read, interpret, explain, and preach these texts. Often, hermeneutics and the art of politics are not clearly distinguished.

Third world hermeneutics refers to the way countries with a background of colonialism, exploitation, and a missionary history try to understand what has happened to them. An example is the book by R. S. Sugirtharajah *Voices from the Margin, Interpreting the Bible in the Third World*, which looks at Africa, Latin America, India, and Indonesia, among others. *Third world hermeneutics* develops from the perspective of colonialism, poverty, underdevelopment, economic exploitation, and cultural victimization. The third world is, however, such a large and complex concept that one has to distinguish different contexts and histories. And yet, for our present purposes, to narrow *Third world hermeneutics* down to Africa does not simplify the task. Hermeneutics in Africa cannot be separated from black theology in the Americas or in Africa, because of the ongoing reciprocal influence between these continents.

Although African hermeneutics overlaps with Latin American hermeneutics, and black hermeneutics, there are also specific distinctions to be made. It is, how-ever, inevitable that this paper will refer to and deal with the whole concept of hermeneutics in the liberation context. I will try not to overlap too much with what has already been said.

Black hermeneutics refers, according to Thiselton (1992, pp. 419–420), to three distinct contexts: (1) black theology in South Africa focused on issues pertaining to colonial history and apartheid; (2) North American black theology finding its distinctive expression in the historical memory of slavery and its aftermath; (3) African hermeneutics in Africa mainly concerned with *contextualization* and the relation between the Bible and African cultures. Although the black theology of one North American, James Cone, has especially influenced black theology in South Africa, Cone's context and approach are different from this present under-taking. Thiselton (1992, p. 423) has correctly indicated that it is tempting but sim-plistic to suggest that African hermeneutics stresses contextualization, where Latin Americans speak of praxis, and North American black theology speaks of black experience. All these movements stress experience and struggle as *contexts* of hermeneutics.

Black theology in South Africa, although it took its example from Afro-Amer-ican forerunners, has predominantly been a truly South African phenomenon, pro-moted by people like Basil Moore, Manas Buthelezi, Steve Biko, Allan Boesak, Frank Chikane, Desmond Tutu, Mokgeti Mothlabi, and many others. The emer-gence of this phenomenon has involved many struggles. Many African theolo-gians have felt that black theology has put too much emphasis on political and economic liberation at the expense of the spiritual component. Black theologians have been equally critical of African theology, feeling that they encouraged a cheap alliance between African culture and Christ. In the apartheid era it was felt that promoting the uniqueness of African theology might promote the idea of apartheid. It was also feared that some indigenous church groups might concentrate on Africanization to the detriment of the liberation struggle.

A reconciliation between black theology and African theology came about in 1977 in Accra, Ghana, with the Pan-African Conference of Third World Theologians, when James Cone indicated that they were not as different as had previously been suggested (Schoffeleers 1988, pp. 109–110).

Developments in Afro-American and liberation hermeneutics influence African hermeneutics, and vice versa. Africa remains, however, only one elliptic point for Afro-American hermeneutics, the other being the Afro-Americans' own history and experience of enslavement. It is, however, not limited to these issues. Afro-American hermeneutics is also concerned about its place in a post-Christian, postmodern, pluralistic, and global context (Coleman 1993, p. 69). According to Coleman (1993, p. 71), black theology in America developed as a conscious discipline in the mid-1960s, and entered a second phase between 1970 and 1975, when African-American theologians took their case to Euro-American colleges and seminaries. A third phase focused on global issues affecting blacks, and they have now embarked upon the fourth phase encompassing the utilization of indigenous resources in concert with interdisciplinary strategies in their theological discourse. This specifically includes researching the religious past of African people for expressions of faith that may be translated into the present. While they concentrated in the 1970s and 1980s on Marxist social analysis, they are now concentrating on developing interdisciplinary skills to examine and appropriate multilayered discourses within the cultural history, by examining what Coleman (1993, p. 75–76) calls "tribal talk." This process is mediated through African hermeneutics, exploring African folklore, traditions, and practices.

In the present quest within Africa for recovering African identity and redefining African theology, one cannot ignore the important influence of Afro-Americans on African theologians. It would, however, be destructive to the development of African theology if its agenda were to be determined by Afro-American issues, just as would be the case with Eurocentric issues. The social contexts of Afro-Americans and their ensuing hermeneutics, in trying to link their Christian and African roots, are quite dissimilar from those of Africa. This is not to say that mutual exchange cannot be productive, as the case of black theology has shown.

African hermeneutics per se is predominantly concerned with ways to reconstruct African theology independently from *all* Western theological influences. It is the effort to understand and interpret the religious significance of African culture and to determine the theological character of African traditional religions. Present-day African theologians are aware of the pressures imposed on African hermeneutics during the liberation period, but do not focus exclusively on it. They concentrate on the anticolonial struggle and on postcolonial reconstruction, trying to find what is typical of Africa and searching for an African intellectual self-definition. The quest for an African hermeneutics testifies to the need for thinking autonomously and creatively in a context of political threat, economic need, and the ongoing presence of Western influences.

This essay tries to come to grips with developments during the last two decades, during which African theologians have started to make a decisive effort to recover what is most typical of African theology. There are several ways in which this is done. My current concern is not with those thinkers who wanted to recover African religions without taking notice of the influence of Christianity, but with those who took the total African religious reality as their point of departure. Thinkers like J. B. Sanquah and Okot p'Bitek prepared the way by concentrating on what African traditional religions are all about (see Awolalu 1991, pp. 129–131).

African hermeneutics obviously cannot refer to a single approach in interpreting and understanding African religions. There are also different degrees to which theologians accept the world-view, ideas, and practices of African traditional religions. African theology cannot be practiced in isolation, nor by ignoring the very formidable presence of Christianity in Africa. It is easier to agree on commonalities like the influence of colonialism, the impact missionary work had on Africa, the common struggle against poverty, illiteracy, underdevelopment, and so on, than to agree precisely on how to integrate African traditional religions into an African theology.

Many African theologians are very critical of those who endeavor to synthesize African traditional religions with any other religious tradition. Onunwa (1991, pp. 120–121) for example, refers to the debates, conferences, and polemics of the mid-1950s and early 1960s on "indigenization," "Africanization," "Theologia Africana" or "Black Theology," which were concerned with practical methods of making Christianity an authentic "African Religion," using some elements of the traditional religions, in order to make Christianity relevant to the traditional situation. Christianity had to be interpreted in the context of traditional religious experience, language, and culture. For Onunwa this means that subscribing to the idea of Christianity being superior to the traditional religions, despite efforts to show the traditional religions as a people's search for ultimate meaning. For theologians like Onunwa, it is simply not acceptable when Christians, or any other interest group, use African traditional religions as a means to their own end.

THE DISTINCTIVENESS OF AFRICAN HERMENEUTICS

It is unwise to restrict African hermeneutics to any specific characteristic. Yet, a more precise delineation may become possible as this hermeneutics develops and is studied. It includes the reactionary and sociocritical. For the purpose of this contribution I shall define African hermeneutics as the effort to rid Africa of the unacceptable legacy of colonialism, to recover African traditional ideas, and to indicate how this is as important a source as the Bible in providing Africans with their specific spirituality.

Hermeneutics Without a Book but Not Without a Text:
The African Way of Reading Life

The text that African hermeneutics tries to understand is much wider than the Biblical text, or Western-oriented theology, since it includes the African world as text. As Awolalu (1991, p.131) puts it, "African traditional religion has no written scriptures or records, yet we can say that it is written everywhere for those who have eyes to see." Religion permeates every aspect of people's lives and can be found in their riddles and proverbs, songs and dancing, rites and ceremonies, myths and folk-tales, shrines and sacred places, and in their artistic designs.

African hermeneutics is a contextual hermeneutics, aware of the legacy of colonialism, the history of African oppression and exploitation, but determined to recover African identity and formulate a theology which takes cognizance of African culture and African traditional religions. African hermeneutics is an understanding of Africa by Africans, for Africans. John Pobee (1996, p. 54) quoted Ela in this regard, saying that one of the primary tasks of Christian reflection in black Africa is to reformulate our basic faith through the mediation of African culture. African symbolism must replace the cultural presuppositions of Western Christianity, namely *logos* and *ratio*.

In the postcolonial era African hermeneutics has seemed to be more concerned with Africanization than with liberation, although the latter is not excluded. For Pobee (1996, p. 57) African theology must restore the identity and ethos of *homo africanus*. But there is resistance to this approach, which is seen by Muthukya (quoted by Pobee 1996, p. 56) as the heathenization of the church.

> This is what they mean by African Christianity. No mention of the one and only saving Gospel of Our Lord Jesus Christ. No mention of sin. No place for the authority of an inspired Bible. Instead their arguments are based on the traditional background of the African people, their culture, customs, and belief. If natural culture and religious customs are acceptable to God, why did Christ send his disciples to preach the Gospel to every creature in the uttermost part of the earth?

African hermeneutics is a hermeneutics without a book but not without a text— the text is of African suffering and dependence. The Bible (book) is read with this text in mind. As Ela (1991, p. 259) puts it:

> The colonized peoples never had a complete view of Christianity exactly because they were restricted to the "book" without the "text." Bereft of a historical, critical sensitivity that would relate the salvation message to a particular context of colonial domination, the missionary church kept Africans in line with taboos and sanctions instead of launching them into the historical adventure of liberation—where, precisely, the living God is revealed.

African hermeneutics *differs* from hermeneutics in the West, but not because rules determining understanding in one context are not valid in another. It is a question of different emphases, a different language and culture, a different self-understanding and world view. Hermeneutics depends on the specific concept of truth one has, the emphasis placed on the written or the spoken word, the way people integrate theory and practice, one's critical aptitude, and so on.

Onwu (1985, pp. 146–150) has already stressed the problems of language and world-view as specific problems of African hermeneutics. Many biblical concepts simply do not exist in African culture, or have a totally different meaning. This especially concerns the personality of Christ, who can be labeled within the African world-view as Black Christ, African Chief, Elder Brother, Great Ancestor. While we know that the African world-view easily assimilates the Old Testament world-view, the Bible was brought to Africa framed in a Western world-view. Onwu (1985, p. 150–153) mentions the fact that, by the time Christianity was introduced into sub-Saharan Africa in the mid-nineteenth century, the world-view of the Christian theologians was only reminiscent of the biblical one. Under the influence of the Enlightenment they had already outgrown the Biblical (as well as African) world-view. They could hardly still make sense of the biblical references to demon possession, and to angels and spiritual forces operating in the affairs of human beings. These, however, fitted perfectly well within African cosmology, which believed that spiritual forces, both evil and good, operated in the world—a world of charms and amulets, sacrifices, ancestral worship, witches, and wizards.

Protest Hermeneutics

Theological hermeneutics would be sterile if it ignored the physical constraints influencing people's experience. African hermeneutics can be typified as a hermeneutics of protest against factors crippling the African peoples. African hermeneutics is a reactionary hermeneutics, trying to come to grips with postcolonial Africa. Part of this postcolonial process concerns the effort to understand and deal with the impact of a postmissionary era. For Ela (1991, p. 257) the God of missionary preaching was a distant God, foreign to the history of the colonized peoples. Exploited and oppressed, they found it difficult to identify this missionary God with the God of Exodus. The primary role of the Bible, and especially the Old Testament, in current African religious movements is to express the reaction and revolt of African Christians.

Hermeneutics of Sociocritical Theory

According to Thiselton (1992, p. 379) sociocritical hermeneutics can be defined as an approach to texts, traditions, and institutions which seeks to penetrate beneath their apparent function to expose their role as instruments of power, domination, and social manipulation. The goal underlying this kind of hermeneutics is to achieve the liberation of those over whom power or social manipulation is exercised. Sociocritical theory provides the theoretical framework for liberation hermeneutics, which includes on a metacritical level African and black hermeneutics.

Sociocritical hermeneutics becomes imperative in a context of oppression where texts, and especially religious texts, are subservient to the existing dominant ideologies. Radical critique of knowledge, for Habermas, is only possible as social theory (Thiselton 1992, pp. 282–283). Hermeneutical understanding as social critique must test traditions in relation to their embodiment of social forces and epistemological distortions.

The real challenge for Africa is the ongoing development of an African hermeneutics and an African religion in which the reinterpretation and critical accommodation of African Christianity, African traditional religions, and other factors of importance, will be determinative of a future theological profile. This may prove to be much more important to African identity than the more global liberation theology was. This process cannot, however, be artificially constructed by any group of theologians with specific blueprints in mind. Instead, one can expect this process to develop spontaneously, unflanked by developments within the African Initiated Churches. These developments may be similar to religious developments all over the world where one finds the accommodation of a multiplicity of religious styles existing in juxtaposition.

For Itumeleng Mosala only a materialist reading of biblical texts, which takes up the conflicting social and political forces and interests, can constitute a genuinely sociocritical hermeneutic (see Thiselton 1992, p. 425). In Mosala's own words (1989, p. 5–6)

> The notion that the Bible is simply the revealed "Word of God" is an example of an exegetical framework that is rooted in an idealist epistemology. I criticize that position in this study because it leads to a false notion of the Bible as nonideological, which can cause political paralysis in the oppressed people who read it.

However, Thiselton (1992, p. 429) rightly warns against the danger that any selective use of texts to encourage the oppressed in the end mirrors the strategy of the hermeneutical method of the oppressors, who use texts to reenforce and reaffirm their corporate identity and interests.

Can the Bible be the *neutral* Word of God?

There is a close relationship between the biblical world and that of traditional Africa. Parratt (1983, p. 90) has remarked that the world of traditional Africa, like that of the Gospels, is one in which supernatural powers impinge on the human world in every respect, since every aspect of life is subject to spiritual powers. The biblical references to demon possession, the healings and miracles performed by

Jesus and the apostles, fit perfectly well into the African world-view. However this is true not only of the apocalyptic background of the New Testament. It is the AICs, in particular, who have shown a considerable preference for the Old Testament. This can be ascribed to many factors, especially the similarities in world-view, the Exodus tradition, the emphasis on the poor, and the fact that the Old Testament deals with so many aspects of life, like the social, agricultural, family, and ritual aspects, all important to African religion (Parratt 1983, p. 91).

Special reflection should be given to the question of whether the Bible can be the neutral word of God. Uka (1991, p. 153ff) challenges the idea that African theology has to be rooted in the Bible as well as the idea that there cannot be a valid theology of African traditional religions. African theology is not theology if it is Christian theology or imported theology. He is also critical of the way in which African theologians in the past simply interpreted Christianity in African terms. This sentiment is underscored by Maluleke (1996, p. 6) when he discusses Bediako, who said that the Christianization of the pre-Christian tradition of Africa could be seen as one of the most important achievements of African theology. Africanization, however, should not be confused with indigenization, which has already been achieved by the African Initiated Churches. What is at stake is the intellectual question of how African Christianity, employing Christian tools, can set about mending the torn fabric of African identity and hopefully point the way to a fuller and unfettered African humanity and personality. For Uka (1991, p. 154) African theology is the theology of African traditional or indigenous religions—not the African theology that tries to solve the problems of indigenization of a new and foreign religion. African traditional religions must be freed from those Western concepts which have for a long time restricted and imprisoned them. It remains, however, to be seen how Uka will employ "Christian tools" to mend African identity.

In this connection a debate is raging concerning the equation of the Bible with the Word of God. For Maluleke (1996, p. 12) the equation of the Bible with the "Word of God" is not only naive, but a dangerous form of naivete. He sees this equation as being debilitating for black and African theologies and as much more harmful than the equation of colonialism with Christianity, or of the African past with Christianity. The reason is that this equation has been used to legitimate the demonization of African traditional culture and religions. The point is that the equation of the Bible with the Word of God implies that it is possible to appropriate the Bible without an ideology. For Maluleke (1996, p. 11) the equation of the Bible with the Word of God has been the most consistent tool used by those questioning the validity of both African Christianity and African theology.

It is African theology's reference to African traditional religions and black theology's reference to liberation that has caused both to be dismissed on the basis of lack of Biblical grounding. This dispute is fundamental in determining the nature of African hermeneutics. From an African point of view, this exclusive stance has caused divided loyalties since Africans have had to deny the importance and appeal that their very own traditions and customs have had and still do have for them. From a Western point of view this stance has offered the opportunity to impose Western ethics, world-view, and theology on Africa. Although there is a case to be made that the Bible is often intolerant, Western hermeneutics itself had to relativize this to accommodate the multiplicity of diverging truth claims from its own traditions.

There is, however, more to the issue. What then is the status of the Bible in Africa if it is not to be seen as the Word of God? This is once again the peculiar character of African thought. It does consider the Bible the Word of God, but not so as to exclude many ideas, customs, and rites from African culture and tradi- tional religion. Africa knows the secret of accommodating (not indigenizing) divergent ideas. In a holistic manner all things are integrated. African thought does not operate on the level of Western metaphysics, where a substantial ontol- ogy determines the detached nature of things as they exist in and for themselves. One has to differ from the oft-quoted remark by Leopold Senghor that reason is Hellenist and emotion is Negroid[1] (see Serequeberhan 1994, p. 6). Elsewhere Serequeberhan (1994, p. 45) quotes Senghor as follows:

> White reason is analytic through utilization: Negro reason is intuitive through participation. European is empiric, the African mystic. The European takes pleasure in recognizing the world through the reproduction of the object...the African from knowing it vitally he feels that he feels, he feels his *existence*, he feels himself; and because he feels the Other, to be reborn in knowledge of the world.

Africa does not separate in a Cartesian manner the mind from the body, or reason from emotion, as is often done in the West. African thought is rational and emo- tional. African hermeneutics favors a relational ontology where life-giving inter- actions determine what is considered important and true. By this criterion the Bible has become important to them, but in a way that it does not exclude the simultaneous influences of past traditions.

The continued growth of African Christianity in its unique way does not depend on, or ask for, Western acknowledgment. The insistence of Western-determined norms simply invites reactionary responses as in the case of Maimela, who sug- gested that black theologians should unapologetically base their theology not even on a materialist reading of the Bible (as Mosala does), but on pragmatic and moral arguments that make sense to them (see Maluleke 1996, p. 14). For Maluleke the way out of this trap is to confront not only the Bible, but all other sources and interlocutors of theological discourse precisely at a hermeneutic level. Canaan Banana has proposed that what he calls "oppressive" texts, must be removed from the Bible and that the religious experiences of other peoples ought to be added to the Bible (see Reed 1996, pp. 282–288). It must be stated that the Bible does not belong to the West. It belongs to those who read it and live from it. But the danger is real that in reacting against the abuse of any text, the text may be identified with those misusing it.

THE INFLUENCE OF AFRICAN TRADITIONAL RELIGIONS (ATRS) AND THE AFRICAN INITIATED CHURCHES (AICS) IN CODETERMINING AFRICAN CHRISTIANITY AND THEOLOGICAL HERMENEUTICS

To understand African hermeneutics and the reason why it focuses increasingly on the ATRs, attention must be given to these religions. To determine their importance, statistical information is given below. The numbers of their adherents, however, do not seem to explain their influence sufficiently; the answer can rather be found in the quest for African identity. A watershed point concerning the importance of the ATRs was reached when theologians began to reckon them as a religion and not as pagan. African traditional religions are the mainspring for African customs, narratives, symbols, and rites, indispensable for developing an African theology and hermeneutics. The African Initiated Churches represent the group in which Christianity and African traditional religions came to be integrated in a fascinating way.

Our hermeneutic concern is with the way African theologians understand themselves, African religion, its place in the world of religions, and how they visualize (idealize) its future. The idea is not to idealize or romanticize the ATRs, but to recognize the important influence they have. Sarpong (1991, p. 289) sounds a warning note in this regard when he says that, like all other cultures, African traditional cultures contain several objectionable elements. But this is not to say that they do not or did not fulfill a social function now or in the past. A careful examination of many an African custom, no matter how repulsive it may be to modern people, will reveal that it once played—or even now plays—a meaningful role in the social life of the people.

Geographical Distribution of Adherents of African Traditional Religions in Some African Countries (Percentage Relative to the Population of Each Country)[2]

There has been a dramatic drop in percentage following the ATRs since 1900, as the selected list of statistics below shows. This is because most Africans were converted to Christianity or Islam. Trends displayed are representative of the whole of Africa. If these trends continue one would expect that the ATRs would eventually become insignificant. How is this to be understood in the light of the renewed interest in the ATRs and the fact that most prominent African theologians try to accommodate the ATRs' ideas in their work? One would perhaps be wrong to expect a revival of the ATRs, or to think that they would eventually replace African Christianity. It would perhaps also be a mistake to assume that they will eventually die out as an active religious group, as the statistical trend seems to indicate. Renewed interest and appreciation by theologians for the

Table 1. Geographical Distribution of Adherents to ATRs

Country	1900	Mid-1970	Mid-1975	Mid-1980	Projection for 2000
Botswana	102,900	347,200	362,560	390,910	491,500
% of population	85.7	56.3	52.5	49.2	34.4
Congo	526,500	79,580	76,240	73,240	75,800
% of population	97.5	6.7	5.7	4.8	2.8
Ghana	1,987,000	2,864,000	2,690,000	2,451,400	1,177,500
% of population	90.3	33.2	27.3	21.4	5.6
Lesotho	271,200	137,210	100,310	80,200	61,000
% of population	88.9	13.2	8.7	6.2	3.0
Madagascar	1,556,000	3,408,050	3,859,780	4,390,180	7,591,000
% of population	60.3	49.2	48.1	47	42.7
Malawi	714,000	1,075,200	1,059,800	1,057,400	1,049,000
% of population	95.2	24.7	21.6	19	11
Mozambique	2,504,900	4,757,300	4,832,300	4,963,700	6,197,000
% of population	96.4	57.8	52.3	47.8	35.1
Namibia	129,600	33,100	28,300	27,800	26,400
% of population	91.3	5.2	4.0	3.5	2.0
South Africa	2,793,000	3,889,210	4,189,700	4,534,400	6,519,000
% of population	57	18.1	17	15.9	13.1
Swaziland	79,200	115,700	112,360	113,490	127,260
% of population	99	28.3	24	20.9	13.5
Zimbabwe	479,800	2,469,000	2,729,500	3,034,300	4,440,000
% of population	96	46.5	43.5	40.5	29.3

Note: Data arranged by Chidi Denis Isizoh from the entries made in D.B. Barrett, ed., *World Christian Encyclopedia*, Nairobi, Kenya: Oxford University Press, 1982.

ATRs may even stimulate the ATRs' growth. Although statistics reflect a drop in percentage adherence to the ATRs, membership statistics do not reveal their influence in African life and on African theologians. One can expect that the cause of the ATRs in a democratic and postapartheid South Africa will be promoted by a renewed spirit of nationalism. One can also expect ATR ideas to become more of an academic concern as the process of urbanization speeds up. Theologians favoring ATR ideas are mostly not religiously observant in the ATR context. It is in groups like the AICs that ATR ideas come to fruition (see Schoffeleers 1988, pp. 114–119).

ATR ideas will be influential in the reformulation of African Christianity. They give access to African culture, and provide African theologians with material to develop an African Christian theology. Schoffeleers (1988, p. 103) states that African religions are essentially monotheistic and in that fundamental respect are fully in accordance with biblical revelation. He believes that Christianity can borrow suitable ideas from the ATRs and vice versa.

The Quest for African Identity

Many African theologians today have taken up the task of formulating a truly African religion, based on African traditions and influenced by the history of Christianity in Africa. This is a holistic hermeneutics which wants to read the African text in its interrelated plurality in the African world. Holism does not negate differences but accommodates them. African hermeneutics is an endeavor to understand and interpret the many paradoxes—the competing, and even opposing, elements determining African life. Although some African thinkers want to rid Africa of all foreign influences, foreign gods, and practices, this is not possible. Not only is it difficult to determine what these influences are and "extract" them from African life—the current interdependence of all countries at the economic and technological levels makes this simply impossible.

There remains, however, much to be done in regaining African identity. In precolonial times, non-Africans wondered and wrote about African religion. Africans were seen mostly as spiritually lost, wicked, and wilful sinners. African religion was negatively portrayed as ancestor-worship, animism, idolatry, fetishism, paganism, polytheism, and the like. During colonial and postcolonial times Africans writing about their religion were over-dependent on Western Christian influences. A postcolonial African hermeneutics seeks to rectify this situation by writing a theology of the people, by the people, and for the people (see Uka 1991, p. 161).

But is it possible to know exactly what African identity actually was, before colonialism, and do the majority of people want to restore this former identity? *Root searching* and *root thinking* do not impress everyone. For example, Kristeva (1993, pp. 2–3) sees the cult of origins as a hate reaction, hatred of those others who do not share my origins and who affront me personally, economically, and culturally—I then move back among "my own," I stick to an archaic, primitive, "common denominator." These are difficult questions and one realizes that the quest for African identity is a focal point of the very complex process of cultural reinterpretation. It seems that the strongest rationale behind the wish to recover African identity is the urge to rid Africa of its negative self-image, mind set of dependency, its poverty, and underdevelopment. Poverty has become a very sinister part of African identity (Pobee 1993, p. 397).

The quest for identity can often be linked to a context in which people's identity has been threatened and deformed. In the case of Africa, colonialism, and continued economic and other forms of dependence on the West can be identified as such threats. Anger has always been a consequence of the denial of identity. Africa has reason, in this regard, to be angry. Violence is seen by some as a way to freedom, as part of the struggle for a changed self-image, which takes place both among the subjugated and against the dominator (Taylor 1994, p. 65). The history of liberation struggles exemplifies this point of view.

From a Western perspective the search for African identity may be experienced as pragmatically inconvenient, and inhibiting the process of development. This is because the promotion of African culture is wrongly perceived as preventing the development of a technological society in Africa. The lack of technological advancement must be ascribed, rather, to the general underprivileged background of black communities and the lack of appropriate education from the preschool level onwards. There is a strong recognition that Africa needs development and that this goal seems to be impossible in isolation from Western aid, ideas, and involvement. But apart from this, the question is whether development—which is inconceivable without science, technology, and industry—can also be purely African. If a so-called Afrocentrism (there are many African identities) is to be promoted, it cannot be done by isolating Africa.

The recovering of African identity is often described by the metaphor of finding one's roots. Finding one's roots is determined by what one is looking for, and how one appropriates what one finds. The quest for identity is in many cases (such as in South Africa) highly politicized and cannot be carried out without dealing with the past. Although the past can never be restored, it remains important for under-standing oneself in the present. *Root thinking* can give direction to the present. There may be recognition, insight, and identification when encountering one's past. Root thinking can be stimulated, but should not be artificially forced upon communities. Africans need not excavate too deeply to find roots to affirm and appropriate.

The African world-view is naturally oriented more towards the glorious, per-fect, primordial state of the past and less to an unknown, uncertain future. The world of the ancestors is always the best, closer to the perfect origin, and it there-fore has more potency than the present or the future. The best in life lies in the past, the world of the ancestors and the origin. Anything passed down from the ancestors—such as culture, religion, and technology—must be maintained and protected and passed on to the next generation. This moral obligation to retain and continue traditions and conventions overrides the desire for change (Turaki 1991, pp. 134–135).

In contrast, the Western identity is an open identity. It excludes the idea of a fixed and stable identity and replaces it with the notion of a continuous and dynamic process of redefinition. The Western notion of identity is linked to one's mentality or attitude, which indicates the volatile nature of Western identity. This does not mean that the West has no identity or that it is not interested in identity. The very process of continuous reidentification and of relating to a multiplicity of identities emphasizes the importance of identity to the West.

Pobee considers that Africa's identity is not to be found solely in Africa. The search for African identity is not wholesale acceptance of either an African or a European oriented culture. Rather, it is an acceptance of what is good, presumably for the dignity and well-being of *homo africanus* (1993, p. 394). And there is not one African identity. This complicates the quest for African identity, especially in its ethnic and cultural nature. African identity is local and contextual, bound to issues occupying a given community's mind and influencing that community's world-view. African identity differs not only from community to community, but is quite different north and south of the Sahara (Bloch-Hoell 1992, p. 101).

There is no going back to some supposedly pristine African identity (Pobee 1993, p. 390). Pobee finds Africa's identity in its present characteristics. African identities are tied to the question of who people are, and these questions are directly linked to their relationship with God (1993, p. 392). This relationship has been inhibited by colonial attitudes. For the growth of a genuine African identity, Africa must be exorcized not only of the spirit of colonialism but also of missionary paternalism. Africa must develop authentic African theologies (1993, pp. 393, 395). Africa must find its identity in the religion typical of Africa. The development of authentic African theologies is a necessary undergirding of African identities (1993, p. 395). Pobee identifies some characteristics typical of *homo africanus* (1993, pp. 396–398): the view of the sacred and secular as one; a communitarian epistemology and ontology; a unique sense of finitude, bound up with Africa's vulnerability and high mortality rate; the experience of reality through song, dance, and ritual; and the culture of poverty (see Pasteur and Toldson 1982, p. 93).

Africa must reject all factors that render African spiritual resources impotent. This means that, to a large extent, rationalistic Western theologies and ecclesiastic initiatives must be rejected. In this matter, the difference between the spiritualities of the African Initiated Churches and that of the black mainline churches is conspicuous.

The ATRs as Source of Present African Theology: Reading the African Text

As we have seen, the effort to develop and reformulate an African theology depends heavily upon African traditional religion which gives access to African lifestyles, myths, narratives, practices, rites, and the broad oral tradition. The ATRs' world-view, their view on God, nature, the ancestors, community life, medicine and healing, the past and future, and so forth, all provide the lens through which traditional Christian doctrines about God and human beings, Christ and sin, protology and eschatology, and the like are being reinterpreted. Apart from the Bible as source for African theology, the ATRs provide the complementary source, without which the present African theology is unthinkable. ATR ideas are, however, not used in a syncretic or eclectic manner, nor does the concept of indigenization[3] fit the hermeneutical processes active in African theology. Bediako (1995, p. 82) confirms in this regard that the struggle for the indigenization of the church by the Christianization of the pre-Christian heritage has passed. The debate will now rage over the abiding relevance of the old religions in the transition to the new Christianity in Africa. The practice of using culture as a determinative factor in formulating theology is foreign to the history of any Christian theology which alleges to use the Bible as the only source of God's revelation.

To understand the development of African theology it is imperative to know African world view and culture, especially as represented by the ATRs. A few remarks will be made in this regard.

An interesting question is whether an implicit theology exists for the ATRs. Uka (1991, pp. 156–160) applied six determinative theological criteria (which Macquarie identified[4]) to traditional religion, to indicate its theological nature.

First, one could be critical of the approach to use criteria offered by a Western scholar against which to measure African religion. The norm remains Western even if African religion fulfills it in a unique way. African traditional religions simply do not have a theology in the sense that theology is known in Christianity. What they do have is a very rich religious experience and tradition, myths, symbols, rites, and so on. These have been interpreted in the past by Westerners in an anthropological and not in a theological manner. It remains to be seen how African theologians will develop an African Christian theology which uses the ATRs as one source among others. It remains, however, almost impossible not to compare or equate religions with one another. It is just as impossible not to use identical or analogous terms, metaphors, symbols, and so on to describe a specific religion. However, this should not be done with a feeling of inferiority or subservience to religious traditions other than one's own.

Although African traditional religion fits the criteria of Macquarie, it does so in a unique way, which requires a specific hermeneutics to accompany this specific theology. Macquarie's criteria are: experience, revelation, scripture, tradition, culture, and reason.

- *Religious experience*: The African as *homo Africanus* knows and encounters the numinous and mystical dimension of life—which forms the basis of the religion. This experience is reflected in its cosmogonic and other myths.
- *Revelation*: African religion is not a religion-of-the-book and lacks such a primary theological source. Africa is not, however, without its experience of revelation. The holy is revealed in nature, at special places, and through symbols, idols, and myths.
- Scripture: The text of African traditional religion is not written. Its oral sources include songs, arts and symbols, wisdom sayings, myths, legends, beliefs and customs, prayers, riddles, names of people and places, and so forth (Uka 1991, p. 157; Parratt 1983, p. 90).
- Like scripture, the *traditions* of the ATRs have been in the main *orally transmitted,* from generation to generation. African hermeneutics cannot be understood apart from the story-telling typical of its oral tradition. Oral theology has been described as theology in the open air, unrecorded theology, generally lost to libraries (Uka 1991, p. 163).

- African *reason* is integrated with all other faculties of the human being. The Africans believe in God and spirits but they are not interested in rationally defining these realities, and most theological terms which display a rational preference mean nothing to them (see Uka 1991, p. 160).

Although these factors may be present in the ATRs, they do not as yet constitute a theology. This comes only to the fore to the extent that African theologians, coming from a Christian background, use these characteristics to formulate a uniquely African theology. Bediako (1994, p. 94; 1995, p. 262) underscores the idea that it is in African Christianity that the primal heritage in Africa is likely to acquire a more enduring place. In this sense the ATR has become the *praeparatio theologia* in the African context. What remains fascinating is the much over-looked fact that ATR actually explains why Christianity has found fertile ground in Africa. The ATR has been an important preparation for the gospel in Africa and forms the major religious substrate for the idiom and existential experience of Christianity in African life (Bediako 1995, pp. 82–83). This implies that, on the one hand, African traditional religions should no longer be regarded as pagan or idolatrous, and on the other hand that this propensity of the ATRs for the gospel implies that Christianity can no longer be dismissed as a foreign religion. Instead, Christianity could be regarded as a natural complement of indigenous religious traditions (Schoffeleers 1988, p. 103).

The fear that Christianity will disappear from the African continent, or be replaced by the ATRs, is unfounded. One can expect, however, to find in future a very unique form of Christianity in Africa. In this regard Mbiti (see Bediako 1995, p. 82) even speaks of a new era in African theology, in which African theo-logians themselves realize that the Christian way of life is in Africa to stay. The Ecumenical Association of Third World Theologians (EATWOT) and the Fel-lowship of Mission Theologians from the Two-Thirds World are embodiments of this realization.

ATR Ideas Influencing the Hermeneutics of African Theology

To understand the impact of ATR on African theology, reference is made to the nature of the primal world-view as explicated by H. W. Turner (quoted in Bediako 1995, pp. 93–96). The following features are mentioned with reference to and in critique of analogical notions in the West (and in Western theology):

- A sense of kinship with nature in which animals and plants, like human beings, have their own spiritual existence and place in the universe as inter-dependent parts of a whole. African ontology considers God, spirits, human, animals, plants, and inanimate creation to be one. To break up this unity is to destroy one or more of these modes of existence, and to destroy one is in effect to destroy all of them (see Bediako 1995, p. 102). The idea of the interdependence and interrelatedness of all of creation is increasingly acknowledged in Western world-view and cosmology. This "ecological aspect" of primal religions explains the religious approach to the placing of human beings in the world. This attitude explains the current appeal of ecotheology, which is receiving renewed interest in the West.

- Human beings are finite, weak and impure or sinful, and stand in need of a power beyond their own. This conviction can be linked to the Christian idea of the sinful nature of human beings, but without the associated notion of guilt.
- Human beings are not alone in the universe and must respect the spiritual world of powers or beings more powerful and ultimate than themselves. Humans can enter into a relationship with the benevolent spirit-world and share in its powers and blessings and receive protection against evil forces. This belief can be related to Christian pneumatology, but sharply criticizes Western autonomy and self-centeredness. Such awareness is sadly lacking in Western science and technology and is a prerequisite for the revival of spirituality.
- There is an acute sense of the reality of the afterlife, which explains the important place of ancestors. This openness towards life after death has become foreign to a Western closed and rationalistic world-view. The belief in the ancestors has interesting links with Christology.
- Humans live in a sacramental universe where there is no sharp division between the physical and the spiritual. One set of powers, principles, and patterns runs through all things on earth and in the heavens and welds them into a unified cosmic system. There is also a new appreciation for these ideas in the Western world. A new biology, and a renewed interest in human consciousness and its relatedness to ideas from quantum physics, have brought this to our attention. The work of Pauli, Bohm and others testifies to this.
- The primal religious world-view is decidedly *this-worldly*. This *this-worldliness* encompasses God and humans in an abiding relationship which is the divine destiny of humankind, and the purpose of the universe (Bediako 1995, p. 101). This holistic approach proposes an answer to Western-style dualism with its unhealthy and often artificial separation between the sacred and the profane.

An Example from the *Ifa* Tradition

Ifa (Eze 1993, p. 266) is a process of seeking knowledge through divination. *Ifa* (also called the Eha process) is closely connected with the Nigerian Yoruba and has occupied an important place among African people for many centuries. The core of *Ifa* is a literary text called *Odu*, comprising thousands of aphorisms, poems, and riddles. *Odu* also contains elaborate exegesis on the text. *Esu* is the *ashé* principle, or the creative Word, as revealed yet hidden in the *Ifa* text (Eze 1993, pp. 273–274). When interpreting the text the *babalawo* (*Ifa*-follower) adopts a "hermeneutic" posture depicting the way of rational reflexivity, under the inspiration of *Esu*. As a way of inquiry, *Ifa* values interpretation as a dialogical event, views knowledge as existential and not disinterested, does not see truth as a set of general principles universally applicable to particular situations but sees truth as a process, and regards rationality as nonhierarchical (Eze 1993, p. 280).

Although the verses of the text are fixed, their interpretation is open. Textual objectivity is seen as submission of one's intuitions to the intersubjective process of inquiry, through which a possible (re)birth of understanding may occur. The meaning of a text is not imposed upon the inquirer who brings his/her preconceptions to determine what is objectively valid. Truth is the dialogue between the text, the Babalawo and the interpreter. *Ifa*-hermeneutics accept that our capacity for understanding is limited. It sees the nature of truth as limited, acknowledging its simultaneous accommodation of truth and untruth, concealment and unconcealment, presence and absence (Eze 1993, pp. 281–283).

These principles are in line with some of the latest ideas found in Western hermeneutics. The advantage of *Ifa* tradition, however, seems to be the existence of a rich textual tradition absent in many parts of Africa. Also, the history of African Biblical hermeneutics seems to lag behind the insights produced by *Ifa* hermeneutics.

Bridging the ATRs and Mainline Christianity: The Role of the African Initiated Churches (AICs)

Sarpong (1991, pp. 288–289) says that the church has not become "African" enough. He refers to the fascinating Vatican directive from *The Congregation for the Propagation of the Faith,* issued in 1659 to missionaries in China and Indo-China, and giving the following guidance:

> Put no obstacles in their way; and for no reason whatever should you persuade these people to change their rites, customs and ways of life unless these are obviously opposed to religion and good morals. For what is more absurd than to bring France and Spain or Italy or any other part of Europe into China? It is not these that you should bring but the faith that does not spurn or reject any peoples' rites and customs, unless they are depraved, but, on the contrary, tries to keep them. Admire and praise what deserves to be respected.

The AICs in South Africa comprise about 7,000 groups of churches, of which the Zion Christian Church is the largest. According to 1991 statistics, the AICs in South Africa represented 31% of the black population, the mainline Christian churches (excluding the AICs) 34 %, and the ATRs and those with no religion 33%. The respective percentages for the 1980 census were 17.7% (AICs), 53% (mainline Christian), and 28.4% (ATRs and no religion). This indicates a dramatic growth for the AICs, and a limited growth for the ATRs and those with no religion. The trend is clearly that of more and more black people leaving the mainline Christian churches for the AICs.

The AICs play a very important role on the African religious scene. They resemble at this stage, for many African theologians, the best example of the direction in which African religion should develop since they incorporate traditional and Christian (predominantly Pentecostal) ideas. They attract predominantly disadvantaged people from the black working class.

The important place the Bible takes among them is well known. The booklet *Speaking for Ourselves,* states:

> We [the AICs] read the Bible as a book that comes from God and we take every word in the Bible seriously. Some people will say that we are therefore "fundamentalists." We do not know whether that word applies to us or not but we are not interested in any interpretation of the Bible that softens or waters down its message. We do not have the same problems about the Bible as White people have with their scientific mentality (quoted by West 1991, p. 158).

Their knowledge of the Bible is of an oral nature. The Bible as text makes no sense to them. Mosala, quoted by West (1991, pp. 159–160), argues that they do not appropriate the Bible in terms of what it says, but in terms of what it stands for—a canonical authority. Their hermeneutical weapons are drawn from the sense of mystery generated by the authority of a basically unknown Bible. They appropriate the mysteries of the Bible and of traditional society in order to cope with their perception/sense of being as a subordinate class. The "mystery" of the symbols of the Bible is important in this hermeneutics of mystification. Mosala (West 1991, p. 160) further indicates that race, gender, and class are absent as hermeneutical factors in the AICs appropriation of the Bible, while African symbols and discourses are very much part thereof.

HERMENEUTICAL APPROACHES OF SOME AFRICAN THEOLOGIANS: CONFLICTING OPINIONS ON THE SOURCE FOR AFRICAN THEOLOGY

The African hermeneutical identity depends to a large extent on the theologians practicing this hermeneutics within the process of doing their theology. Instead of concentrating on only one or two names we will try to give a picture of how some of the players approach the task. African theologians, as can be expected, differ in their hermeneutical approaches to African religion. Although it is a generalization, one can distinguish two groups. The first might be referred to as the "old guard" and includes well-known theologians such as E. W. Fashole-Luke, Bolaji Idowu, John Mbiti, Iturneleng Mosala, and Harry Sawyer. The "new guard" includes such theologians as Eboussi Boulaga, JeanMarc Ela, Ambrose Moyo, Kwame Bediako, and Mercy Oduyoye (Rogers 1994, pp. 245–246).

Most African theologians involve themselves, to a greater or lesser extent, in liberation issues and the postcolonial urge to find what is typical of African religion. As can be expected, their theologies are dynamic and this especially comes to the fore in the work of the younger theologians who have been more exposed to postcolonial conditions. Their work should not be considered definitive on any specific theological topics. As articulated by Sarpong (1991, p. 288), the African can pursue a particular cause or act in a definite pattern for twenty years or so, and when the Westerner concludes that he will continue to do so for the rest of his life, the African suddenly breaks this pattern.

Old-guard theologians have taken Western Christian theology, developed it in African terms, and called it "indigenization." African traditional values and experiences have become a passive partner, subordinated to a presumably superior Western theology. They practice a Western form of hermeneutics which does not suit or serve the African context. They stress the centrality of the Bible and see it as the basic source for the development of African Christian theology. They see the Old Testament, in particular, as a source for developing a *Theologia Afticana*. Fashole-Luke, while favoring African traditional religion as a source of nourishment for African people, warns against the notion that African traditional religion is a preparation for the gospel (see Rogers 1994, p. 247). Mbiti's approach is to take biblical themes, compare them to the African world-view and culture, and discuss the question whether biblical themes can be apprehended by Africans. As an example, the African forms of concepts like time and history cannot appropriate directly the biblical understanding of eschatology, because the African world-view is cyclical and the rhythm of nature ensures that the world will never come to an end. Idowu sees African traditional religion as a *praeparatio evangelica* in the sense that he believes that God has not left himself without witness in any nation, and that it is therefore necessary to find out what God has done, in what way he has been known and approached in Nigerian history and upon what, traditionally, Nigerians base their faith now and their hope for the afterlife (quoted in Rogers 1994, p. 249).

New-guard theologians reject the indigenization process, affirming African traditional values, and avoiding what have been called Western bourgeois values. Their primary work was produced in the 1980s, in response to the call for liberation in South African religious circles. Ogku Kalu and Manas Buthelezi (one of the leading figures in promoting black theology in South Africa, along with Basil Moore) were calling for scholars to use the hermeneutical perspective of liberation when interpreting the Bible. In their view, the content of the biblical message must be transposed from the first-century situation to that of the hearer in such a way that the biblical situational and indigenous elements are replaced by those of the twentieth-century hearer in South Africa (Rogers 1994, pp. 252–253).

In 1984 the Congress of African and European Theologians convened in Cameroon to consider the appropriate forms of theology for African people. They stressed the need for a new hermeneutic biblical tradition reflecting political realities (Rogers 1994, pp. 253–258). Theologians such as Marc Ela, Mercy Oduyoye, Eboussi Boulage, and Ambrose Moyo supported this approach. Boulage distrusted even the name "African Christianity" because it symbolized African acceptance of the domination of Africa by the West on social, political, economic, and scientific levels. He still accepts the Bible as part of Christianity from within an African perspective, and he favors an "aesthetic Christianity" that responds to biblical themes of a universal nature. He sees the contribution of African Christians to African civilization as still to come. Ela concentrates on an African reading of Exodus and voices his suspicions toward enculturation/indigenization. Africa has to develop its own models of faith. Mercy Oduyoye stresses that Christian theology in Africa must be constructed from the vantage point of the "underside of history." For her, the Old Testament provides the key to an authentic African theology. Moyo calls for dialogue between Christianity and African traditional religion. ATR should not take precedence over biblical revelation. He wants to liberate the church in Africa from the white missionary establishment. The AICs are already free from this domination.

Rogers (1994, pp. 258–260) concludes that while the Old Guard theologians were reluctant to enter the political realm, the New Guard is strongly committed to a hermeneutic that responds to the current oppressive regime where and whenever it occurs. The Old Guard was open to indigenization whereas the New Guard follows a style of confrontation. The Old Guard saw African traditional religion as *praeparatio evangelica,* whereas the New Guard considers the ATRs in their own right. However, both Old and New Guard theologians agree that an African perspective on the Bible is essential to buttress a "living theology" appropriate for African Christian experience. African traditional religion is considered a worthy source from which to understand African religiosity.

AFRICAN HERMENEUTICS INTO THE FUTURE

An exciting future, presenting many challenges, awaits African hermeneutics. One could expect the liberation theme to remain important, but shift its emphasis to economic progress and African politics. The task of developing an African religion, integrating Christian and African traditional ideas, is far from complete.

No single hermeneutic or methodological approach seems to fit the African context perfectly. A poly-method and multi-hermeneutic approach seems the best way to go. In the past the search for an appropriate approach was influenced by the idea that African religion is so different, with its ethnic and preliterate context, that it can be studied only anthropologically. Evans-Pritchard (quoted by Metuh 1991, pp. 147–148) has warned against the danger of reductionism in using any categorical approach to study African religion. African religious concepts and categories need not be forced into the well-known Western categories of monotheism, polytheism, pantheism, and animism.

The vibrancy of African theology and hermeneutics will be determined not by the theologians, but by the spiritual reality of everyday life. This was the secret of African religion in the past and will be its strength in the future.

NOTES

1. In the past little serious attention was given by African theologians to the problem of Biblical hermeneutics. Fasholé-Luke (quoted in Parratt 1983, p. 91) indicated that historically the missionary penetration of Africa was done by male Europeans with a fundamentalist view of the Bible, and until fairly recently this factor has tended to circumscribe biblical studies on this continent.

2. Thornton (1996, pp. 144–145) mentions that the South African condition is more postmodern than it is postcolonial. In contemporary South Africa there are literally no names, no vocabulary, to discuss major aspects and parts of its political situation. There is no agreement on what are the boundaries of "black" or "white." No one knows whether to refer to "tribes," "ethnic groups," "language groups," "peoples," or "races."

3. Bediako (1995, p. 82) confirms in this regard that the struggle for the indigenization of the church by the Christianization of the pre-Christian heritage has passed. The debate will now rage over the abiding relevance of the old religions in the transition to the new Christianity in Africa.

4. One could be critical of the approach to once again use Western criteria against which to measure African religion. The norm remains Western even if African religion fulfills it in a peculiar way. African Traditional Religions simply do not have a theology as it is known in Christianity. What they do have is a very rich religious experience and tradition, myths, symbols, rites, and so on. These have been interpreted in the past by Westerners in an anthropological and not a theological manner. It remains to be seen how African theologians will develop an African Christian theology that uses the ATRs as one source among others. It remains, however, almost impossible not to compare or equate religions with one other. It is just as impossible not to use identical or analogues terms, metaphors, symbols, and so on, to describe a specific religion. This should not be done with a feeling of inferiority or subservience to religious traditions other than one's own.

REFERENCES

Awolalu, J. O. 1991. "African traditional religion as an academic discipline." Pp. 123–138 in *Readings in African traditional religion: structure, meaning relevance, future*, edited by E. M. Uka. NY: Peter Lang.

Bediako, K. 1994. "Jesus in African culture." Pp. 93–126 in *Emerging voices in global Christian theology*, edited by W. A. Dyrness. Grand Rapids, MI: Zondervan.

Bediako, K. 1995. *Christianity in Africa. The renewal of a non-Western religion*. Edinburgh: Orbis Books.

Bloch-Hoell, N. E. 1992. African identity. European invention or genuine African character? *Mission Studies ix* (1), 98–107.

Coleman, W. 1993. Tribal talk: Black theology in postmodern configuration. *Theology Today*, L/1, 68–77.

Ela, J. M. 1991. "A black African perspective: an African reading of Exodus." Pp. 256–266 in *Voices from the margin: interpreting the Bible in the Third World* , edited by R. S. Sugirtharajah. Edinburgh: Orbis Books.

Eze, E. C. 1993. Rationality and the debates about African philosophy. *Dissertation Abstracts International*, Publication AAT 9403294. http://wwwlib.umi.com/dissertations/.

Kristeva, J. 1993. *Nations without nationalism*. NY: Columbia University Press.

Maluleke, T. S. 1996. Black and African theologies in the New World order: a time to drink from our own wells. *Journal of Theology for Southern Africa, 96*, 3–19.

Metuh, E. 1991. "Methodology for the study of African religion." Pp. 139–150 in *Readings in African traditional religion: Structure, meaning, relevance, future*, edited by E. M. Uka. NY: Peter Lang.

Mosala, I. J. 1989. *Biblical hermeneutics and black theology in South Africa*. Grand Rapids, MI: Eerdmans.

Onunwa, U. R. 1991. "African traditional religion in African scholarship: a historical analysis." Pp. 109–122 in *Readings in African traditional religion. Structure, meaning, relevance, future* edited by E. M. Uka. NY: Peter Lang.

Onwu, N. 1985. The hermeneutical model: The dilemma of the African theologian. In *African Theological Journal, 14*(2), 145–160.

Parratt, J. 1983. African theology and biblical hermeneutics. *African Theological Journal, 12*(2), 88–94.

Pasteur, A. B. and I. L. Toldson. 1982. *Roots of soul: The psychology of black expressiveness*. NY: Anchor Press.

Pobee, J. S. 1993. "Africa in search of identity." Pp. 387–398 in *The ecumenical movement tomorrow*, edited by M. Reuver, F. Solms, and G. Huizer. Kampen: Kok.

Pobee, J. S. 1996. "A Passover of language: an African perspective." Pp. 53–58 in *Mission in bold humility*, edited by W. Saayman and K. Kritzinger. NY: Maryknoll.

Reed, S. A. 1996. Critique of Canaan Banana's call to rewrite the Bible. *Religion and Theology, 3*(3), 282–288.

Ricoeur, P. 1974. *The conflict of interpretations*. Evanston, IL: Northwestern University Press.

Rogers, R. G. 1994. "Biblical hermeneutics and contemporary African theology." Pp. 245–260 in *Uncovering ancient stones* edited by L. M. Hopfe. IN: Eisenbrauns.

Sarpong, P. K. 1991. "Christianity meets traditional African cultures." Pp. 287–296 in *Readings in African traditional religion: Structure, meaning, relevance, future* edited by E. M. Uka. NY: Peter Lang.

Schoffeleers, M. 1988. Black and African theology in Southern African: a controversy reexamined. *Journal of Religion in Africa, xviii*(1), 99–123.

Serequeberhan, T. 1994. *The hermeneutics of African philosophy*. London: Routledge.

Sugirtharajah, R. S. (Ed.). 1991. *Voices from the margin. Interpreting the Bible in the Third World*. NY: Orbis.

Taylor, C. 1994. "The politics of recognition." Pp. 25–74 in *Multiculturalism: Examining the politics of recognition*, edited by A. Gutman. Princeton, NJ: Princeton University Press.

Thiselton, A. C. 1992. *New horizons in hermeneutics*. London: Harper Collins.

Thornton, R. 1996. "The potentials of boundaries in South Africa: Steps towards a theory of the social edge." Pp. 136–156 in *Postcolonial identities in Africa*, edited by R. Werbner and T. Ranger. London: Zed.

Turaki, Y. 1991. "Culture and modernization in Africa: a methodological approach." Pp. 123–144 in *Cultural diversity in Africa: Embarrassment or opportunity?* Potchetstroom: PU vir CHO.

Uka, E. M. 1991. "Theology of African traditional religion: A review." Pp. 153–166 in *Readings in African traditional religion. Structure, meaning, relevance, future*, edited by E. M. Uka. NY: Peter Lang.

West, G. 1991. *Biblical hermeneutics of liberation. Models of reading the Bible in the South African context*. Pietermaritzburg: Cluster.

RELIGIOUS MINORITIES DURING RUSSIA'S TRANSITION FROM ATHEISM TO SECULARISM

Alexander Agadjanian

ABSTRACT

This paper describes the religious "market" in post-U.S.S.R. Russia, with the most attention to religious minorities. In Russia, as well as in some other post-communist countries, the new situation does not fit in any existing typology of religious life. On the one hand, there is a "rehabilitation" of religion after decades of an antireligious sociopolitical environment. On the other hand, there is the process of accommodating to a new global postreligious modernity that presumes religious pluralism within a secularized setting. The paper especially considers the situation of minority religions in a country dominated by one powerful denomination, Russian Orthodoxy. This study is based on a series of interviews conducted in 1995 and 1996 among leaders and ordinary members of several minority communities including Pentecostals, Lutherans, *Rosa* (Dew) Church[1], and New Apostolic Church, all in Moscow.

Research in the Social Scientific Study of Religion, Volume 11, pages 65-79.
Copyright © 2000 by JAI Press Inc.
ISBN: 0-7623-0656-4

INTRODUCTION: THE PROBLEM
AND METHODOLOGY

The changes that have occurred in Russia within the last decade are fundamental. These changes of course extend to the question of religion. At the same time the social transition is still far from being completed, and the patterns of the new society cannot be identified with certainty. In this situation social sciences perhaps should abstain from generalizations and treat identified trends and processes only as emerging hypotheses.

At the same time this cognitive uncertainty gives more opportunities for theoretical experimentation. In Russia, as well as in some other postcommunist countries, the new situation doesn't fit in any existing typology of religious life. On the one hand, we witness a "rehabilitation" of religion after decades of an antireligious (or, to be accurate, pseudoreligious) sociopolitical environment. On the other hand, we see an accommodation to a new global postreligious modernity that presumes religious pluralism within a secularized setting.

It is this unique situation that requires treatment from several different points of view. In this paper I shall consider some general premises, suggested by recent polls, and then concentrate more closely on some minority religious groups. I direct my attention to the minority religions in a country dominated by one powerful denomination, Russian Orthodoxy. These minorities deserve more scholarly attention for their own sake than they have received so far. At the same time, this analytical approach will also contribute to a better understanding of general trends, as explained below.

This study is based on a series of interviews I conducted in 1995 and 1996 among leaders and ordinary members of several minority communities including Pentecostals, Lutherans, *Rosa* (Dew) Church[1], and New Apostolic Church, all in Moscow. To be introduced to a community, I first made appointments with the pastors. The interviews with them included both a general overview of the community in question, and the leaders' personal opinions about the present religious situation, as well as their own religious life story. Then I met with several ordinary members of each community. In total I interviewed twenty people, including four pastors and one Orthodox priest.

All the interviews with ordinary church members contained the same set of questions (see below), although posed in varying order and sometimes worded differently. I intentionally avoided absolute uniformity, for my experience, as well as that of my colleagues, has found absolute fidelity to a standardized questionnaire is not useful for a study of such subtle matters as religion. The ensuing reduction in rigor is balanced by a deeper perception (and sometimes, at least, a respondent's cooperation). This is an ambiguity proper to any qualitative research.

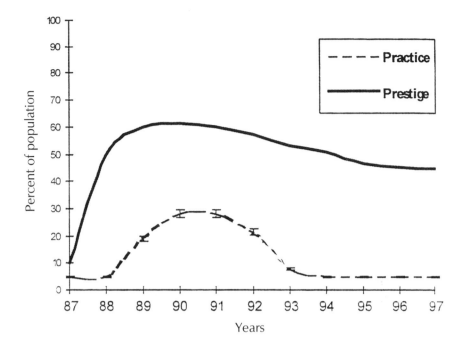

Figure 1. Religiosity Dynamic: "Practice" and "Prestige" Compared

I also was trying to present myself as not only a sociologist doing a "survey" but also as a person involved in the same social environment, speaking the same language, and sharing the same perplexities of identity within a changing society. This relational attitude was further supported by my participant–observation both during the sacral ceremonies and the postceremonial interaction, such as shared meals, and so forth.

Nevertheless, the major questions were always the same: personal history of conversion; self-perception within the community (with special attention to individual–group relations); self-identification within the Russian religious field (with the emphasis on the minority person's attitude toward the Orthodox Church); and finally, self-perception in the changing world of the Russian postcommunist reforms.

My previous study of Eastern cult communities in Russia (Agadjanian 1993), carried out in 1993–1994, was also used for the purpose of comparison.

NEW RELIGIOUS SETTING IN RUSSIA: TRANSITION FROM IMPOSED ATHEISM TO MODERN SECULARISM

The most striking feature of the recent statistics on Russian religiosity is a wide gap between data regarding the evident respect toward religion and everything related to it, on the one hand, and the low level of religious practice and real religious zeal, on the other.

As *Figure 1* illustrates, the general *prestige* of religion among Russians attains the level of most "religious" countries: in one of the most recent and reliable surveys, carried out in 1996, forty-seven percent of respondents answered "yes" to the question "do you believe in God;" fifty-five percent supported the importance of religious guidance in moral questions, and sixty-three percent in spiritual questions.[2]

Figures for *practice*, however, after a noticeable rise in the late 1980s and early 1990s, go down to the lowest level known in the world: only five to seven percent attend religious ceremonies at least once a month, and only two percent attend once a week.[3]

How can we explain this gap? It seems that the explanation lies in the specific relationship between these two variables—"prestige" of (or "respect" for) religion and the "real practice" of it. In most countries these two variables tend to correlate, as both form part of the general logic of development of a system of values. Either religion is both highly respected and practiced as an important traditional system incorporated in a society on the everyday life level (e.g., in Ireland or India)[4], or secularization has worked as a systemic process of changing values, which process narrows the space for religion both in general attitudes and in practice (e.g., in Finland or Sweden).

My hypothesis is that in the case of postcommunist Russia the "respect for religion" and the "real religiousness" are following separate developmental paths and different logics. I suggest that 70 years of imposed atheism have produced a unique situation where the notion of religion became related to at least two different fields of references—first, general public field, and second, practical functional field.

In communist Russia "practical" religion (institution, believers, morals, rituals) existed separately as an underground reality, while the "public" religion was officially and effectively discredited, repressed, and banished from public life. What we have observed in the first postcommunist years was a continuation of this functional separation. The public references of religion have changed completely and dramatically. Beginning with the first waves of *glasnost* and the official celebration of the millennium of Russian Christianity in 1988, religion came to the fore of political and cultural discussions as one of the core values unjustly forgotten and urgently wanted for the "new Russia." On this wave a new "Law of Freedom of Conscience" was adopted in 1990. This promoted both an open religious propaganda of traditional churches and the emergence of hundreds of new religious organizations. As a result, a sort of "religious boom" occurred in the early 1990s. In that period the functional separation mentioned above was barely noticeable. Yet today we can interpret this "boom" in terms of this separation.

Thus, *symbolically*, religion became a publicly recognized ideological alternative. Clearly, it had become an alternative to communism as an antireligious society. At the same time, and more importantly, it was an alternative to the ideological vacuum and/or anarchy that emerged after the Marxist/Soviet system of values was officially abolished. First of all, religion became "popular" and "fashionable" because it was a fresh ideology, as opposed to discredited communism and socialism. Second, it was conveniently used and instrumentalized as a symbol of a new national and personal identity that was strongly needed[5]. Finally, religion was viewed, in a very deductive but *impressionistic* way (i.e., without going into much detail), as an image of a coherent and traditionally legitimized order that is lacking on earth (especially in the times of troubles). All these factors explain the prestige and respect toward religion reflected in 1990s surveys.

At the same time, *in terms of practice*, the situation was and remains quite different. To be sure, a "practice" boom has also been registered in the surveys. The number of child and adult baptisms in the early 1990s were strikingly high. The numerical growth of restored Orthodox parishes and new religious communities was, perhaps, unprecedented in recent world history[6]. A closer look, however, reveals that this did not bring deep changes in real religiousness. "Real" religion of "true" believers, as the recent figures show, has mostly been immune to this boom and remained at the same level as before.

This means, in my view, that any reported figures of massive religious practice are mostly based in the phenomenon of public symbolism. Baptisms, weddings and holy days' attendance rates fall in the same range as the rates of calling oneself a "believer" and approving of the important role religion plays in spiritual life. All these symbolic actions, as well as symbolic utterances, have little in common with sustained belief and real ongoing religious involvement[7].

According to many observations, the religious "boom" that coincided with the most difficult and shocking period of reforms apparently slowed down in 1993, and practically came to an end in 1994–1996[8]. Nevertheless, the gap between the symbolic and *praxis* dimensions of religion remains. However, this phenomenon has evolved as well. The most important change is that in recent public discourse religion has been viewed as less relevant to the social and political fields; with only twenty-two percent of the 1996 survey respondents agreed that religion "gives answers to social problems." Political activity of the Church and religion is now rarely reported in mass media. The only lines of thought where religion has won major positions (and for a long time in my opinion) are moral education and spiritual questions.

The importance attributed by respondents to religion stands below such values as *family* and *work* (without going into detail of what precisely "work" or "family" mean for Russians). The *family* is important for 96 percent of respondents, *work* for 84 percent, while only 32 percent of respondents consider *religion* important for their lives. It is worth noting that this figure is also lower than the percentage of self-proclaimed "believers."

Generally speaking, after many decades of the imposed dominance of a single ideology, Russians are mostly skeptical and suspicious of any kind of ideology that goes beyond the level of simple pragmatic values of self-satisfaction. The younger generations are particularly distrustful of *any* global ideology and/or big institution (Western societies have acquired such skepticism much earlier). Although the first years of shocking changes and ideological upheaval moved many Russians to such new systems of values as nationalism, liberalism, or religion (or, more properly, to different kinds of *faiths*), Russians also acquired a seductive freedom that came from a general loosening of social control. Ultimately, this latter trend has become dominant in the form of a "me–first" attitude, "optional ethics" (Davie 1996) and pragmatic narcissism (Agadjanian 1993)[9]. Currently most Russians adhere to traditional nuclear values like "the family" and "work," rather than more general value systems, which might require participation in broader social bodies like a nation, a class, or a church.

In view of these points, the *religious prestige* versus *religious practice* gap becomes more understandable and less surprising. Still, the phenomenon is remarkable and meaningful, illustrating, as we can say now, the separation of abstract symbolic expectations that people assign to religion, and their empirical *real* attachment to it.

While drawing this conclusion, we have to keep in mind the fact of an incontestable dominance by Russian Orthodoxy in the Russian religious field. The 1996 random survey revealed that 65 percent of self-proclaimed believers belonged to this denomination. The prestige–practice gap is endemic to this largest religious sector, where the purely symbolic statement "I believe" has no vital religious consequences. As I showed earlier "true believers" with an intrinsic religious orientation, comprise a small percent of population as a whole. However within religious minorities the proportions of symbolic and true believers are quite different, as is their *kind* of religiousness. In this sense the analysis of minorities, to which I now turn, seems to be of special importance.

MINORITY AS AN ANALYTICAL TOUCHSTONE AND A SOCIAL PATTERN

For an understanding of religious life of this rapidly changing society, an analysis of minority religions is most revealing. First, the status of minorities is an indicator of to what degree marginal phenomena are being legitimized in a new societal setting, and hence, how far the freedom of heterodoxy and its legal protection extend. Second, their more or less precarious status (whatever legal framework may maintain their equal freedom over against a dominant church), requires some innovative efforts and thus they accumulate new experiences of religious life.

Third, the minority situation requires a special commitment from the members, thus attracting neophytes of high conviction, who are seriously preoccupied with their religious experiences.

Hundreds of minuscule religious minority groups appeared in Russia when religious freedom was proclaimed in 1990. These were Protestant communities of both established and new origins, "Eastern" cults and sects, new religious movements, and so forth[10]. In the early 1990s these groups were mostly "imported" from Western Europe and the United States. In the course of time, however, these "imported" religions have been profoundly modified to fit the Russian context, and communities of indigenous origin have also appeared in large numbers.

Still, the problem of tolerance toward these new (or newly recognized) religious agents surfaced as soon as the law of 1990 was adopted, and until now the problem has remained unsolved. Minorities retain a more or less evident imprint of being foreign, different and/or alien. This deeply internalized bias of Russian society is nourished from at least three sources. The first is the official conservatism of the Russian Orthodox Church hierarchy, which is concerned with keeping its traditional dominance. The second is massive religious illiteracy and a simplified set of identity criteria, leading to a sort of xenophobic syndrome against any heterodoxy or simply against uncommon things. And the third is the new Russian state's use of *the* dominant religion as a legitimization instrument.

The last point contains some ambiguity. The new regime, balancing between liberal reforms and imperial traditions of the Russian state, supports religious freedom, on the one hand, and manipulates the "official" Orthodox symbols, on the other. Within the ruling elite of the 1990s there is a permanent split between "liberals" and those who are lobbying for more uniformity and control, and for exclusive rights for the dominant church. This split is replicated in society at large where conservatives have a clear majority, in contrast to the elite level[11].

While freedom is always vulnerable in a society with moral, legal, and institutional dysfunctions, the freedom of minorities is the first to be affected. Religious minorities in Russia have had to be on permanent alert, for the implementation of even liberal laws is problematic in a loose society with weak mechanisms of law implementation and enforcement.

Religious minorities deserve a special attention, finally, because they form a *new social pattern*, as well as a *new sociological object*, in Russian society. They are in fact an experimental ground for a society undergoing change. The status that they have is something new in recent Russian history. The structures they maintain are unusual in many respects, including their size, their internal organization, and their relationships with the outside world. As a result of this uniqueness and newness, religious minorities are more likely to attract into their orbit dynamic people from new social strata, who are less involved with networks rooted in the *ancien regime* and more apt to create new types of social networks. In this sense, religious minorities can be seen as a touchstone for understanding the development of the civic society in posttotalitarian culture.

PERSONAL AND GROUP IDENTITY IN
MINORITY RELIGIONS

Members of minority groups have an especially strong commitment to their direct communities, in comparison to members of the Orthodox Church, with its parochial organization based on geographic boundaries. A small religion unites highly devoted people regardless of their place of residence. People from such communities enter these groups in two ways—either by a long family tradition, or as neophytes after a certain time of religious search. The former category is composed of people of different ages who have been long attached, for example, to a Pentecostal or Baptist community, or to one of small sects derived from them. Either they came to the church through their families, growing up in a religious context, or sometimes individually. In this latter case they refer to their parents as atheists. But always, in all such cases, there is a kind of self-identification based on a multigenerational memory (whether it is real or invented). They recall their ancestors as belonging either to a religious community (in most cases, however, the Russian Orthodox), or to an ethnic minority, such as Scandinavian or German or Polish. These memories provide legitimization for belonging to a religious minority of Protestant (or Catholic) type.

Recent neophytes are quite different. In most, albeit not all, cases they are younger and their explicit motivation and the roots of their religiosity are different. Most of them in the interviews *emphasized* a total lack of previous religious experience within their family heritage as well as on their own. This emphasis is by itself very significant. By this they mean that their conversion is self-made and individually motivated, being a clear negation of the atheism of their family tradition. Psychologically, it sounds like a challenge to *the society* the parents belonged to. Thus, compared to the first category, the ground of their religiosity is antitraditional.

The neophytes come from a social stratum that has grown significantly in the years of postcommunist troubles. This is a large group of young urban people who live as spiritual nomads roaming from one sect, club, or group to another in a persistent identity quest. For most of them, the religious search is largely a socialization quest, and most of them eventually give up any religious interest. Only a few of them, who have a deeper dissatisfaction with secular values, become permanent believers.

In both cases, tradition-based or antitraditional, the final result is a comparatively strong and motivated commitment. We deal here with a phenomenon quite different from the massive "temporary" conversions to the Orthodox Church, registered in the polls of the early 1990s. To be sure, this kind of deep commitment is also found in the dominant church. But while in the Orthodox Church its rate of occurrence is exceptional[12] (compared to the widespread rate of symbolical affiliation), within religious minorities such commitment is almost the absolute rule.

Another side of this contrast is linked to the distinction between *liturgical* unity of a religious group and *social* unity. In the former case the group identity is felt during the religious rite, but the feeling usually disappears as soon as the rite comes to the end. This temporary identity brings people together only for a short time in the Orthodox liturgy. Although there usually exists a core of faithfully attending parishioners, the flock is usually fluctuating and mixed, especially on religious holy days, when most of people don't know each other and go home as soon as the ceremony is over. In small minority religions the group identity goes beyond the ritual practices, and in most cases beyond the walls of a church. The chorus rehearsals, the postceremonial meals (or tea), the continuing friendly contacts in the home are very common for all the communities I studied. In this respect the holy days are not very much different from the regular services.

To be sure, the extent and the forms of group commitment vary from one community to another: obligatory collectivist participation in charismatic Christian groups and some of the Eastern communities would seem excessive to Lutherans or members of inclusive NRMs, although the latter stress, as some of my respondents did, that they feel very well integrated in a community while enjoying their right to keep their individual distance. In fact, this possibility to feel at the same time both a self-sustained individuality and an affiliation with a specific community seems to be at the core of the religious belonging we discuss here. Members of minorities, therefore, would say they belong to their particular local group, while an average Orthodox believer would more likely identify himself with the Russian Orthodox Church as a whole.

SELF-PERCEPTION IN THE OUTSIDE WORLD: A BASIC CONTRADICTION

As we have seen, the minorities are usually more conscious of the boundary that separates them from the outside world, and particularly, the larger religious world. This perception of a strict boundary is mostly positive, based on positive feelings for an immediate community they belong to. But at the same time they also feel, to a lesser extent however, some of solidarity with each other in opposition to the dominant Church, as well as to irreligious society as a whole.

The members of all communities I have studied in 1996 refer to themselves as belonging to "churches of a Protestant kind," although they are more likely to speak of themselves as just "Christians." In contrast, an Orthodox believer would more likely say he or she is *pravoslavnyi* (Orthodox). In many cases, however, this is a tenuous distinction, because for many Russians *pravoslavnyi* means the same as "Christian."

However, the precarious status of the minorities dictates that they endorse an explicit position of liberalism and tolerance. To survive in a situation of yet uncertain religious pluralism, which is often questioned in many respects, religious minorities need to profess more liberal attitudes than the average. These attitudes sometimes sharply contradict their general religious conservatism and organizational rigidity.

Let us look in some detail at this basic contradiction. It is hardly possible to imagine a minority religion whose members were not supporters of the recent liberal reforms in general, and religious freedom in particular. To be sure, they usually speak of the reforms with some restraint, and with some bitter moral critique, but they nonetheless endorse the long-term changes. Their rejection of the prereform communist regime is indisputable.

It is also the case for most of Orthodox believers and self-proclaimed Orthodox. But for them the denial of communism does not mean the acceptance of liberal principles. In contrast, for minorities this reciprocal relationship is evident. The best example is the question of religious legislation. The liberal law of religious freedom adopted in 1990 was the legal foundation for hundreds of small religious groups and a guarantee of their free activities. Consequently, these groups are very sensitive to any attempt to reconsider the legislation. Another example is their effusive phraseology of outside openness, ecumenism and tolerance, and the respect they express, as a matter of principle, to the Russian Church. This sort of discourse is found in most small religions, with the exception of several exclusive sects.

In view of this explicit liberalism one would be somewhat surprised to know the opposing attitudes which can also be found. Because of the same precarious status, the members of minorities feel a need to maintain their boundaries and identity in a world that seems to be still alien. One of the common means of self-definition is the criticism of the dominant church, which is, in their view, corrupted, archaic, ambitious, xenophobic, and intolerant. Such statements stand in contrast to the words of respect that are mostly superficial. A pastor said that among Orthodox people there are very few of those who "really know God," and that religious revival can come to Orthodoxy only if it rejects its traditional method of "achieving unanimity by the ax." A member of a Pentecostal community argued that the Russian Church has been too involved with the state, and "thus has lost its spiritual basis." For young people of the NRM and Christian minorities, the Russian Church is most unacceptable because of the lack of free and ongoing member communication, that is, socialization motives. In this respect their own immediate communities are by far more convenient for socialization.

A second self-defining attitude used by religious minorities is accusations against the "godless society." Religious people share rather ambiguous attitudes toward the recent changes in society. While the general result of "overcoming the satanic power" (i.e. Soviet regime) is highly appreciated, there appears some reluctance to accept *the way* in which liberal reforms are implemented by the ruling power. Here we can find a whole spectrum of opinions found in the society at large. One common reservation is that freedom without God (or without

Krishna's truth, for example) is dangerous for morality: As one of respondents put it, "the right to choose is not yet the ability to choose right."

Another reservation is that no effective change is at all possible until the ruling elite is composed of true believers. By this same token, democracy is viewed with some suspicion. As for the market economy reforms, their controversial results are criticized from the perspective of religious priorities in values.

There is a consensus about the priority of spiritual gains. But the range of attitudes towards material achievements is noteworthy. In this respect Orthodox and, for example, Pentecostal respondents are similar in their criticism of democracy and the market economy, and especially of the new social differentiation. Pentecostals are in this respect even more critical that the Orthodox. One respondent openly decried as "diabolic perversions" such terms as "Christian democracy" and "Christian business."

Generally, however, younger people are more neutral and even positive, as are almost all young members of NRM and of minor Christian communities. A *Rosa* pastor was telling me about the blessing for those who work hard, and that he hoped to see Russian Christian millionaires appear. He also argued that Christian politics are quite possible. Another respondent said money is viewed positively in the Bible, and the family well-being is religiously recommended in order to acquire God's blessing[13].

The organizational structure of small communities tends to be as rigid as needed to maintain viability. The informal power is typically concentrated in the leader's hands. The schedule of religious and other activities is routinized and punctually adhered to. A "central" event is usually reproduced in smaller territorial groups, led by some "ordained" members of the central core. All this is in contrast to the way an average urban Orthodox parish is organized: fluctuating composition of attendants, lack of extra-service parochial traditions and rules, lack of spontaneous organization of the flock, a loose calendar for nonritual events and activities, and so forth.

The attitudes of minority members are by far more conservative than it might seem at the first sight. All opinions of the adepts have a strong religious subtext. In the interviews they made frequent references to religious evaluations and norms while commenting on different life situations and political events (see examples above). In this respect they are as conservative as fully practicing Orthodox believers, although surely less intolerant of different religious denominations.

The minorities also share a common *underground* mentality inherited from the Soviet times, when their predecessors (and some of today's veterans) held clandestine meetings outside the cities, hiding their beliefs and rituals, and suffering socially and even administratively when disclosed. This complex of oppression and heroism makes some of them feel suspicious and skeptical of the surrounding "liberal" setting, and they try to go on playing the role of dissidents[14]. Although this complex is most widespread among older people (especially from Pentecostal circles), its impact is also strong on younger members, who still feel that their religion is viewed at least as "strange" by their compatriots.

These details make the basic contradiction clear: being tolerant in views but tight in structure (both organizationally and mentally). Both qualities are necessary to any minority to maintain its identity and self-protection. This kind of antithesis is, generally, quite different from what the dominant church looks like, where we witness the opposite combination: On the one hand, we observe a more articulated outward-looking conservatism and even authoritarianism by the official hierarchy, with a restrained attitude toward liberal religious legislation, and an indisputable liturgical orthodoxy. On the other hand, we find a loose and fluid parochial structure and composition (in urban parishes), a less intensive extra-ritual networking, and by consequence, a less expressed sense of primary social belonging.

CONCLUSION. A PATTERN OF SECULARIZED SOCIETY?

Let us assume that the general trend of postcommunist transition in Russia is toward an emergence of the elements of civil society, which include structural pluralism, separation of the private and public fields, free intensive networks at grass-roots level, and individualization (mostly seen in urban areas). If this assumption is true, the minority religious groups, with the exception of several exclusive sects inclined toward totalitarian forms, represent a pattern of this new and still developing social setting.

Let us consider this pattern in several respects. *Politically*, minorities, as opposed to the dominant Orthodox hierarchy, represent a type of relationship with the state that could never exist under the communist power and that is close to the common Western pattern: a strict separation, independence from public money, depoliticalization and deideologization[15]. *Socially*, the minorities, unlike the average practitioners of the dominant Church, are composed of relatively young people, with more equal gender ratio, coming from middle and lower-middle class urban professional groups, having better education and broader world-outlooks than the general population[16]. *Organizationally*, minorities usually have a well-established group structure and intensive group activities, which involve all members and which are focused on different kinds of active participation in common life. There are some elements of a free civil association and even of a small private enterprise, in this type of organization. *Psychologically,* minorities maintain a much stronger sense of group identity and individual belonging, and this sense is surely combined with, and based upon, religious beliefs. The participation in a dense network gives a feeling of a common achievement orientation. In the case of these religious groups the goals to be achieved appear to be therapeutic, self-perfection, or, finally, salvation.

As a matter of fact, the traits I have just listed are related to how religion exists in modern (or postmodern) secular society. Religion moves out of public life; it becomes privatized and subject to arbitrary eclectic interpretations; around it appears a crowd of para- and quasi-religious phenomena; the institutional and ritual participation is massively abandoned or becomes occasional—and finally, religion in a strict sense of the word, remains embodied in *small active communities based on strong immediate attachment*. Thus, the religious minorities I studied play the role of a live experiment, where people learn both how *to be* religious and how *to deal with* religion in a postatheist secular society.

By comparison, the massive formal (symbolic) affiliation with Orthodoxy, revealed in the surveys of the 1990s, is a phenomenon of a quite different kind. Stemming from the general identity crisis, this type of affiliation seems to be a state of collective mind and is not likely to have deep structural consequences. At the same time, this state of mind can persist for a long time, being encouraged and manipulated by politicians. Orthodoxy remains an important source of national identity, as is the case with, for example, Irish Catholicism or Iranian Shi'ism, although compared to these latter, Orthodoxy's fundament of "living" beliefs is much weaker.

Nevertheless, whatever exceptional status they keep because of their dominant position and symbolic significance, the Orthodox parishes, composed of both *real* believers and nominal belongers, will perhaps gradually move in the same direction as do the minorities. This has already happened with some groups within the Orthodox Church as they adjust themselves to the new secular world. However, this possibility strongly depends on whether the ruling Church hierarchy is able to imagine and carry out a profound *aggiornamento*.

NOTES

1.   The *Rosa* is an original Russian community, created by a Russian pastor with Pentecostal roots, and thus with evident charismatic accents, and gathering mostly young people at a big movie theater twice a week. After two hours of prophecies, the believers take part in an open, public communion ceremony. The Church has some territorial structure, although the hierarchy seems not to be excessive. Some of the members come from different Pentecostal sects widespread in the Russian South and Ukraine, but the majority come from nonreligious parents.

2.   For example, the last variable is very close to the highest figures in World Value Study of 1991, which are found in both Irelands and the United States, and is practically similar to the level of Italy and Austria.

In another recent survey conducted by the Institute for System Studies and Sociology in Moscow, 44 percent of the 1200 Muscovites polled said they believed in God. The majority of Muscovites, 59.5 percent thought that the state should support the church and 69 percent that Orthodox services should be broadcast on television. Half did not object to religious teaching in schools and 82 percent said that the destroyed churches have to be restored (Moscow News #4 1996)

These figures are supported, with a range from about 45 percent to 60 percent of self-declared believers, by the previous studies carried out since 1990: for example, Greeley, 1994; The Simple

Soviet Man, 1993; a survey by the Analytical Center of the Russian Academy of Sciences in 1990 and 1991; comments published in *Voprosy Filosofii* (Problems of Philosophy), 7, 1992.

It is remarkable, that these figures have not really changed during 1990s.

3.   Church attendance is the most commonly recognized measure of religious practice. In more general terms, practice means both ritual participation and institutional attachment.

4.   For example, the share of those who support the moral and spiritual guidance of religion is very close to the highest levels found in both Irelands and the United States, and equal to the level of Italy and Austria. All comparisons are drawn from the World Value Studies program of 1991.

5.   The place of religion in the quest for the "Russian idea" constitutes a topic of special interest. The subject of "national idea" has been in the center of Russian discourse since the mid-nineteenth century. While an expression like the "French idea" or the "American idea" sounds very strange, the problem of the "Russian idea" is a very common and widely discussed notion. In the postcommunist years the discussion restarted with a new pace. Religion (in this case, Russian Orthodoxy) is one of the most frequent elements of these discussions of the "Russian idea."

6.   In 1996 the total number of registered religious communities in Russia was 13,078, compared to 5,501 in 1990, before the Law of Freedom of Conscience was adopted. So the figure more than doubled. Interestingly, the percentage of Russian Orthodox communities in these two listings decreased from 63 percent to 55 percent. (see *Religioznye ob'edineniia* 1996).

7.   The gap between nominal and real references to religion is also supported indirectly by several variables in the surveys. While 47 percent say they "believe in God," only 22 percent say that "God exists," 24 percent believe in life after death, 24 percent believe in heaven, and so on. Why are those who "believe in God" twice as many as those who say "God exists"? Perhaps because to say "I believe" means to choose a symbolic vector, a self-identification with an abstract idea, a symbol, while to say "God exists" means to share a particular religious knowledge, representation, and tradition. The same reasoning might apply to such concrete notions as life after death or heaven.

8.   1993 was a landmark year as reported by members of different denominations of my sample. About 70 percent of respondents converted in the years 1990–1993, and this group includes people of all ages. An Orthodox priest reported a tremendous rise in the number of baptisms in 1989–1991, and that sometimes there were 50–60 people in his church each Sunday, only 5–10 percent of them babies. The *Rosa* pastor recalls that the peak was in 1991–1992, when about 300 people might "make confession" (i.e. be converted) in one day. The Lutheran pastor said the rise of attendance in 1990–1991 was quite unexpected, as was the later drop in 1993–1994. Massive ceremonies of conversion accompanied the visits of renown Eastern cultists like Ole Nidal in 1991–1992.

Later came a stabilization of attendance at levels which are currently much lower than in the critical years of 1989–1993 (see Figure 1).

9.   The Russian form of narcissism and a "me-first" attitude is partly a psychological response to communistic, *Orwellian* collectivism that dominated before. However, it bears some close resemblance to the selfish individualism and institutional erosion that are common in the Western societies today.

10.   In principle, it is necessary to include in this list the minority groups within the Russian Orthodox Church itself. I mean not only several churches separated from the Moscow Patriarchy and maintaining institutional independence, but also several communities *within* the jurisdiction of the Moscow Patriarchy, especially the so-called "Orthodox brotherhoods" ("*pravoslavnye bratstva*") of different orientations, that profess a cohesive religiosity with strong feeling of belonging. These communities deserve special analysis and are not included in this study.

11.   The conceptual controversies finally become explicit in purely legal issues. The old Russian parliament (the Supreme Soviet) was going to adopt in 1993 an amendment practically discarding the principle of equality supported by the law of 1990; eventually it did not because it was dismissed by the president. A new wave of legal discussions began in 1995–1996 in the state *Duma* (the new parliament), going in the same direction: more state control, fewer guarantees for freedom of faith, some unequivocal (although not direct) points of preferences towards the dominant church (see, for

example, the discussion in *Moscow News* #43 1996). In July of 1997 the new, less liberal, bill passed in the *Duma* by the vast majority. It was then vetoed by the president after a storm of domestic and international critique, thus provoking for the first time a clear crisis in state–church relations. Two months later, it was passed again and signed by the president in a slightly changed version. The new 1997 law introduced many clauses that are not favorable for minorities.

12.   This kind of affiliation is found among Orthodox brotherhoods (see Note 10), as well as in some other parishes placed in exceptional situations. For example, a Moscow Orthodox priest I interviewed reported of his thoroughly unified community set up during the restoration works in his church. The priest himself qualified this case as exceptional.

13.   The question of differences in attitudes towards work and wealth cannot be elaborated here in full detail.

14.   As one of the respondents puts it, "many of us still retain something from this psychology of the 'catacomb Christianity,' when we were in permanent stress." Some of the interviewed community leaders were well aware of this predisposition but yet unable to overcome it.

15.   Most of my respondents tried to be politically indifferent, either because of their essential escapism, as in NRM, or by dependence on Paul's statement that "no authority exists without God's permission" (Rom.13,1), as in Protestant groups.

At the same time, it is just minorities, not the Russian Orthodox Church, who made attempts at participating in party politics in the beginning of 1990s, and later, in the parliamentary elections of 1995. These attempts had little success: the Christian–Democratic Union supported by Russian Protestants, mostly Baptists, received less than 1 percent of the votes. After that religious politics have been practically nonexistent. The Orthodox Church, without engaging in organized political activity, supplies its support by fragments to the state, to nationalist opposition, and, to a far lesser extent, to democratic political groups.

16.   Typically, members of Moscow minority groups such as Eastern cults, Protestant-like new sects (such as *Rosa*, for example), most of the NRMs, and the "modernist" Orthodox communities are between 20–40 years of age. This figure is definitely younger that the practicing Orthodox, on average. They typically come from the families of urban low-middle professionals and most of them have higher education (except traditional Pentecostals).

REFERENCES

Agadjanian, A. 1993. Les cultes orientaux et la nouvelle religiosite en Russie. *Revue d'etudes comparatives Est–Ouest*, 3–4, (septembre–decembre), 155–177.

Davie, G. 1996. Religion in Europe. *Archives des sciences sociales des religions*, 94, 7–8.

Greeley A. 1994. A religious revival in Russia? *Journal for the Scientific Study of Religion, 33*(3), 253–272.

Furman D. and K. Kaariainen. 1997. *Believers, Atheists and Others: Evolution of Russian Religiosity.* Voprosy filosofii (Problems of Philosophy). Moscow, *6*, 35–52 (in Russian).

Religioznye ob'edineniia 1996. *Guide of Religious Organizations of the Russian Federation.* Moscow,1996 (in Russian).

The Simple Soviet Man. 1993. *The Simple Soviet Man: Essays in the Social Portrait in the Beginning of 90s.* Moscow: Nauka Publishers (in Russian).

AN EMPIRICAL ASSESSMENT OF
THE WAGNER–MODIFIED HOUTS
QUESTIONNAIRE
A SPIRITUAL GIFTS INVENTORY

Judith V. Kehe

ABSTRACT

The use of spiritual gift inventories in empirical religious research is becoming more prevalent. However, the psychometric properties of these inventories and the discrepancy in the number of underlying dimensions that these inventories purport to measure have raised questions about their use. This study investigated the potential usefulness and the psychometric properties of the Wagner–Modified Houts Questionnaire, a spiritual gifts inventory. Participants in this study were 108 pastoral counselors and 36 clergy. Descriptive statistics revealed gender differences among certain spiritual gifts. Males had significantly higher mean scores on the gifts of evangelism, helps, knowledge, pastor, poverty, service, and teaching. Moderate success was attained in predicting seven of eleven hypothesized gifts among pastoral counselors with clergy having consistently higher mean scores than lay persons. Exploratory factor analysis using oblique oblimin rotation produced a three-factor structure. This inventory appears to be a promising tool for further development.

Research in the Social Scientific Study of Religion, Volume 11, pages 81-98.
Copyright © 2000 by JAI Press Inc.
All rights of reproduction in any form reserved.
ISBN: 0-7623-0656-4

81

Designed primarily to assist Christians in discovering their unique and diverse gifts, spiritual gift inventories are based in the New Testament passages which point to the varied gifts among members of the church (Romans 12:4–8; 1 Corinthians 12:6–10, 28–31; 1 Corinthians 14:1–19; Ephesians 4:11–12 and 1 Peter 4:11). The overall purpose of these gifts in the edification of the body of Christ, the Church, is readily apparent in these scriptures. From a Christian perspective, spiritual or charismatic gifts can be readily understood as gifts that are divinely bestowed. The source of these gifts is the Holy Spirit and these gifts "are not the result of human initiative, effort or merit" (Hocking 1975 p. 2).

On an empirical level, measuring spiritual gifts has been a somewhat more tenuous undertaking. Not only is there criticism about the inventories themselves, but the empirical research cannot occur without addressing certain theoretical and theological concerns. The issue of whether spiritual gifts should be construed as literary devices is one such concern, as well as the continued debate around differentiating between spiritual gifts and natural talents (Cooper and Blakeman, 1994). These authors also cited 1 Peter 4:11 as providing the basis for yet another debate among the empirical literature: whether the two gifts cited in this New Testament book (serving and speaking) are two additional spiritual gifts, or whether these are two broad categories of spiritual gifts.

Cooper and Blakeman (1994) summarized that two major criticisms exist with the use of spiritual gift inventories in research. First, the psychometric properties of these inventories are considered less than robust, with poor internal and external reliabilities, and therefore lack the rigor of standardized tests. Second, the inventories have been criticized for the overlapping of spiritual gifts; hence the number of underlying gifts that these inventories purport to measure has been questioned. Further compounding this issue is the fact that the number of spiritual gifts has indeed varied from inventory to inventory and gender differences have been found. Ledbetter and Foster (1989) summarized some of these variations among the various spiritual gifts: Baxter (1983) identified 11 gifts, Bennett and Bennett (1971) 10 gifts, Blanchard (1983) 22 gifts, Currah (1972) 21 gifts, Gangel (1983) 20 gifts, Hocking (1975) 14 gifts, and Wagner (1979) 27 gifts.

Previous studies (Cooper and Blakeman 1994; Ledbetter and Foster 1989) revealed gender differences among the spiritual gifts of administration, helping, prophecy, discernment, teaching, knowledge, and leadership. Among the participants in Ledbetter and Foster's study, females scored higher in helping and males scored higher on prophecy, discernment, teaching, knowledge, and leadership. In Cooper and Blakeman's study, males had higher mean scores than females on the gift of administration. However, the overall sample sizes in these studies (less than 100) with unequal gender cells limit their potential generalizability.

In factor analyzing the Hocking spiritual gifts inventory, Ledbetter and Foster (1989) produced three factors of Serving, Speaking, and Governing. This inventory was designed to measure 14 spiritual gifts. Hocking (1975) distinguished between gifts from Jesus Christ that represented four distinct individuals (apostles, prophets, evangelists, and pastors who were equated as teachers) and those gifts that were given by the Holy Spirit. The gifts of the Holy Spirit were placed in three categories and consisted of the speaking gifts (prophecy, teaching, exhortation, word of wisdom, and word of knowledge), the serving gifts (ministering or helps, giving, ruling, discernment of spirits) and the supernatural gifts (faith, healing, working of miracles, interpretation of tongues, and the gift of speaking in tongues).

Factor analysis of the Hocking Spiritual Gift Inventory by Ledbetter and Foster (1989) revealed that the spiritual gifts of mercy and helps loaded on the serving factor and the gifts of discernment, wisdom, prophecy, serving, knowledge, teaching, and exhortation loaded on the speaking factor. This latter cluster of spiritual gifts can be readily identified among Hocking's (1975) theoretical clustering of "speaking gifts." Ledbetter and Foster's findings lent support to previous findings (Bruce 1971; Frederickson 1985; McRae, 1976) of a two factor solution with an additional third factor of "governing" identified and which included the two gifts of leadership and administration. The content and construct validity of the Hocking Spiritual Inventory was, however, found to be questionable.

While supporting Currah's (1972) finding of a third factor, Ledbetter and Foster's third factor (governing) did not correspond to Currah's gifts of intellect, faith, and tongues, but seem to more closely match Blanchard's (1983) category of "office." Currah's third category seemed to more closely match Hocking's (1975) supernatural category, which included the gifts of faith, miracles, tongues, and the interpretation of tongues. While there seems to be some congruence in the possibility of three underlying numbers of factors, predicting what gifts would cluster on one factor poses a challenge to assessing the psychometric properties of spiritual gift inventories.

Cooper and Blakeman (1994) examined the psychometric properties of the Objective Questionnaire Testing (OQT) set of the Motivational Spiritual Gifts Inventory (MGI) which was developed by Fortune and Fortune (1987). The secular version of this inventory included 175 items to identify seven motivational gifts of perceiver, server, teacher, exhorted, giver, administration, and compassion. In addition to the previously mentioned motivational gifts (those gifts that one possesses and which serve as the motivational source for our lives), Fortune and Fortune delineated two other categories of gifts: manifestation and ministry gifts. Manifestation gifts, those gifts that included the supernatural manifestations of the Holy Spirit, included the gifts of knowledge, faith, healing, miracles, and prophecy, discerning of spirits, the gift of tongues, and the interpretation of tongues. This list closely matches Hocking's (1975) category of supernatural gifts. Ministry gifts, according to Fortune and Fortune, are those gifts that equip one for ministry and include the spiritual gifts of apostle, prophet, evangelist, pastor, and teacher. These gifts are comparable to Hocking's (1975) category gifts from Jesus Christ.

The aforementioned empirical studies (Cooper and Blakeman 1994; Ledbetter and Foster 1989) have provided us with some insight into the psychometric properties of spiritual gift inventories and have also provided a springboard for further exploratory and comparative studies with spiritual gifts. Evidence was provided to support the existence of gender differences; however given the prevalence of other spiritual gifts inventories and their increasing use within the church, there is a dearth of research that has explored clergy and lay differences as well as the potential use of spiritual gift inventories among pastoral counselors.

The purpose of this study was threefold. First, this inventory was used to predict what spiritual gifts pastoral counselors are more likely to possess based on the theoretical review of the literature; second, gender differences were explored to support previous findings; and third, this study explored whether exploratory factor analysis of the Wagner–Modified Houts Questionnaire, an inventory that is readily available, will support a three factor solution.

HYPOTHESIZED PATTERNS OF SPIRITUAL GIFTS AMONG PASTORAL COUNSELORS

While one would expect to find varied spiritual gifts among pastoral counselors, it was hypothesized that the mean scores on the following 11 spiritual gifts— discernment, exhortation, faith, healing, helps, knowledge, mercy, pastor, prophecy, service, and wisdom would be higher than the other 14 gifts of the total 25 gifts that the Wagner–Modified Houts Questionnaire (Wagner 1995) purports to measure. These eleven spiritual gifts were selected based on exploration of the theoretical and empirical literature that highlights the traits and functions of a pastoral counselor.

Wicks (1983), in his definition of pastoral counseling, has argued for the gift of *discernment* where the pastoral counselor has to focus his or her eye on God in the therapeutic relationship. Discernment is also one of the five spiritual gifts that Tan (1991) postulated that the lay counselor should have. The other four were *wisdom, knowledge, mercy,* and *healing.* Tan argued that the counselor should be "...a spirit-filled, mature Christian who has knowledge of scripture, wisdom in applying scripture to life, and a regular prayer life" (p. 101).

Many of the current definitions of the pastoral counselor have their roots within pastoral care. Clebsch and Jaekle (1964) outlined four pastoral functions—guiding, reconciling, healing, and sustaining. The guiding function, as well the recognition of pastoral counselors as pastors, are captured in Blanchette's (1991) definition of the pastoral counselor: "The genuine pastoral counselor can be said to be a *pastor* in every sense of the word" since the pastoral counselor is one who "shepherds persons into a new grazing land, leads people to cooler waters" (p. 31) towards making confident choices. In clarifying aspects of his definition of the pastoral counselor, Estadt (1993) concluded, "as pastoral counselors we are instinctively interested in the spiritual dimension of our clients" (p. 2). The pastoral function of healing is readily apparent in this clarification. Clebsch and Jaekle (1964) described healing as the "restoration to a condition of wholeness, on the assumption that this restoration achieves also a new level of spiritual insight and welfare" (p. 8). The *healing* function of pastoral counseling was previously cited as one of the spiritual gifts among counselors (Tan 1991). Within this healing dimension of pastoral counseling, one can easily envision a helping relationship where one seeks help from someone who is perceived as being able to provide that help; hence the selection of the gift of *helps*.

Some of the hypothesized spiritual gifts for the pastoral counselor are highlighted in the process of pastoral counseling. Within the therapeutic relationship, the gift of *exhortation* or encouragement has been found to be a characteristic of Christian counselors (De Vries II 1994). De Vries II also found significant intercorrelations between *exhortation, wisdom,* and *knowledge.* Gerkin (1984) has argued for the integration of *faith* and praxis in the pastoral counseling process in order for pastoral counseling to be both an authentically theological and a scientifically psychological discipline. Oates (1951) previously emphasized the gift of *faith* by commenting that *faith* and the gift of *discernment* are the two most desirable traits of the pastoral counselor. Oates had suggested that any counselor who has faith in the presence of God in counseling and who deeply perceives God as present in the pastoral process is doing pastoral counseling. Hendrix (1977) has proposed that pastoral counseling have both a priestly and a *prophetic* dimension. Rooted in the traditional view of the prophet, Hendrix described the pastoral counselor as one who is extraordinarily sensitive to evil.

The notion of pastoral counseling as a ministry to which one is called is salient among pastoral counselors (Kehe et al. 1998). Hence, the gift of *service* is at the heart of ministry. "The Basic English definition of the word (Ministry) is simply *service*" (Messer 1989, p. 28).

HYPOTHESIZED GENDER DIFFERENCES

In this present study, it was hypothesized that if any significant gender differences were found that they would be among the following gifts: administration, discernment, knowledge, helping, prophecy, and teaching to support findings from the aforementioned studies (Cooper and Blakeman 1994; Ledbetter and Foster 1989). Based on these findings, males were expected to score higher on the gifts of administration, prophecy, discernment, teaching, leadership, and knowledge; and females were expected to score higher on the gift of help. However, since the questionnaire, which was used in this study, is different from those of the aforementioned studies, caution would be exercised in making generalizations.

PSYCHOMETRIC DIMENSIONS OF SPIRITUAL GIFTS

One of the major areas of debate with spiritual gift inventories is their poor construct validity. Despite the number of gifts that these inventories purport to measure, factor analysis has revealed three underlying factor solutions (Cooper and Blakeman 1994; Ledbetter and Foster 1989). It was hypothesized that gifts which loaded on any one factor in these cited two studies would load either on similar factors or would cluster together based on some logical theoretical categorical fit such as Hocking's (1975) gifts from Jesus Christ or gifts from the Holy Spirit (speaking gifts, serving gifts, and the supernatural gifts) or Fortune and Fortune's (1987) manifestation or ministry gifts.

METHOD

Measures

The Wagner-Modified Houts Questionnaire (Wagner 1995) has been developed in connection with Fuller Seminary, California. Initially, Wagner (1979) identified 20 gifts, but later added five additional spiritual gifts from the New Testament and two Old Testament gifts (Ledbetter and Foster, 1989) for a total of 27 gifts. This modified questionnaire is comprised of 125 items on which the participant assesses the truthfulness of each item as it pertains to his or her life. From the 125 items on this questionnaire, 25 scales measure 25 Biblical or spiritual gifts that have been identified: Administration, Celibacy, Discernment of Spirits, Evangelist, Exhortation, Exorcism, Faith, Giving, Healing, Helping, Hospitality, Intercession, Interpretation, Knowledge, Leadership, Mercy, Miracles, Missionary, Pastor, Prophecy, Service, Teaching, Tongues, Voluntary Poverty, and Wisdom. These gifts are describes as follows (pp. 111–117):

Administration. The gift of administration is the special ability that God gives to certain members of the Body of Christ to understand clearly the immediate and long-range goals of a particular unit of the Body of Christ and to devise and execute effective plans for the accomplishment of those goals.

Celibacy. The gift of celibacy is the special ability that God gives to certain members of the Body of Christ to remain single and enjoy it; to be unmarried and not suffer undue sexual temptations.

Discerning of Spirits. The gift of the discerning of the spirits is the special ability that God gives to certain members of the Body of Christ to know with assurance whether certain behavior is purported to be of God is in reality divine, human, or satanic.

Evangelist. The gift of evangelist is the special ability that God gives to certain members of the Body of Christ to share the gospel with unbelievers in such a way that men and women become Jesus' disciples and responsible members of the Body of Christ.

Exhortation. The gift of exhortation is the special ability that God gives to certain members of the Body of Christ to minister words of comfort, consolation, encouragement, and counsel to other members of the Body in such a way that they feel helped and healed.

Exorcism. The gift of exorcism is the special ability that God gives to certain members of the Body of Christ to cast out demons and evil spirits.

Faith. The gift of faith is the special ability that God gives to certain members of the Body of Christ to discern with extraordinary confidence the will and purposes of God for his work.

Giving. The gift of the giving of the spirits is the special ability that God gives to certain members of the Body of Christ to contribute their material resources to the work of the Lord with liberality and cheerfulness.

Healing. The gift of healing is the special ability that God gives to certain members of the Body of Christ to serve as human intermediaries through whom it pleases God to cure illness and restore health apart from the use of natural means.

Helps. The gift of helps is the special ability that God gives to certain members of the Body of Christ to invest the talents they have in the life and ministry of other members of the Body, with thus enabling those others to increase the effectiveness of their own spiritual gifts.

Hospitality. The gift of hospitality is the special ability that God gives to certain members of the Body of Christ to provide an open house and a warm welcome to those in need of food and lodging.

Intercession. The gift of intercession is the special ability that God gives to certain members of the Body of Christ to pray for extended periods of time on a regular basis and see frequent and specific answers to their prayers, to a degree much greater than that which is expected of the average Christian.

Interpretation. The gift of interpretation is the special ability that God gives to certain members of the Body of Christ to make known in the vernacular the message of one who speaks in tongues.

Knowledge. The gift of knowledge is the special ability that God gives to certain members of the Body of Christ to discover, accumulate, analyze, and clarify information and ideas which are pertinent to the well-being of the Body.

Leadership. The gift of leadership is the special ability that God gives to certain members of the Body of Christ to set goals in accordance with God's purpose for the future and to communicate these goals to others in such a way that they voluntarily and harmoniously work together to accomplish those goals for the glory of God.

Mercy. The gift of mercy is the special ability that God gives to certain members of the Body of Christ to feel genuine empathy and compassion for individuals (both Christian and non-Christian) who suffer distressing physical, mental, or emotional problems, and to translate that compassion into cheerfully done deeds that reflect Christ's love and alleviate the suffering.

Miracles. The gift of miracles is the special ability that God gives to certain members of the Body of Christ to serve as human intermediaries through whom it pleases God to perform powerful acts that are perceived by observers to have altered the ordinary course of nature.

Missionary. The gift of missionary is the special ability that God gives to certain members of the Body of Christ to minister whatever other spiritual gifts they have in a second culture.

Pastor. The gift of pastor is the special ability that God gives to certain members of the Body of Christ to assume a long-term personal responsibility for the spiritual welfare of a group of believers.

Prophecy. The gift of prophecy is the special ability that God gives to certain members of the Body of Christ to receive and communicate an immediate message of God to His people through a divinely anointed utterance.

Service. The gift of service is the special ability that God gives to certain members of the Body of Christ to identify the unmet needs involved in a task related to God's work, and to make use of available resources to meet those needs and help accomplish the desired results.

Teaching. The gift of teaching is the special ability that God gives to certain members of the Body of Christ to communicate information relevant to the health and ministry of the Body and its members in such a way that others will learn.

Tongues. The gift of healing is the special ability that God gives to certain members of the Body of Christ (a) to speak to God in a language they have never learned and/or (b) to receive and communicate an immediate message of God to His people through a divinely anointed utterance in a language they never learned.

Voluntary Poverty. The gift of voluntary poverty is the special ability that God gives to certain members of the Body of Christ to renounce material comfort and luxury and adopt a personal lifestyle equivalent to those living at the poverty level in a given society in order to serve God more efficiently.

Wisdom. The gift of wisdom is the special ability that God gives to certain members of the Body of Christ to know the mind of the Holy Spirit in such a way as to receive insight into how given knowledge may best be applied to specific needs arising in the Body of Christ.

Subjects

The sample population was comprised of 108 pastoral counselors (61 current enrollees at the master's level and 47 post master's degree students in a pastoral counseling training program in the Baltimore -Washington area). Thirty-six ordained ministers who were never enrolled in a formal pastoral counseling program were used as a comparison group. The overall sample size was 144 subjects, 67 males and 75 females (no gender was indicated by 2 participants). Lay pastoral counselors represented 69 percent of the pastoral counseling sample. Religious denominations represented were Roman Catholics (47.9 percent); Protestants of various denominations (Anglican, Adventist, Religious Science, Lutheran, Episcopalian, Church of Christ, Methodist, Quaker, African-Methodist, United Methodist, Baptist, Presbyterian, and Christian Church) represented 50.7 percent, and the remaining 1.4 percent comprised a category of "other" and included participants of the Unitarian–Universalist and the Jewish faith.

Procedure

Pastoral counselors' participation was solicited through classroom presentations and through personal invitations. Some graduate pastoral counselors with local addresses were selected from an alumni directory for geographic convenience. All churches listed in a local newspaper were contacted for clergy participation. In addition, clergy participation was also solicited through acquaintances. Informed consents were obtained for participation in the study, and the instrument was completed at participants' convenience. Because the New Testament book is the primary source for spiritual gift inventories, participants whose faith denomination did not endorse this book were given the option not to complete the spiritual gift questionnaire. The instrument was the last item to be completed in a package, which comprised of demographic information, an exploratory questionnaire, and scales to assess spiritual dimensions. A total of 135 questionnaires were completed.

For the analysis of the data, participants were classified in the following groups based on ordained status and pastoral counseling training:

Group 1 was comprised of clergy who were never enrolled in a formal pastoral counseling program. Group 2, clergy who were currently enrolled in the Master's Degree program in Pastoral Counseling. Group 3, clergy who had a Master's Degree in Pastoral Counseling. Group 4, lay persons who were currently enrolled in the Master's Degree program, and Group 5, lay persons who had a Master's Degree in Pastoral Counseling. Fourteen of the pastoral counseling students classified themselves as "vowed religious" and for the data analysis, they were categorized as "lay" to make up a sample size of 64 ordained and 71 lay persons.

Table 1.   Group Means and Standard Deviations: Spiritual Gifts

Spiritual Gifts	GRP 1	GRP 2	GRP 3	GRP 4	GRP 5
Administration	11.50 (2.38)	10.62 (2.90)	9.71 (3.69)	8.23 (3.03)	8.72 (3.14)
Celibacy	3.44 (4.18)	4.69 (4.29)	5.14 (4.38)	4.05 (4.84)	2.48 (4.03)
Discernment*	6.53 (3.03)	6.38 (2.75)	6.14 (3.55)	4.23 (2.85)	2.72 (2.07)
Evangelism	8.68 (3.06)	8.85 (2.15)	8.00 (3.86)	5.38 (3.03)	4.60 (2.92)
Exhortation*	11.12 (2.89)	11.77 (2.13)	10.79 (3.77)	10.10 (2.09)	9.28 (2.72)
Exorcism	1.12 (1.77)	1.08 (2.22)	2.36 (3.61)	.68 (1.69)	.24 (.60)
Faith*	9.39 (3.40)	9.77 (2.28)	8.50 (4.24)	7.29 (3.18)	8.28 (2.78)
Giving	9.21 (3.49)	9.54 (3.07)	8.14 (4.28)	7.39 (3.19)	6.45 (2.75)
Healing*	5.01 (2.88)	5.08 (2.81)	5.29 (3.15)	3.38 (3.38)	2.96 (1.72)
Helps*	11.13 (2.43)	11.85 (1.99)	10.57 (2.95)	8.81 (2.91)	8.16 (2.81)
Inter. Tongues	.68 (2.31)	1.23 (2.86)	1.71 (2.73)	1.00 (2.30)	.24 (1.01)
Intercession	7.82 (3.01)	7.62 (1.80)	8.29 (3.83)	6.06 (3.40)	5.43 (2.88)
Knowledge*	10.87 (3.16)	11.54 (2.07)	10.86 (3.01)	8.56 (3.27)	8.00 (2.74)
Leadership	10.25 (2.42)	10.62 (2.33)	8.57 (3.41)	8.14 (2.75)	8.52 (2.62)
Mercy*	11.10 (2.68)	11.00 (2.52)	10.59 (3.25)	10.29 (2.85)	9.32 (2.61)
Miracles	5.24 (3.02)	5.38 (2.02)	5.00 (3.98)	3.64 (2.79)	3.16 (1.72)
Missionary	9.47 (2.86)	11.54 (2.03)	9.50 (2.59)	8.38 (3.03)	7.32 (2.17)
Pastor*	10.96 (2.71)	10.92 (2.63)	11.43 (3.55)	7.76 (3.03)	7.32 (2.17)
Poverty	5.99 (2.93)	8.62 (3.82)	6.75 (3.96)	6.51 (3.45)	5.32 (3.30)
Prophecy*	7.40 (3.04)	6.77 (3.35)	5.93 (3.85)	4.72 (3.46)	3.76 (2.79)
Service*	9.43 (2.84)	8.38 (2.10)	8.21 (4.08)	7.45 (2.81)	5.60 (2.47)
Teaching	11.57 (3.01)	12.08 (2.29)	11.64 (3.34)	8.28 (3.62)	7.56 (3.74)
Wisdom*	10.90 (2.71)	10.54 (2.88)	10.64 (3.05)	9.23 (2.70)	8.72 (2.46)

Note: * = hypothesized gifts
GRP 1 = ordained clergy with no formal training
GRP 2 = ordained clergy enrolled in MS Program
GRP 3 = ordained clergy with MS Degree
GRP 4 = lay counselors enrolled in MS Program
GRP 5 = lay pastoral counselors with MS Degree

RESULTS

Descriptive Statistics

Table 1 presents the mean scores and standard deviations for the varying groups. As can be seen, ordained clergy with no formal training in pastoral counseling (Group 1) and Groups 2 and 3 (clergy who are currently enrolled in MS program in pastoral counseling and clergy with MS degrees in pastoral counseling) scored consistently above the means on most of the spiritual gifts. An asterisk ("*") indicates the eleven hypothesized gifts. Seven of the eleven hypothesized gifts—exhortation, faith, helps, pastor, mercy, knowledge, and wisdom were

Table 2.   Ranked Mean Scores of Groups

Group 1	Group 2	Group 3	Group 4	Group 5
Teaching (11.57)	Teaching (12.08)	Teaching (11.64)	Exhortation (10.10)	Mercy (9.32)
Administ (11.50)	Helps (11.85)	Pastor (11.43)	Mercy (10.29)	Exhortation (9.28)
Helps (11.13)	Exhortation (11.77)	Knowledge (10.86)	Wisdom (9.23)	Administration (8.72)
Exhortation (11.12)	Knowledge (11.54)	Exhortation (10.79)	Helps (8.81)	Wisdom (8.72)
Mercy (11.10)	Missionary (11.54)	Wisdom (10.64)	Knowledge (8.56)	Missionary (8.68)
Pastor (10.96)	Mercy (11.00)	Mercy (10.59)	Missionary (8.38)	Leadership (8.52)
Wisdom (10.90)	Pastor (10.92)	Helps (10.57)	Teaching (8.28)	Faith (8.28)
Knowledge (10.87)	Administration (10.62)	Administration (9.71)	Hospitality (8.24)	Helps (8.16)
Leadership (10.27)	Leadership (10 54)	Missionary (9.50)	Administration (8.23)	
Missionary (9.47)	Wisdom (10.54)	Faith (8.50)	Leadership (8.14)	
Service (9.43)	Hospitality (10.31)	Hospitality (8.28)		
Faith (9.39)	Faith (9.77)	Leadership (8.57)		
Giving (9.21)	Giving (9.54)	Faith (8.50)		
Hospitality (8.70)	Evangelism (8.85)	Intercession (8.29)		
Fvangelism (8.68)	Poverty (8.62)	Hospitality (8.28)		
	Service (8.38)	Service (8.21)		

among those that had high mean scores (mean scores greater than 8 out of a possible 15). Table 2 provides a rank order of the groups' mean scores.

Mercy and exhortation (two of the hypothesized gifts) had the highest mean scores. The gifts of teaching, administration, and missionary, which were not in the hypothesized cluster of gifts, also had high mean scores. The scores on the gifts of exorcism, speaking in tongues, and the interpretation of tongues were skewed. A closer examination revealed that some of the items on these three categories were not fully completed.

The Discriminant Function Analysis in table 3 demonstrates that nine of the eleven previously hypothesized spiritual gifts for both lay and ordained pastoral

Table 3.   Canonical Discriminant Function Analysis:
Lay and Ordained Pastoral Counselors Structure matrix:
pooled within-groups correlations between discriminating
variables and canonical discriminant functions

	Function 1	Function 2	Function 3
Pastor	.56333*	.10259	−.17012
Teaching	.50451*	.13003	−.02244
Evangelism	.50255*	.15578	.04841
Knowledge	.44034*	.11675	.03542
Helps	.43843*	.13788	.13933
Discernment	.42756*	.33227	−.01676
Mission	.35128*	−.07646	.27559
Healing	.30414*	.09299	−.07943
Intercession	.30017*	.12848	−.14026
Miracle	.29529*	.11054	.02036
Prophecy	.27472*	.17264	.07563
Giving	.25915*	.17125	.15838
Wisdom	.25761*	.11768	−.05519
Administration	.25666*	−.09671	.08114
Exhortation	.25142*	.17710	.12755
Faith	.21792*	−.19431	.13536
Poverty	.21761*	.19593	.21053
Service	.24587	.39191*	.00426
Tongues	.01727	.34622*	−.12532
Celibacy	.14543	.21478*	−.05945
Interpretation	.15227	.21454*	−.11457
Mercy	.14354	.20738*	.05180
Exorcism	.26227	.14693	−.32803*
Leadership	.22687	−.09206	.29020*
Hospitality	.19759	.10638	.26298*

Note: *denotes largest absolute correlation between each variable and any discriminant
function.

counselors clustered on function 1, which explained 55.06 percent of the variance
with function 2 explaining 25.03 percent of the variance.

Independent sample t-tests revealed significant clergy and gender differences
with the spiritual gift inventory. In table 4 significant mean differences were
found when clergy were compared with lay persons. Clergy had significantly
higher mean scores at p<.05 and at p<.005 levels. Table 5 illustrates significant
gender differences. Males scored significantly higher than females on the following gifts: evangelism, helps, knowledge, pastor, poverty, service, and teaching.
No significant female differences were found. The three gifts (exorcism, gifts of
tongues, and the interpretation of tongues) that were found to be skewed in this

Table 4. Means (M) and Standard Deviations (SD) of Spiritual Gifts: Ordained and Lay Pastoral Counselors

Spiritual Gift	Ordained		Lay		Total	
	M	SD	M	SD	M	SD
Administration	**10.87	(2.95)	8.55	(3.23)	**9.62**	(3.21)
Celebacy	**3.78	(4.02)	2.02	(3.95)	**3.76**	(4.42)
Discernment	**6.32	(3.03)	3.83	(2.73)	**4.98**	(3.17)
Evangelism	**8.41	(3.03)	5.39	(3.11)	**4.98**	(3.17)
Exhortation	11.13	(2.97)	9.81	(2.69)	**9.28**	(2.72)
Faith	**9.05	(3.42)	8.32	(3.11)	**8.44**	(3.31)
Giving	*9.10	(3.44)	7.08	(2.85)	**8.00**	(3.45)
Healing	**5.07	(2.87)	3.88	(3.24)	**4.12**	(3.00)
Helps	**11.14	(2.38)	8.67	(2.81)	**9.82**	(2.98)
Hospitality	8.78	(3.21)	7.81	(3.22)	**8.46**	(3.22)
Intercession	*7.85	(3.56)	5.53	(3.39)	**6.82**	(3.25)
Knowledge	**10.98	(2.90)	8.60	(3.36)	**9.64**	(3.26)
Leadership	*9.94	(2.64)	8.51	(2.89)	**9.09**	(2.82)
Mercy	11.11	(2.62)	9.92	(2.88)	**10.42**	(2.80)
Miracles	**5.22	(3.07)	3.75	(2.50)	**4.31**	(2.87)
Missionary	*9.82	(2.69)	8.43	(2.66)	**9.18**	(2.87)
Pastor	**10.96	(2.83)	7.69	(2.97)	**9.27**	(3.28)
Poverty	**6.55	(3.33)	5.46	(3.05)	**6.38**	(3.45)
Prophecy	**7.05	(3.25)	4.79	(3.32)	**5.60**	(3.50)
Service	**8.91	(2.83)	7.03	(2.81)	**7.80**	(3.11)
Teaching	**11.56	(2.92)	8.18	(4.03)	**9.79**	(3.79)
Wisdom	*10.74	(2.69)	9.25	(2.79)	**9.87**	(2.82)

Notes: Independent Samples T-Test (N = 118). Ordained (N = 60); Lay persons (N = 58).
  * Significant at $p < .05$; ** significant at $p < .005$

study were not included in this analysis. Table 5 summarizes the t-test for equality of means with significance at .05 and .005 levels respectively.

Exploratory Factor Analysis

Cronbach's alpha for the Wagner–Modified Houts Questionnaire was .97. Interscale coefficient between items was .92. Many significant correlations occurred between the spiritual gifts, which hints at the potential overlapping of items. In factor analyzing this inventory, both criteria of at least 5 individuals for each subscale and a sample of over 100 were met as suggested by Gorsuch (1983). Principal axes factoring that minimizes error variance (Kline 1994) with oblique oblimin rotation yielded 3 factors. Factors were analyzed using scree plots. The

Table 5.   Means (M) and Standard Deviations (SD) of
Spiritual Gifts by Gender

Spiritual Gift	Men		Women	
	M	SD	M	SD
Administration	9.89	(3.12)	9.46	(3.39)
Celibacy	3.81	(4.51)	3.71	(4.31)
Discernment	5.12	(3.03)	4.63	(3.21)
Evangelism	**7.61	(3.49)	5.73	(3.26)
Exhortation	10.74	(3.14)	10.10	(2.52)
Faith	8.44	(3.51)	8.37	(3.25)
Giving	8.54	(3.60)	7.61	(3.07)
Healing	4.46	(2.96)	3.88	(3.15)
Helps	*10.31	(3.15)	8.93	(3.32)
Hospitality	8.72	(3.42)	8.18	(2.99)
Intercession	6.88	(3.56)	6.52	(3.18)
Knowledge	*10.25	(3.15)	8.93	(3.32)
Leadership	9.51	(2.93)	8.75	(2.75)
Mercy	10.78	(2.85)	10.23	(2.66)
Miracles	4.43	(2.94)	3.08	(2.80)
Missionary	9.47	(2.95)	8.81	(2.68)
Pastor	**10.20	(3.17)	8.14	(3.25)
Poverty	6.98	(3.44)	5.79	(3.25)
Prophecy	5.79	(3.28)	5.28	(3.71)
Service	*8.54	(3.16)	7.38	(2.89)
Teaching	**10.95	(3.27)	8.56	(4.02)
Wisdom	10.27	(2.87)	9.37	(2.72)

Notes: Independent Samples T-Test (N = 137). Males (N = 66); Females (N = 71).
 * Significant at $p < .05$; ** significant at $p < .005$.

percentages of variance accounted for by each factor, factor loadings, and eigen values of the three factors are presented in Table 6. The identification of the three factors explained 64 percent of the variance.

DISCUSSION

Predicting Spiritual Gifts among Pastoral Counselors

The finding that seven of the eleven hypothesized gifts had higher mean scores among pastoral counselors is promising. However, this inventory seems to be a better discriminating tool for use among clergy who had consistently higher mean scores than lay persons. The gifts of mercy and exhortation had the highest mean

Table 6. Summary of Factor Loading for Oblimin Three-Factor Solution for the Wagner Modified Houts Questionnaire

Item	Factor Loading		
	1	2	3
Teaching	.87	.17	.32
Wisdom	.86	.17	.26
Knowledge	.84	.18	.27
Exhortation	.82	.12	.39
Pastoring	.82	.19	.26
Faith	.77	.14	.15
Evangelism	.77	.14	.15
Prophecy	.77	.37	.12
Discernment	.75	.35	.32
Miracle	.73	.43	.24
Leadership	.72	.02	.17
Helps	.71	−.03	.49
Administration	.69	−.04	.19
Intercession	.68	.21	.56
Giving	.66	.47	.16
Healing	.63	.47	.16
Service	.63	−.02	.53
Mission	.63	−.13	.53
Interpretation	.18	.87	−.08
Tongues	.18	.80	.08
Exorcism	.38	.51	.12
Poverty	.37	.03	.86
Mercy	.52	−.07	.64
Hospitality	.48	−.25	.56
Celibacy	.05	.09	.51
	Factor Correlations		
Factor 1	—		
Factor 2	.16	—	
Factor 3	.35	.18	—

scores and may indicate that among the sample population the cornerstone of being "pastoral" may lie in the possession of these two spiritual gifts. De Vries (1994) had found that the gift of exhortation or encouragement was prevalent among Christian counselors.

The definition of "mercy" as used in the leader's manual for this inventory includes the key word "empathy" which is at the crux of the helping relationship and is described by Wagner (1995) as the "...ability to feel genuine empathy and compassion for individuals..." (p. 113). Empathy has also been found to be positively correlated with religious integration (Lyons and Zingle 1990) and Muse and colleagues (1994) found that pastoral counseling students were more empathic when compared to both clinical counseling and business students. One can therefore envision that as pastoral counselors help their clients to discover the truth about themselves that mercy may be at the crux of this pastoral relationship. The biblical passage as found in Psalms 85:10: *Mercy and truth are met together; righteousness and peace have kissed each other* seems quite apropos here.

The low mean scores that were found with the gift of discernment among all participants was surprising and could hint at a discrepancy in the conceptual understanding of the word "discernment" as applied to the counseling dyad as compared to its definition as a spiritual gift. This finding points to the need for a comparative study between clergy, pastoral counselors, and spiritual directors to see if the gift of discernment is more salient among spiritual directors.

Gender Differences Among the Spiritual Gifts

Gender differences were found in this study and supported previous findings of gender differences among spiritual gifts. In this sample, males were found to score higher than females on the spiritual gifts of teaching and knowledge—two of Hocking's (1975) "speaking" gifts and this finding lends support to previous gender differences that were found in the two benchmark studies that were discussed previously. In this study, there were also significant differences found on the gifts of evangelism, helps, pastor, poverty, and service. The gifts of evangelism and pastors are two of the four gifts that Hocking postulated are given from Jesus Christ and which represented four distinct individuals. (The other two were prophets and apostles). Since pastors were equated to teachers, in Hocking's framework, it was not surprising that the male population also scored highly on teaching.

The gender differences that were found in this study could have been confounded by a clergy effect in that clergy, who were predominantly male, could have contributed to the significant male differences especially on the gifts of pastor and evangelism. High scores on the gift of poverty could again be attributed to the ordained and religious population, some of whom may have taken the vows of poverty along with the vows of celibacy and chastity. A further limitation of these findings is that the possession of certain spiritual gifts may be more socially desirable among this highly religious population. Further studies that would utilize a more heterogeneous population of diverse religious and vocational backgrounds are clearly indicated. Could the scale predict as well among nonreligious populations and also among other helping professionals? Would gender differences be found among a nonreligious population?

Psychometric Properties of the Wagner–Modified Houts Questionnaire

The reliabilities found in this inventory are rather encouraging and suggest that this inventory may be a worthwhile tool for further development in empirical research. The overlapping of many items and the finding of three underlying factors hint at the continued need for both exploratory and confirmatory factor analysis in researching spiritual gifts. The finding of three factors in this study and in previous studies also forces one to look at the conceptual understanding of spiritual gifts and the exploration of whether the information found in the biblical passage of 1Peter 4: 11 supports the notion of two broad categories of spiritual gifts. Do spiritual gifts illustrate the uniqueness and diversity of an individual's gifts, a qualitative distinction, or are spiritual gifts better understood as merely a quantitative concept?

One of the most interesting findings in this study is the potential use of the Wagner–Modified Houts Questionnaire as a discriminating tool among clergy and pastoral counselors. The high scores that were found among clergy hint at its potential usefulness among clergy. Studies that correlated spiritual gifts with personality styles as well as with spiritual assessments could prove beneficial in the avocation process. This study supports the further exploration of the spiritual gifts of mercy and exhortation as being the cornerstone of being "pastoral."

REFERENCES

Baxter, R. E. 1983. *Gifts of the Spirit*. Grand Rapids: Kregel.

Bennett, D., and R. Bennett 1971. *The Holy Spirit and You*. Plainfield, NJ: Logos International.

Blanchette, M. 1991. In B. Estadt, M. Blanchette and J. Compton (Eds.), *Pastoral Counseling*, 2nd edition. NJ: Prentice Hall.

Blanchard, T. 1983. *A practical guide to finding and using your spiritual gifts*. Wheaton, IL: Tyndale House.

Bruce, F. F. 1971. *I and II Corinthians*. Grand Rapids, Eerdmans.

Clebsch, W. A. and C. R. Jaeckle 1964. *Pastoral Care in Historical Perspective*. NY: Jason Aronson.

Cooper, S. E. and S. Blakeman. 1994. "Spiritual Gifts: A Psychometric Extension." *Journal of Psychology and Theology, 22*(1), 39–44.

Currah, G. J. 1972. *The New Testament Spiritual Gifts defined and described*. Unpublished master's thesis, Western Conservative Baptist Seminary, Portland, OR.

De Vries II, R. J. 1994. *Is it a gift? The Relationship between Therapeutic Competence and Individual Therapist's Characteristics of Experience, Personality and Spirituality*. Unpublished doctoral dissertation, Fuller Theological Seminary.

Estadt, B. K. 1993. In Pursuit of Freedom. *Psychology of Religion Newsletter*, American Psychological Association, Division 36, *18*(1).

Fortune, D. and K. Fortune. 1987. *Discovering Your God-given Gifts*. Old Tappen, NJ: Fleming H. Revell Company.

Fredrickson, S. E. 1985. *The Construction and Preliminary Validation of the Spiritual Gifts Inventory, Research Version*. Unpublished doctoral dissertation, Western Conservative Baptist Seminary, Portland, OR.

Gangel, K. O. 1983. *Unwrap Your Spiritual Gift*. Wheaton, IL: Victor.

Gerkin, C. V. 1986. "Faith and Praxis: Pastoral Counseling's Hermeneutical Problem." *Pastoral Psychology, 35*(1), 3–15.

Gorsuch, R. L. 1983. *Factor Analysis* (2nd ed.). Hillsdale, NJ: Lawrence Earlbaum Associates.

Hendrix, H. 1977. Pastoral Counseling: In Search of a New Paradigm. *Pastoral Psychology, 25*(3), 157–172.

Hocking, D. L.1975. *Spiritual Gifts*. Long Beach, CA: Sounds of Grace Ministries.

Kehe, J., J. Ciarrochi, J. Greer, and R. Wicks. 1998. "The Pastoral Counselor in the Nineties: The Quest for Spirituality among Religious Integration and Pastoral Care Functions." *American Journal of Pastoral Counseling.* Vol. 1(4).

Kline, P. 1994. *An Easy Guide to Factor Analysis*. New York & London: Routledge.

Ledbetter, M. J. and J. D. Foster. 1989. "Measuring Spiritual Giftedness: A Factor Analytic study of a Spiritual Gifts Inventory." *Journal of Psychology and Theology, 17*(3), 274–283.

Lyons, P. and H. Zingle. 1990. *Journal of Psychology and Theology, 18*(4), 375–380.

Messer, D. 1989. *Contemporary Images of Christian Ministry*. Nashville: Abingdon.

McRae, W. J. 1976. *The Dynamics of Spiritual Gifts*. Grand Rapids: Zondervan.

Muse, J. S., B. K. Estadt, J. M. Greer, and S. Cheston. 1994. Are Religiously Integrated Therapists More Empathetic? *Journal of Pastoral Care, 48*(1), 14–23.

Oates, W. 1951. *The Christian Pastor*. Third edition, Revised. Louisville, KY: Westminster Press.

Tan, S. 1991. *Lay Counseling: Equipping Christians for a Helping Ministry*. Michegan: Zondervan Publishing House.

Wagner, C. P. 1995. *Your Spiritual Gifts Can Help Your Church Grow*. CA: Gospel Light.

Wicks, R. J. 1983. *Self-Ministry Through Self-Understanding: A Guide to Christian Introspection*. Chicago: Loyola University Press.

THE FRANCIS–LOUDEN MYSTICAL
ORIENTATION SCALE (MOS)
A STUDY AMONG ROMAN CATHOLIC PRIESTS

Leslie J. Francis and Stephen H. Louden

ABSTRACT

A new measure of Mystical Orientation is developed using a sample of 1,468 Roman Catholic priests. The measure operationalizes the seven aspects of mysticism identified by Happold (1963): ineffability, noesis, transiency, passivity, oneness, timelessness, and true ego. The scale is shown to possess good psychometric properties. In terms of Eysenck's dimensional model of personality, mystical orientation is shown to be positively related to extraversion, but independent of both neuroticism and psychoticism.

Research in the Social Scientific Study of Religion, Volume 11, pages 99-116.
Copyright © 2000 by JAI Press Inc.
All rights of reproduction in any form reserved.
ISBN: 0-7623-0656-4

INTRODUCTION

Defining Mysticism

Various theoretical perspectives offer definitions as to what constitutes mysticism. Contrary to earlier assumptions that mysticism in all its forms is one and the same (Huxley 1954), it is now generally agreed that there is no such thing as mysticism-in-general. Rather there are only particular mystical systems and individuals, Buddhist, Christian, Greek and Hellenistic, Hebrew and Jewish, Hindu, Islamic, Taoist and Confucian, and so forth.

The focus in this paper is upon mystical orientation which is based within a Christian context. However, any extensive consideration of mysticism must also include nature–mysticism, which refers to the kind of intense experience whereby a subject experiences a merging with cosmic totality. In the context of a culture shaped by the Christian tradition, an awareness of nature with quintessentially mystical overtones is epitomised in the poetry of William Blake, Alfred Lord Tennyson, and William Wordsworth, and the painting of William Blake and Joseph Turner (Zaehner 1961, p. 36). Denial of *any* resemblance between the intense unifying experience of nature and that of a transcendent presence has been deemed absurd (Dupré 1987), especially in light of the support of correlational studies by Greeley (1975) and Hood (1978), in which nature experiences are among the most commonly cited triggers of religious experiences, and especially of those that appear spontaneously (Hood 1995, p. 593).

Mystical experiences resulting from narcotically induced states and their induction of religious–mystical states, as well as mystical experiences resulting associated with pathological psychic conditions, such as manic depression and hysteria, cannot *per se* be excluded from consideration of the mystical (Zaehner 1961; Dupré 1987).

From an etymological perspective the English word *mystical* is derived from a Latin transliteration of the Greek word *musterion*, a word akin to the Greek *mustes*—"close mouthed" from the Greek verb *muo*—"I shut my mouth." As a noun, therefore, *musterion* came to be used to refer to an initiate into a religious mystery-cult, membership of which often involved an obligation of secrecy (Partridge 1958, p. 424). For the purpose of this study, etymology is of limited value; already by the end of the nineteenth century, Dean Inge (1899) listed no fewer than 26 definitions of mysticism.

In the nontheistic context, mysticism concerns union with some principle or other (James 1982) and in Christian terminology mysticism means union with God (Otto 1950; Underhill 1960; Zaehner 1961). In other words, mystical experience may be defined as a sense of union or identity with something other than oneself. Mysticism belongs to the core of all religion, insofar as religion implies belief in a transcendent reality with which in some way communication through direct experience is possible. Mysticism, then, has a history of experience in which the mystic claims to have been in immediate contact with the Ground of Being, known in a way that is free from imaginative content and incapable of normal conceptualization (Corbishley 1967). This is the paradox at the heart of mystical experience. Those of mystical insight say that, although their consciousness of a Presence is more real to them than anything else that they know, they are unable to describe it unless by symbols, images, and approximations and furthermore do not know it as they know other things (Happold 1963). Hence the perennial difficulty experienced by mystics of transmitting their experiences in language that is readily meaningful to those who have not had such experiences.

Parrinder (1976), on the one hand, equates mysticism more closely with everyday religious experience, emphasising that the religious experience of the ordinary believer is in the same class as that of the mystic. The difference according to this perception of mysticism between "union" and "communion" is a matter of degree, not of kind (Poloma 1995). Berger (1979), in contrast, assumes that most people do not have intense religious experiences; he sums up in the assertion that "modern consciousness is not conducive to close contact with the gods" (Berger 1979, p. 89). In contrast to this view of Berger, Poloma (1995) adduced "fledgling efforts" at gaining evidence from Gallup surveys among others of the widespread nature of mystical experience in American society, and according to Hood (1976) the nonmystical, nonreligious language context in which such reports are expressed is a factor in its frequency of acknowledgement. The mystical is experienced but is not reported in mystical or religious language (Back and Bourque 1970; Greeley 1974).

The transcendental experience of the content of mysticism is described by Otto (1950) as *mysterium tremendum et fascinans*. The complex "feeling state" of mysticism is characterised in terms of its object, the *mysterium,* which is at one and the same time awesome, majestic, powerful—*mysterium tremendum*—and appealing, fascinating, alluring—*mysterium fascinans* (Wulff 1995). In mysticism, according to Stace (1960), *fascinans* triumphs over *tremendum,* where human individuals engage with an entity that is both intrinsically fearsome yet ultimately captivating.

Underlying this study is the presupposition that a claim to mystical experience at whatever level is not incompatible with an attempt at some empirical measurement of the phenomenon of mystical experience. Measurement, however, presupposes clarity of definition. One fruitful tradition concerned with the definition of mysticism, which can form an appropriate basis for operationalization of the construct, attempts to identify the key characteristic component of the mystical experience. This tradition has its roots in the pioneering work of William James.

In the opinion of James (1982) there are four characteristics of mysticism. The first, *ineffability,* is a negative description emphasising the private or incommunicable quality of the experience. The subject of this state of mind says that, "it defies expression, that no adequate report of its contents can be given in words" (James 1982, p. 380). It appears to follow that this characteristic or quality of mysticism must be directly experienced with the consequence that mystical states are more like states of feeling than like states of intellect. As with the ineffability of the experience of being-in-love, which literature worldwide is strewn with both successful and unsuccessful attempts to encapsulate in words, so with mystical experience.

The second of James' four marks justifying the calling of an experience mystical is *noesis*. James (1982, p. 380) writes as follows. "Although so similar to states of feeling, mystical states seem to those who experience them to be also states of knowledge." This noetic quality pertains to states of insight into levels of truth inaccessible to the discursive intellect. "They are illuminations, revelations, full of significance and importance, all inarticulate though they remain; and as a rule they carry with them a curious sense of authority after-time" (James 1982, p. 380–381).

The third characteristic entitling a state to be called mystical in the opinion of James is *transiency* which describes the brief, inconstant, and intermittent nature of the experience. Mystical states do not endure for long though they may recur "and from one recurrence to another it is susceptible of continuous development in what is felt as inner richness and importance" (James 1982, p. 381).

His fourth attribute of a state to be looked upon as mystical is *passivity,* emphasising both the experience of being controlled by a superior power as well as the undeserved, gratuitous nature of the mystical experience. James differentiates mystical states, strictly so called, from allied occurrences of what he refers to as prophetic speech, automatic writing, and mediumistic trance. Whereas the latter may be looked upon as an interruption, an invasion of the subject's inner life with no residual recollection or significance, mystical states are never merely interruptive. Both memory of the content of mystical experiences and a profound sense of their importance remains with the subject (James 1982, p. 381).

Happold (1963) attributes to mystical states not four but seven marked characteristics. In addition to the previously mentioned four characteristics of *ineffability, noesis, transiency,* and *passivity* described by James (1982), Happold adds *consciousness of the oneness of everything,* in which existence is perceived as a unity. In theistic mysticism, God is felt to be in everything and everything to exist in God. In ancient Chinese philosophy this consciousness of oneness is perceived to be a restoration of a primal meaning and unity which is achieved by escaping from the pulling asunder by the polar opposites of *yang* (light) and *yin* (darkness). Though it may be expressed in different ways by Hindu, Sufi, and Christian contemplatives, the resolution of the dilemma of duality through this sense of the oneness of everything "is at the heart of the most highly developed mystical consciousness" (Happold 1963, p. 47).

Happold's sixth characteristic of mystical experience is a *sense of timelessness.* Ordinarily, life is experienced as falling into the past, present or future. This relationship between events is inexorably changing and can be measured by what is known as clock-time. There are, however, according to the mystics, experiences that appear to have a timeless quality, which is in an entirely different dimension from that of any known sense of time.

Happold's seventh characteristic of mystical experience is what may be called *true ego,* described as "the conviction that the familiar phenomenal *ego* is not the real *I*" (Happold 1963, p. 48). "By the *self* Jung does not mean what we normally mean by the word. Rather, it has affinities with the self of Hindu psychology" (Happold 1963, p. 50). In Hinduism the *true self* is called *Atman* which is immortal, constant, unchanging, and not bound by space–time. In Christian mysticism, the notion of true ego has been given several names, the *spark,* the *soul spark,* the *center,* the *apex of the soul,* the *ground of the spirit.* Whatever the nature of this entity, it has been described as closely akin to the divine and sharing in the life of God.

The Hood Mysticism Scale

The best known attempt to provide a psychometric assessment of mystical orientation is the Hood Mysticism Scale developed by Hood (1975). This instrument is concerned with identifying and measuring forms of reported religious experience termed "transcendent experience." It was constructed using the eight conceptual categories of Stace (1960) as a framework for generating an initial pool of 108 scale items in a self-report questionnaire. The final 32 items retained were those items which through several revisions proved to be most clearly understood while retaining face validity in terms of Stace's conceptualization, and at the same time showed good empirical properties of discrimination between high and low scorers. The two best positively experienced and the two best negatively experienced items were selected for each of Stace's eight categories.

As described by Hood (1975) the scale categories are first, *ego quality* (E) referring to the experience of a loss of sense of self while consciousness is nevertheless maintained. The loss of self is commonly experienced as an absorption into something greater than the mere empirical ego. The second category, *unifying quality* (U) refers to the experience of the multiplicity of objects of perception as nevertheless united. Everything is perceived as "One." The third category, *inner subjective quality* (Is) refers to the perception of an inner subjectivity to all things, even those usually experienced in purely material forms. The fourth category, *temporal/spatial quality* (T) refers to the temporal and spatial parameters of the experience. Essentially both time and space are modified with the extreme being one of an experience that is both "timeless" and "spaceless." The fifth category, *noetic quality* (N) refers to the experience as a source of valid knowledge. Emphasis is on a nonrational, intuitive, insightful experience that is nevertheless recognised as not merely subjective. The sixth category, *ineffability* (I) refers to the impossibility of expressing the experience in conventional language. The experience simply cannot be put into words due to the nature of the experience itself and not because of any deficit in the linguistic capacity of the subject. The seventh category, *positive affect* (P) refers to the positive affective quality of the experience. Typically the experience is of joy or blissful happiness. The eighth category, *religious quality* (R) refers to the intrinsic sacredness of the experience. This includes feelings of mystery, awe, and reverence that may nevertheless be expressed independently of traditional religious language.

In his foundational study, Hood (1975) discussed both the properties of an overall 32 item mysticism scale and the properties of two subscales identified by factor analysis: a general mystical experience factor of 20 items and a religious interpretation factor of 12 items. In a subsequent factor analytic study, Caird (1988) identified both a two factor solution and a three factor solution, using oblique rotations. In Hood's original two factor solution, a correlation of .47 was found between the factors. In Caird's two factor solution a correlation of .46 was found between the factors. In a further replication of the two factor solution, Reinert and Stifler (1993) found a correlation of .53 between the factors. This study also reported an alpha coefficient of .93 for the 32 item scale.

The Hood Mysticism Scale (1975) has been used in a number of studies, for example, to measure: future church participation (Hood 1976); the eliciting of mystical states of consciousness (Hood 1978); personality correlates of the report of mystical experience (Hood, Hall, Watson, and Biderman 1979); religious and unity criteria of Baptists and those reporting no religious affiliation in reports of mystical experience (Morris and Hood 1980); mysticism and intense experiences—a Finnish study (Holm 1982); the relationship of mystical experience and creativity (Cowling 1985); contemplative prayer as an adjunct to psychotherapy (Finney and Malony 1985); glossolalia as learned behaviour (Spanos, Cross, Lepage, and Coristine 1986); correlates of mystical and diabolical experiences (Spanos and Moretti 1988); prayer experience and religious orientation (Hood, Morris, and Watson 1989) and the discriminability of reported mystical experiences from psychosis (Stifler, Greer, Sneck, and Dovenmuehle 1993).

Personality and Mysticism

In his initial attempt to validate the Hood Mysticism scale, Hood (1975) reported correlations between the mysticism scale and various indices concerned with aspects either of religiosity or of personality. Correlational studies included Hoge's (1972) intrinsic religious motivation scale, Taft's (1970) measure of ego permissiveness, and the MMPI (Bohrnstedt, Borgatta, and Evans 1968). The difficulty in such an approach to construct validation lies in the need to distinguish between the anticipated correlations of mysticism with the general characteristics of religiosity more widely conceived. Eysenck's dimensional model of personality may be able to generate new insights into this distinction.

In recent years a considerable number of empirical studies have explored the relationship between Eysenck's dimensional model of personality (Eysenck and Eysenck 1985) and different aspects of religion (Eysenck 1998). Eysenck's dimensional model of personality argues that individual differences can be most adequately and economically summarised in terms of the three higher order factors of extraversion, neuroticism, and psychoticism. The high scorer on the extraversion scale could be described as sociable, carefree, and optimistic. The high scorer on the neuroticism scale could be characterized in a single word, as a worrier. The high scorer on the psychoticism scale could be described as cold, impersonal, and insensitive. The low scorers on each of these dimensions are characterised by opposite sets of traits.

These three higher order factors, together with a lie scale, have been operationalized in the Eysenck Personality Questionnaire (Eysenck and Eysenck 1975), the Revised Eysenck Personality Questionnaire (Eysenck, Eysenck, and Barrett 1985), the Junior Eysenck Personality Questionnaire (Eysenck and Eysenck 1975) and the Revised Junior Eysenck Personality Questionnaire (Corulla 1990). Abbreviated forms of the revised instruments are also available for use among adults (Francis, Brown, and Philipchalk 1992) and children (Francis 1996). Various editions of the Eysenck instruments have been used alongside different measures of religion. The indices of religion used include the Siegman (1962) religious attitude scale, the Thurstone and Chave (1929) scale of attitude towards the reality of God and the Foa (1948) Sabbath observance scale (Siegman 1963), the Allport, Vernon, and Lindzey (1960) study of values inventory (Chlewinski 1981), the Allport and Ross (1967) religious orientation inventory (Johnson, Danko, Darvill, Bochner, Bowers, Huang, Park, Pecjac, Rahim, and Pennington 1989; Chau, Johnson, Bowers, Darvill, and Danko 1990; Robinson 1990); the Wilson and Patterson (1968) conservatism scale (Wilson and Brazendale 1973; Nias 1973b; Pearson and Sheffield 1976), the Wilson, Nias, and Insel (1972) children's scale of social attitudes (Nias 1973a; Powell and Stewart 1978), the Wilson (1975) attitude inventory (Egan 1989), the Batson and Ventis (1982) measure of means, end, and quest orientations of religiosity (Watson, Morris, Foster, and Hood 1986), the Braithwaite and Law (1985) value survey (Heaven 1990), the Katz and Schmida (1992) student religiosity questionnaire (Francis and Katz 1992), the Josey (1950) scale of religious development (Biegel and Lester 1990), and the Francis (1989) scale of attitude toward Christianity (Francis, Lewis, Brown, Philipchalk and Lester 1995).

Two main conclusions emerge from the existing pool of studies concerned with the relationship between religion and Eysenck's dimensional model of personality. The first conclusion is that different patterns of correlations emerge between personality and different aspects of religiosity. In this sense, personality theory may be helpful to distinguish between empirical assessments of different aspects of religion. The second conclusion is that psychoticism is the dimension of personality which predicts most clearly and consistently the difference between being religious and being irreligious. In this sense, indices which distinguish most clearly between *degrees* of religiosity might be predicted to correlate most closely with psychoticism scores, while indices which distinguish most clearly between *ways* of being religious might be predicted to correlate most closely with other dimensions of personality.

Just three previous studies have specifically explored the relationship between Eysenck's dimensional model of personality and mysticism. Caird (1987) administered the Hood Mysticism Scale (Hood 1975) alongside the Eysenck Personality Questionnaire (Eysenck and Eysenck 1975) among a sample of 115 first year religious studies students at the University of Queensland. In this study no significant correlations were found between mysticism and extraversion, neuroticism, psychoticism, or lie scale scores. Caird (1987) set these nonsignificant findings against two conflicting views regarding the potential theoretical relationship between mysticism and Eysenck's dimensional model of personality. On the one hand, Caird cited the Group for the Advancement of Psychiatry (1976) as regarding mystical experiences as essentially introvert, with neurotic and psychotic sufferers especially tempted to seek relief through such experiences. On the other hand, Caird cited Maslow (1964) as identifying mystical experiences with peak experiences, more characteristic of health than of neurosis or psychosis. Caird's original study was partly replicated by Spanos and Moretti (1988) who administered the Hood Mysticism Scale alongside the neuroticism scale of the Eysenck Personality Inventory (Eysenck and Eysenck 1964) among a sample of 124 female university students. In this study once again no significant correlation was found between mysticism and neuroticism scores.

In a third study, Francis and Thomas (1996) constructed a nine item Likert type scale of mysticism, predicated on Happold's (1963) identification of mysticism as characterised by the following seven qualities: ineffability, noesis, transiency, passivity, consciousness of the oneness of everything, sense of timelessness, and true ego. They administered this scale alongside the short form Revised Eysenck Personality Questionnaire (Eysenck, Eysenck, and Barrett 1985) among a sample of 222 male Anglican clergy. In this study the data demonstrated a significant positive correlation between mysticism and extraversion but no relationship between mysticism and either neuroticism or psychoticism. Francis and Thomas (1996) set the significant correlation between mysticism and extraversion against the suggestion of the Group for the Advancement of Psychiatry's (1976) view that mystical experiences are essentially introvert and the Jungian model of spirituality which associates the spiritual life with the shadow side of personality (Michael and Norrisey 1984; Duncan 1993; Goldsmith 1994).

Mystical Orientation and Priesthood

In order to explore the relationship between aspects of personality and different *ways* of being religious, there are clear advantages of conducting research among populations which may be expected to be generally proreligious. Roman Catholic priests may provide an example of such a population. Moreover, a strong historical link may exist between mysticism and priesthood, since many notable mystics were in holy orders or were hermits, monks, or nuns, although little legitimate empirical research appears to describe the link. During the early Middle Ages the most dominant influence on Western mysticism was of Augustine (345–430), while the teachings of John Cassian (c360–c435), Gregory the Great (540–604), and Bernard of Clairvaux (1091–1153) were influential within the Benedictine monasteries where monks maintained a high ascetical ideal (Spencer 1963). Francis of Assisi (1181–1226) was the founder and inspiration of Franciscan mysticism, while two of the most significant mystics influencing the Dominican Order were the Italian, Thomas Aquinas (1225–1274) and the German, Johannes (Meister) Eckhart (1260–1329), both prominent Dominicans. The *Spiritual Exercises*, a vital work in the training of members of the Society of Jesus, was written by Ignatius Loyola (1491–1556) the founder in 1540 of the Jesuit Order. Also notable are the writings and ascetical influence of John of the Cross (1542–1591) a Spanish Carmelite monk whose poetic *Noche oscura del alma* (Dark night of the soul) has passed into universal language, and of Teresa of Avila (1515–1582) a Spanish Carmelite nun whose autobiography *The Way of Perfection* and mystical treatise *The Interior Castle* have extended their influence far beyond the boundaries of Spain and of the ancient Carmelite order.

Mysticism may therefore be looked upon as one way of expressing religiosity consistent with the wider Catholic tradition. As seminarians during their six-year training, priest aspirants undertake a formal study of mysticism as well as engage in the practice of half an hour daily meditation. As ordained clergy, priests may be called "full-time professionally religious men." Though it is assumed that priests may express their religiosity in different ways, some of them might reasonably be expected to express their religiosity in ways that are open to the mystical orientation.

Research Agenda

In spite of its clear strengths, closer inspection of the items which constitute the Hood Mysticism Scale suggests two possible areas of weakness. The first weakness concerns the length and complexity of some of the items. Item four, for example, reads "I have had an experience in which everything seemed to disappear from my mind until I was conscious only of a void." Complex items may provoke resistance or carelessness among more able respondents and confusion among less able respondents. The first aim of the present study, therefore, was to propose and test a somewhat less complex set of items. The second weakness concerns Hood's dependence on Stace's broad definition of mysticism, with the consequence that some of the individual items may reflect general moods or wider religious responses. Item five, for example, reads "I have experienced profound joy," while item nine reads, "I have never had an experience which seemed holy to me." At face value these items may simply help to identify the happy atheist. The second aim of the present study, therefore, was to anchor the operationalization of mystical orientation within the seven categories proposed by Happold (1963).

METHOD

Sample

Using a database of addresses generated from the semi-official Catholic Directory of England and Wales, a total of 3,581 questionnaires were dispatched to the regular and secular parochial priests in England and Wales. Of these 3,518 were successfully mailed. A total of 1,468 questionnaires were returned useful for analysis of mystical orientation, giving a satisfactory response rate of 42 percent. Of the respondents, 2 percent were under the age of thirty, 13 percent were in their thirties, 20 percent were in their forties, 25 percent were in their fifties, 26 percent were in their sixties, 12 percent were in their seventies and 2 percent were in their eighties.

Measures

Personality was assessed by the Eysenck Personality Questionnaire (Eysenck and Eysenck 1975). This questionnaire provides a 21 item index of extraversion, a 23 item index of neuroticism, a 25 item index of psychoticism, and a 21 item lie scale index. Each item is scored on a dichotomous scale: *yes* and *no*.

Mystical orientation was assessed by a 21 item scale, whose items were embedded in a battery of 66 items concerned with different aspects of religious experience. Respondents were asked "how important are the following experiences to your faith?" They were requested to rate each item by circling a number on a five point scale, ranging from 1–*not at all* to 5–*a great deal*.

Data Analysis

Data analysis was by means of the SPSS statistical package (SPSS Inc. 1988), using the frequency, reliability, and correlation routines.

RESULTS

Table 1 presents the twenty one items of the scale of mystical orientation ordered into the seven categories proposed by Happold (1963), together with the correlation coefficients of each item with the rest of test. These correlation coefficients ranged between 0.42 and 0.75 which indicated that all the 21 items contribute appropriately to the overall scale score. The item with the highest correlation with

Table 1. Scale of Mystical Orientation: Correlation Coefficients for Each Item with the Rest of Test, Factor Loadings and Item Endorsement

Item	r with Rest of Test	factor Loadings	% Important
Ineffiability			
experiencing something I could not put into words	0.6499	0.6890	47.1
feeling moved by a power beyond description	0.7003	0.7397	22.9
being aware of more than I could ever describe	0.5580	0.5995	62.6
Noesis			
sensing God in the beauty of nature	0.4211	0.4627	73.0
knowing I was surrounded by a presence	0.6912	0.7318	46.7
hearing God speak to me	0.5669	0.6130	33.6
Transiency			
brief glimpses into the heart of things	0.6238	0.6639	53.1
transient visions of the transcendental	0.4204	0.4618	21.1
passing moments of divine revelation	0.7158	0.7513	43.0
Passivity			
being overwhelmed by a sense of wonder	0.6652	0.7061	39.7
being in a state of mystery outside my body	0.6041	0.6475	9.1
being grasped by a power beyond my control	0.6267	0.6412	33.6
Oneness			
feeling at one with the universe	0.6688	0.7122	29.2
feeling at one with all living beings	0.6318	0.6762	34.4
sensing the unity in all things	0.6588	0.7010	35.6
Timelessness			
losing a sense of time, place and person	0.6345	0.6778	16.4
being conscious only of timelessness and eternity	0.6437	0.6864	15.7
the merging of past, present and future	0.5391	0.5835	24.0
True ago			
being absorbed within the divine	0.6974	0.7355	34.1
losing my everyday self in a greater being	0.6607	0.7031	28.1
feeling my everyday self absorbed in the depths of being	0.7525	0.7878	28.2

the sum of the other 20 items reads "feeling my everyday self absorbed in the depths of being." The scale achieved the satisfactory alpha reliability coefficient of 0.94 (Cronbach 1951). These statistics confirm that the items cohere to produce a satisfactory homogenous scale.

The second column in table 1 presents the factor loadings identified in the first factor of the unrotated solution by principal component analysis. These loadings ranged between 0.46 and 0.79. The first factor explained 45.1 of the variance, while the second factor explained only 7.3 of the variance. These statistics confirm the basic unidimensionality of the scale.

The third column in table 1 presents the proportions of the 1,468 participating priests who rated each experience as 4 or 5 (important) on a five point scale. These statistics indicate that more than seven out of ten of the priests

Table 2. Correlation Matrix between Personality and
Scale of Mystical Orientation

	Extraversion	Neuroticism	Psychoticism	Lie Scale
mystical orientation	+0.1914	−0.0416	−0.0001	+0.0030
	p < .001	NS	NS	NS
lie scale		−0.1070	−0.2550	−0.0511
		p < .001	p < .001	p < .01
psychoticism			+0.1128	+0.1666
			p < .001	p < .001
neuroticism				−0.1648
				p < .001

report that *sensing God in the beauty of nature* is important to their faith. More than six out of ten of the priests report that *being aware of more than they could ever describe* is important for their faith. More than five out of ten of the priests declare that *brief glimpses into the heart of things* are important to their faith. More than four out of ten of the priests describe *experiencing something they could not put into words; knowing they were surrounded by a presence;* and *passing moments of divine revelation* as important to their faith. More than three out of ten of the priests rate as important to their faith *being overwhelmed by a sense of wonder; being grasped by a power beyond their control; feeling at one with all living beings; sensing a unity in all things; being absorbed within the divine; hearing God speak to them.* More than two out of ten of the priests describe *feeling moved by a power beyond description; having transient visions of the transcendental; feeling at one with the universe; the merging of past, present and future; losing their everyday self in a greater being; feeling their everyday self absorbed in the depths of being.* More than one in ten of the priests rate as important to their faith *losing a sense of time, place, and person* and *being conscious only of timelessness and eternity.* Fewer than one out of ten of the priests report that *being in a state of mystery outside their body* is important for their faith.

Table 2 presents the Pearson correlation coefficients between extraversion, neuroticism, psychoticism, the lie scale and the index of mystical orientation. These statistics show that mystical orientation measure is unrelated to neuroticism, psychoticism, and lie scale scores. It is, however, positively related to extraversion scores. In other words, mystical orientation is associated with extraversion.

Finally, table 3 presents the mean scale scores of mystical orientation according to the age groups of the Catholic priests. No significant association was found between mean scale scores and age ($F = 1.9$, NS).

Table 3.   Mean Scale Scores of Mystical Orientation by Age

Age Group	N	Mean	SD
under 40	211	60.5	16.9
40-49	301	61.1	16.5
50-59	361	61.7	17.6
60-69	372	60.0	19.0
70 and over	183	57.4	19.6

CONCLUSIONS

This study set out to develop a new index of mystical orientation, based on Happold's (1963) conceptualization of mysticism as comprising seven distinctive components, to establish the psychometric properties of this instrument among a sample of Roman Catholic priests, and to establish the location of mystical orientation within the framework of Eysenck's dimensional model of personality. Three main conclusions emerge from the findings.

The first conclusion concerns the psychometric properties of the Francis–Louden Mystical Orientation Scale (MOS). The high alpha coefficient and factor structure of the twenty-one items selected for the scale support the unidimensionality of the instrument and lends empirical weight to Happold's (1963) contention that mysticism is characterised by seven qualities. According to the empirical data the seven identified characteristics, ineffability, noesis, transiency, passivity, oneness, timelessness, and true ego cohere to generate a single unidimensional construct. These data suggest that the Francis–Louden Mystical Orientation Scale provides an appropriate and adequate operationalization of Happold's theoretically derived definition of mysticism. Moreover, the instrument succeeds in doing so through a series of short, simple, and unambiguous phrases. On these grounds the instrument can be commended for further application and exploration.

The second conclusion concerns the extent to which Roman Catholic parochial clergy report awareness of mysticism within their religious experience. This awareness can now be analysed in terms of the seven distinctive components of mysticism identified by Happold (1963) and shown by the present study to cohere within a unidimensional construct. The first characteristic is *ineffability*, a negative description emphasising the private or incommunicable quality of the experience. The data demonstrate that 63 percent of Catholic priests regard as important to their faith the experience of *being aware of more than they could ever describe*, while 47 percent have experienced *something they could not put into words*, and 23 percent have felt *moved by a power beyond description*. The second characteristic of *noesis* describes the quality of illumination or revelation given by the experience. The data demonstrate that 73 percent of Catholic priests regard as important to their faith *sensing God in the beauty of nature,* while 47 percent regard as important *knowing they were surrounded by a presence* and 34 percent *hearing God speak to them*. The third characteristic is *transiency*, describing the brief, inconstant and intermittent nature of the mystical experience. The data demonstrate that 53 percent of Catholic priests regard as important to their faith *brief glimpses into the heart of things*, while 43 percent have sensed *passing moments of divine revelation* and 21 percent have had *transient visions of the transcendental*. The fourth characteristic of *passivity* describes the experience of being controlled by a superior power. The data demonstrate that 40 percent of Catholic priests regard as important to their faith *being overwhelmed by a sense of wonder*, while to 34 percent experiencing *being grasped by a power beyond their control* and to 9 percent *being in a state of mystery outside their body* is important to their faith. The fifth characteristic of *oneness* refers to the perception of everything being as "one." The data demonstrate that 36 percent of Catholic priests regard as important to their faith *sensing the unity in all things* while for 34 percent *feeling at one with all living beings* and for 29 percent *feeling at one with the universe* is important to their faith. The sixth characteristic is *timelessness*, referring to the modification in mystical states of temporal experience. The data demonstrate that 24 percent of Catholic priests regard as important to their faith a sense of *the merging of past, present, and future*, while for 16 percent *losing a sense of time, place, and person*, and for 16 percent *being conscious only of timelessness and eternity* is important to their faith. The seventh characteristic of mysticism is *true ego* referring to the experience of a loss of sense of the self. The data demonstrate that for Catholic priests 34 percent regard as important to their faith *being absorbed within the divine*, while for 28 percent *losing their everyday self in a greater being* and for 28 percent *feeling their everyday self absorbed in the depths of being* is important to their faith.

The third conclusion concerns the location of mystical orientation within Eysenck's dimensional model of personality. While previous studies concerned with broader aspects of religion have demonstrated that psychoticism is the dimension of personality fundamental to individual differences in levels of religiosity (Francis 1992), including features like prayer and church attendance (Francis 1997) and attitude towards Christianity (Francis, Lewis, Brown, Philipchalk, and Lester 1995), the present study suggests that the measure of mystical orientation is quite distinct from the more general assessments of religiosity by finding no significant association between mystical orientation scores and psychoticism scores. This finding is also supported by Caird (1987) and by Francis and Thomas (1996).

While conflicting theoretical perspectives suggest that neuroticism/psychoticism should be either positively (Group for the Advancement of Psychiatry 1976) or negatively (Maslow 1964) associated with mysticism, the present study suggests that mystical orientation is quite independent of emotional stability by finding no significant correlation between mystical orientation scores and neuroticism scores. This finding is supported by those of Caird (1987), by Spanos and Moretti (1988) and by Francis and Thomas (1996).

While the Group for the Advancement of Psychiatry (1976) suggested that mystical experiences are essentially introvert, the present study suggests that mystical orientation is in fact the very opposite of an experience which appeals primarily to introverts by finding a significant positive correlation between mystical orientation scores and extraversion scores. This finding is supported by Francis and Thomas (1996) among Anglican clergy, but not by Caird (1987) among first year religious studies students. Both Francis and Thomas (1996) and the present study provide support for the Jungian model of spirituality which associates the spiritual life with the shadow side of personality (Michael and Norrisey 1984; Duncan 1993; Goldsmith 1994).

Further studies are now needed to check the psychometric properties of the Francis–Louden Mystical Orientation Scale (MOS) and the location of mysticism within Eysenck's dimensional model of personality among other populations and in other cultural contexts.

REFERENCES

Allport, G. W. and J. M. Ross 1967. "Personal religious orientation and prejudice." *Journal of Personality and Social Psychiatry,* 5, 432–446.

Allport, G. W., P. Vernon, and G. Lindzey 1960. *A study of values.* Boston, MA: Houghton Mifflin.

Back, K. W. and L. B. Bourque 1970. "Can feelings be enumerated?" *Behavioral Science,* 15, 489–496.

Batson, C. D. and W. L. Ventis 1982. *The religious experience.* NY: Oxford University Press.

Berger, P. L. 1979. *The heretical imperative: Contemporary possibilities of religious affirmation,* Garden City, NY: Doubleday.

Biegel, K. and D. Lester 1990. "Religiosity and psychological disturbance." *Psychological Reports,* 67, 874.

Bohrnstedt, G. W., E. F. Borgatta, and R. R. Evans 1968. "Religious affiliation, religiosity and MMPI scores." *Journal for the Scientific Study of Religion,* 7, 255–258.

Braithwaite, V. A. and H. Law 1985. "Structure of human values: testing the adequacy of the Rockeach value survey." *Journal of Personality and Social Psychology,* 49, 250–263.

Caird, D. 1987. "Religiosity and personality: are mystics introverted, neurotic, or psychotic?" *British Journal of Social Psychology,* 26, 345–346.

Caird, D. 1988. "The Structure of Hood's Mysticism Scale: A factor-analytic study." *Journal for the Scientific Study of Religion,* 27, 122–126.

Chau, L. L., R. C. Johnson, Bowers, J. K., Darvill, T. J., and G. P. Danko 1990. "Intrinsic and extrinsic religiosity as related to conscience, adjustment and altruism." *Personality and Individual Differences,* 11, 397–400.

Chlewinski, Z. 1981. "Personality and attitude toward religion in Poland." *Personality and Individual Differences,* 2, 243–245.

Corbishley, T. 1967. "Mysticism," in *The New Catholic Encyclopedia,* 10, 175–179, Palatine, IL: Jack Heraty and Associates.

Corrula, W. J. 1990. "A revised version of the psychoticism scale for children." *Personality and Individual Differences,* 11, 65–76.

Cowling, W. R. 1985. "Relationship of mystical experience, differentiation and creativity." *Perceptual and Motor Skills,* 61, 451–456.

Cronbach, L. J. 1951. "Coefficient alpha and the internal structure of tests." *Psychometrika,* 16, 297–334.

Duncan, B. 1993. *Pray your way,* London: Darton, Longman, and Todd.

Dupré, L. 1987. "Mysticism," in M. Eliade (ed.), *The Encyclopedia of Religion,* 10, 246–261. NY: Macmillan.

Egan, V. 1989. "Links between personality, ability, and attitudes in a low-IQ sample." *Personality and Individual Differences,* 10, 997–1001.

Eysenck, H. J. and S. B. G. Eysenck 1964. *Manual of the Eysenck Personality Inventory.* London: University of London Press.

Eysenck, H. J. and S. B. G. Eysenck 1975. *Manual of the Eysenck Personality Questionnaire (adult and junior).* London: Hodder and Stoughton.

Eysenck, H. J. and S. B. G. Eysenck 1985. *Personality and individual differences: A natural science approach.* NY: Plenum Press.

Eysenck, H. J., S. B. G. Eysenck, and P. Barrett 1985. "A revised version of the psychoticism scale." *Personality and Individual Differences,* 6, 21–29.

Eysenck, M. W. 1998. "Personality and the psychology of religion." *Mental Health, Religion and Culture,* 1, 11–19.

Finney, J. R. and N. H. Malony 1995. "An empirical study of contemplative prayer as an adjunct to psychotherapy." *Journal of Psychology and Theology,* 13 (4) 284–290.

Foa, U. G. 1948. "An equal interval scale for the measurement of attitudes towards Sabbath observance." *Journal of Social Psychology,* 27, 273–276.

Francis, L. J. 1989. "Measuring attitude towards Christianity during childhood and adolescence." *Personality and Individual Differences,* 10, 695–698.

Francis, L. J. 1992. "Is psychoticism really a dimension of personality fundamental to religiosity?" *Personality and Individual Differences,* 13, 645–652.

Francis, L. J. 1996. "The development of an abbreviated form of the Revised Junior Eysenck Personality Questionnaire (JEPQR-A) among 13–15 year olds." *Personality and Individual Differences,* 21, 835–844.

Francis, L. J. 1997. "Personality, prayer, and church attendance among undergraduate students." *International Journal for the Psychology of Religion,* 7, 127–132.

Francis, L. J., L. B. Brown, and R. Philipchalk 1992. "The development of an abbreviated form of the Revised Eysenck Personality Questionnaire (EPQR-A): its use among students in England, Canada, the USA, and Australia." *Personality and Individual Differences,* 13, 443–449.

Francis, L. J. and Y. Katz 1992. "The relationship between personality and religiosity in an Israeli sample." *Journal for the Scientific Study of Religion,* 31, 153–162.

Francis, L. J., J. M. Lewis, L. B. Brown, R. Philipchalk, and D. Lester 1995. "Personality and religion among undergraduate students in the United Kingdom, United States, Australia, and Canada." *Journal of Psychology and Christianity,* 14, 250–262.

Francis, L. J. and M. T. Stubbs 1987. "Measuring attitudes towards Christianity: from childhood to adulthood." *Personality and Individual Differences,* 8, 741–743.

Francis, L. J. and T. H. Thomas 1996. "Mystical orientation and personality among Anglican clergy." *Pastoral Psychology,* 45, 99–105.

Goldsmith, M. 1994. *Knowing me knowing God,* London, SPCK.

Greeley, A. 1974. *Ecstasy a way of knowing.* Englewood Cliffs, NJ: Prentice-Hall.

Greeley, A. 1975. *The sociology of the paranormal: a reconnaissance.* Beverley Hills, CA: Sage.

Group for the Advancement of Psychiatry. 1976. *Mysticism: Spiritual Quest or Psychological Disorder?* New York: GAP.

Happold, F. C. 1963. *Mysticism: A study and an Anthology.* Harmondsworth: Penguin.

Heaven, P. C. L. 1990. "Religious values and personality dimensions," *Personality and Individual Differences,* 11, 953–956.

Hoge, D. R. 1972. "A validated intrinsic religious motivation scale." *Journal for the Scientific Study of Religion,* 11, 369–376.

Holm, N. G. 1982. Mysticism and intense experiences, *Journal for the Scientific Study of Religion*, 21, 268–276.

Hood, R. W. 1975. "The construction and preliminary validation of a measure of reported mystical experience." *Journal for the Scientific Study of Religion*, 14, 29–41.

Hood, R. W. 1976. "Mystical experience as related to present and anticipated future church participation." *Psychological Reports*, 39, 1127–1136.

Hood, R. W. 1978. "Eliciting mystical states of consciousness with semistructured nature experiences." *Journal for the Scientific Study of Religion*, 16, 155–163.

Hood, R. W. 1995. "The facilitation of religious experience" in R. W. Hood, Jr. (ed.) *Handbook of Religious Experience*, 568–597. Birmingham, AL: Religious Education Press.

Hood, R. W., J. R. Hall, P. J. Watson and M. Biderman 1979. "Personality correlates of the report of mystical experience." *Psychological Reports*, 44, 804–806.

Hood, R. W., Morris, R.J. and P. J. Watson 1989. "Prayer experience and religious orientation." *Review of Religious Research*, 31, 39–45.

Huxley, A. 1954. *The Doors of Perception*. London: Chatto and Windus.

Inge, W. R. 1899. *Christian Mysticism*. London: Methuen.

James, W. 1982. *The Varieties of Religious Experience*. London: Penguin Books.

Johnson, R.C., G. P. Danko, T. J. Darvill, S. Bochner, J. K. Bowers, Y. H. Huang, J. Y. Park, V. Pecjak, A. R. A. Rahim, and D. Pennington 1989. "Cross cultural assessment of altruism and its correlates." *Personality and Individual Differences*, 10, 855–868.

Josey, C. C. 1950. "A scale of religious development." *American Psychologist*, 5, 281.

Katz, Y. J. and M. Schmida 1992. "Validation of the Student Religiosity Questionnaire." *Educational and Psychological Measurement*, 52, 353–356.

Maslow, A. H. 1964. *Religions, values, and peak-experiences*. Columbus, OH: Ohio State University.

Michael, C. P. and M. C. Norrisey 1984. *Prayer and temperament: different prayer forms for different personality types*. Charlottesville, VA: The Open Book Inc.

Morris, R. J. and R. W. Hood 1980. "Religious and unity criteria of Baptists and nones in reports of mystical experience." *Psychological Reports*, 46, 728–730.

Nias, D. K. B. 1973a. "Measurement and structure of children's attitudes," in G. D. Wilson, (ed.), *The psychology of conservatism* (chapter 6). London: Academic Press.

Nias, D. K. B. 1973b. "Attitudes to the Common Market: a case study in conservatism," in G. D. Wilson, (ed.), *The psychology of conservatism* (chapter 16). London: Academic Press.

Otto, R. 1950. *The idea of the Holy*. Translated by J.W. Harvey. London: Oxford University Press.

Parrinder, G. 1976. *Mysticism in the world's religions*. London: Oxford University Press.

Partridge, E. 1958. *Origins: a short etymological dictionary of modern English*, (4th ed). New York: Macmillan,

Pearson, P. R. and B. F. Sheffield 1976. "Is personality related to social attitudes? An attempt at replication." *Social Behaviour and Personality*, 4, 109–111.

Poloma, M. M. 1995. "The sociological context of religious experience," in R.W. Hood, Jr. (ed.). *Handbook of Religious Experience*, 161–182, Birmingham, AL: Religious Education Press.

Powell, G. E. and R. A. Stewart 1978. "The relationship of age, sex and personality to social attitudes in children aged 8–15 years." *British Journal of Social and Clinical Psychology*, 17, 307–317.

Reinert, D. F. and K. R. Stifler 1993. "Hood's Mysticism scale revisited: a factor-analytic replication." *Journal for the Scientific Study of Religion*, 32, 383–388.

Robinson, T. N. 1990. "Eysenck personality measures and religious orientation." *Personality and Individual Differences*, 11, 915–921.

Siegman, A. W. 1962. "A cross-cultural investigation of the relationship between religiosity, ethnic prejudice, and authoritarianism." *Psychological Reports*, 11, 419–427.

Siegman, A. W. 1963. "A cross cultural investigation of the relationship between introversion, social attitudes, and social behaviour." *British Journal of Social and Clinical Psychology*, 2, 196–208.

Spanos, N. P., W. P. Cross, M. Lepage, and M. Coristine 1986. "Glossolalia as learned behavior: an experimental demonstration." *Journal of Abnormal Psychology,* 95, 21–23.

Spanos, N. P. and P. Moretti 1988. "Correlates of mystical and diabolical experiences in a sample of female university students." *Journal for the Scientific Study of Religion,* 27, 105–116.

Spencer, S. 1963. *Mysticism in World Religion,* Harmondsworth: Pelican Books.

SPSS Inc. 1988. *SPSSX User's Guide.* New York: McGraw-Hill.

Stace, W. T. 1960. *Mysticism and Philosophy.,* Philadelphia, PA: Lippincott.

Stifler, K., J. Greer, W. Sneck, R. Dovenmuehle 1993. "An empirical investigation of the discriminability of reported mystical experiences among religious contemplatives, psychotic inpatients, and normal adults." *Journal for the Scientific Study of Religion,* 32, 366–372.

Taft, R. 1970. "The measurement of the dimensions of ego permissiveness." *Personality: An International Journal,* 1, 163–184.

Thurstone, L. L. and E. J. Chave 1929. *The Measurement of Attitude.* Chicago, IL: University of Chicago Press.

Underhill, E. 1960. *Mysticism.* 12th ed rev. London: Meridian Books. Watson, P. J., R. J. Morris, J. E. Foster, and R. W. Hood 1986. "Religiosity and social desirability." *Journal for the Scientific Study of Religion,* 25, 215–232.

Watson, P. J., R. J. Morris, J. E. Foster, and R. W. Hood. 1986. "Religiosity and social desirability." *Journal for the Scientific Study of Religion* 25: 215–232.

Wilson, G. D. 1975. *Manual for the Wilson–Patterson Attitude Inventory.* Windsor: NFER.

Wilson, G .D. and A. H. Brazendale 1973. "Social attitude correlates of Eysenck's personality dimensions." *Social Behaviour and Personality,* 1, 115–118.

Wilson, G. D., D. K. B. Nias, and P. M. Insel 1972. *Manual for the Children's Scale of Social Attitudes.* London: Children's Studies Ltd.

Wilson, G. D. and G. Patterson 1968. "A new measure of conservatism." *British Journal of Social and Clinical Psychology,* 7, 264–269.

Wulff, D. W. 1995. "Phenomenological Psychology and Religious Experience" in R. W. Hood, Jr. (ed.). *Handbook of Religious Experience,* 183–199, Birmingham, AL: Religious Education Press.

Zaehner, R.C. 1961. *Mysticism sacred and Profane: an inquiry into some varieties of praeternatural experience.* London: Oxford University Press.

AN EVALUATION OF THE INCREMENTAL VALIDITY OF THE SPIRITUAL EXPERIENCE INDEX–REVISED

Richard J. Csarny, Ralph L. Piedmont, William J. Sneck, and Sharon E. Cheston

ABSTRACT

An analysis of the Spiritual Experience Index–Revised confirmed the presence of two distinct dimensions: Spiritual Support and Spiritual Openness. Further analysis examined the incremental validity of each scale in comparison with personality as measured by the Five Factor Model. Spiritual Support correlated with personality agreeableness, religious attendance and prayer frequency, prayer and God satisfaction, and experience of the presence of God. Spiritual Support provided incremental variance over personality in the prediction of most religious variables, racism, sexual attitude tolerance, and life satisfaction. Spiritual Openness correlated with personality Openness to Experience, broad-minded religious self identification, but not with most religious variables. Spiritual Openness provided incremental variance over personality in the prediction of racism and sexual attitude tolerance, but not most religious variables or life satisfactions. These results support the validity and usefulness of the Spiritual Support subscale, but call into question the validity of Spiritual Openness as a spiritual construct.

Research in the Social Scientific Study of Religion, Volume 11, pages 117-131.
Copyright © 2000 by JAI Press Inc.
All rights of reproduction in any form reserved.
ISBN: 0-7623-0656-4

117

One critical problem in religious research and clinical practice is that religious or spirituality measures often reflect creedal beliefs and therefore have limited usefulness with religiously diverse populations. The Spiritual Experience Index (SEI), (Genia 1990; 1991) was developed to address this limitation and provide a measure of spiritual or faith maturity that is independent of denominational beliefs. Genia utilized a developmental criterion-based approach which characterized mature faith as a transcendent relationship to something greater than oneself and openness to spiritually diverse viewpoints. It is not dependent on a particular dogma or formal religious structure but reflects commitment without absolute certainty. Mature faith includes rational and emotional components, lacks egocentricity and magical thinking, demonstrates social interest and humanitarian concern, and is reflected in moral behaviors which reflect values, meaning, and purpose in life.

Genia (1997) has further refined the SEI. She isolated 13 of the original 38 items which describe a factor of Spiritual Support and 10 items representing Spiritual Openness. Spiritual Support (SS) reflects a reliance on spirituality for meaning, sustenance, and support. Spiritual Openness (SO) reflects an inclusive and universal approach to faith. These 23 items constitute the SEI-Revised.

Preliminary analysis of the SEI-Revised (Genia 1997) has shown many strengths including its ability to predict a number of outcomes such as religious and spiritual well-being and satisfaction with one's relationship with God above the influence of Intrinsic religiousness and Quest. While Genia believes her sample adequately represented national norms of religious attendance and self-identified religious importance, she drew her sample of 286 participants from a single university and the resulting narrow demographic ranges limit the generalizability of her results. In addition, the restricted scope of personality measures provided limited ability to establish discriminant and incremental validity with respect to personality.

This present study adds to the validity assessment of the SEI-R by utilizing a nationwide sample with a more diverse age distribution, and it tests an expanded range of outcomes (life satisfaction, racism, and sexual attitudes) that are of interest to both religion and psychology. In addition, this study utilizes a widely used measure of religious maturity, the Faith Maturity Scale (FMS) (Benson, Donahue, and Erickson 1993), following the recommendations of Gorsuch (1984) to compare new scales with already established ones. Finally and most importantly, the present study contributes by using the more comprehensive Five Factor Model (FFM) of personality to more adequately test the incremental validity of the SEI-R.

Such testing of incremental validity is important because in the development and use of spiritual measures a vexing question frequently surfaces: to what extent do these instruments measure distinctly spiritual constructs, or to what extent do they measure personality through the perspective of spiritual terminology? This question has surfaced for years without adequate resolution (see Allport 1950;

Dittes 1969; Francis 1992b; King and Hunt 1971; Kirkpatrick and Hood 1990; Piedmont 1996; and Van Wicklin 1990). However the exposition and current refinement of the Five Factor Model (FFM) now offers an excellent opportunity for religious researchers to systematically assess spiritual or religious constructs in relation to personality.

Because the Five Factor Model presents a robust and adequate taxonomy of personality (Digman 1990; Goldberg 1981; McCrae and Costa 1990; Saucier and Goldberg 1996), it has been characterized by Briggs (1992) as being the model of choice for the researcher who wants to represent the broad domain of personality variables. Because this more comprehensive model of normal personality is now available, the once difficult task of assessing the distinctness of any given spiritual construct apart from personality constructs becomes much easier. This process may be accomplished quantitatively through the use of hierarchical multiple regression methods. That is, for any chosen criterion or outcome variable, a multiple regression is performed which inputs the personality model on step 1 and the selected spiritual construct on step 2. Any significant additional variance appearing in step 2 represents the contribution of the spiritual construct apart from the personality model, and suggests the possibility of a distinct and unique construct.

Through the use of the FFM this study examined the predictive efficacy of the SEI-R over and above the contribution of FFM personality and clarified to what extent SEI-R constructs suggest something uniquely spiritual. It was hypothesized that the SEI-R would exhibit a factor structure similar to that found with Genia's normative sample, exhibit significant correlations with the Faith Maturity Scale and with spiritual behaviors, and provide significant predictive power above FFM personality in the prediction of both spiritual and secular outcomes. If the SEI-R is a valid measure of spiritual maturity free from denominational constraints, it should show itself to be robust with any mainline religious group such as represented in this study's sample.

METHOD

Participants

Three hundred and eighty participants responded to a mailed survey directed to committed members of primarily Roman Catholic Christian religious groups. Religious affiliation was 83 percent Roman Catholic, 11 percent Protestant, 6 percent Other, 0 percent Jewish, 0 percent unaffiliated, as compared to Genia's sample of 34 percent, 29 percent, 7 percent, 13 percent, and 17 percent respectively. Demographics were as follows, with Genia's normative values in parentheses: 90 percent Caucasian (81 percent), 58 percent female (66 percent), 16.6 mean number of years of education (15), and mean age 52 (22). Church attendance was high: 88 percent attended church monthly or more, compared to 48 percent in the normative sample. Almost all participants were from urban areas: 59 percent were from the eastern United States, 20 percent the midwest, 14 percent central, and 6 percent the west. Mean range of household income was $45,000 to 60,000 per year, and 53 percent of the participants were married.

Measures

SEI-R

Developed by Genia (1997), this 23-item questionnaire was designed to measure mature faith and spirituality independent of dogma or formal religious structure. Items are answered on a 6-point scale ranging from (1) *strongly disagree* to (6) *strongly agree*. Two factors, Spiritual Support and Spiritual Openness, were identified. Cronbach's alphas were .79 for SO, .92 for SS, and .89 for the full scale. Genia notes that SS strongly correlates with intrinsic faith, religious well-being, and worship attendance. Spiritual Openness correlates positively with Quest, and negatively with dogmatism. Both subscales are unrelated to depression or self-esteem. Using median splits, Genia developed a four-fold typology for scoring spiritual maturity. Those low on SS and SO are characterized as spiritually *underdeveloped*; high SS and low SO indicates *dogmatic* believers; low SS and high SO are spiritual seekers or *transitionals*; high SS and high SO are *growth-oriented*. Genia believes that SS and SO offer a new and useful way of looking at spiritual maturity.

Faith Maturity Scale (FMS)

The FMS was developed by Benson, Donahue, and Erickson (1993) to measure two metaphorical dimensions of Christian faith maturity: a vertical faith in which a person relates directly to God, and a horizontal faith in which a person discovers God through others. It is a 38-item self report measure utilizing a 7-point scale ranging from (1) *never true* to (7) *always true*. A 12-item short version developed by Donahue was used in this study. Scale reliabilities using Cronbach's alpha were robust across age, gender, respondent type, and denomination, and range from .84 to .90 for the 38-item scale and .88 for the 12-item scale. The correlation between the 12- and 38-item scales is .94 for adults. Considerable evidence supports the validity of the FMS, and it has been used in many studies of congregations across the United States. In addition, it has consistently demonstrated incremental validity apart from personality across a number of variables and populations (Csarny 1998; Piedmont 1996).

NEO-Five Factor Inventory (FFI)

Developed by Costa and McCrae (1992) as a shorter 60 item version of the NEO Personality Inventory–Revised, the FFI operationalizes the major dimensions of personality hypothesized in the Five-Factor Model. The NEO PI-R as well as the earlier NEO-PI was developed through analysis of personality descriptors observed in scientific theories and natural language (the lexical approach), and through factor analytic methods. Measures of five major dimensions or domains of personality were developed: Neuroticism (N), representing emotional vulnerability; Extraversion (E), an indicator of positive energy; Openness to Experience (O), a tendency to seek new knowledge and experience for its own sake; Agreeableness (A), a tendency to tendermindedness, trust and compassion; and Conscientiousness (C), representing orderliness and discipline.

Items are answered on a 5-point scale ranging from (1) *strongly disagree* to (5) *strongly agree*, and scales are balanced to control for acquiescence. Internal consistencies for the five domains ranged from .86 to .95. Long term stability has been well demonstrated. The NEO-PI has been extensively validated (McCrae and Costa 1987; Piedmont, McCrae, and Costa 1992), and it has shown predictive utility with a large number of life outcomes such as somatic complaints, stress coping, well-being, and response to psychotherapy (Costa and McCrae 1992).

Modern Racism Scale (MRS)

Developed by McConahay (1986), the MRS measures a subtle form of racism toward blacks that is rooted in abstract principles and diffuse negative feelings, and which is usually reflected in certain symbolic issues that raise strong ambivalence. For example, one question states, "Over the past few years, blacks have gotten more economically than they deserve." The MRS is a 6-item self-rating measure and questions are answered on a 5-point scale ranging from (1) *strongly disagree* to (5) *strongly agree*.

The MRS has used somewhat different items over the last twenty years, and alpha coefficients for these versions have ranged from .75 to .86, while test retest reliability has ranged from .72 to .93. Validity issues were addressed through comparisons with other measures, behavioral outcomes, and experiment. The MRS has successfully predicted antiblack voting patterns, interracial perceptions and distance, and hiring decisions (McConahay, Hardee, and Batts 1981).

Two additional items in similar form were created by the researcher to measure discrimination against women. For example, one item reads, "Women are getting too demanding in their push for equal rights." These items were included to expand the usefulness of the MRS style of questioning to another issue which often surfaces conflicting feelings.

Valois Sexual Attitude Scale (VSAS)

This instrument was initially designed by Valois and Ory (1988) to evaluate attitude changes in a human sexuality program for university students. It consists of 46 5-point self-rating items addressing nine sexual topics: sexual stereotypes, masturbation, premarital intercourse, homosexuality, sexual communication, abortion, oral–genital sex, birth control, and college marriages. Responses range from *strongly agree* to *strongly disagree*, and a high score indicates more sexual attitude tolerance. Cronbach's alpha for the subscales ranged from .66 to .92. Content validity was addressed through expert review. Valois (1980) reported a 4-month stability coefficient of .85.

Because the Valois Sexual Scale contained no questions on extramarital sexual activity, the researcher added two questions utilizing a similar format to address this issue.

Index of Domain Satisfactions and Index of Overall Life Satisfaction

Developed by Campbell, Converse, and Rodgers (1976), these scales consist of a series of single questions based on one's satisfaction with everyday life domains such as marriage, job, family, and so forth. Additional questions were added by the researcher to address satisfaction with relationship to God, and satisfaction with prayer life. Participants respond according to a 7-point scale ranging from *completely dissatisfied* to *completely satisfied*. Only the two end points and the middle *neutral* point are labeled on the scale. Stability correlations for the original Index ranged from .42 to .67 for individual domains, and .76 for the entire measure.

Campbell and colleagues (1976) note the inherent difficulties in developing reliable and valid measures for life satisfactions, and in establishing reliability coefficients for the scales. They take their estimates as the bottom range. Validity was not directly addressed, but behavioral prediction and assessment of responsiveness to change led them to believe the measures performed well. Andrews and Withey (1976) evaluated the Index of Overall Life Satisfaction and estimated validities to be .73 to .79. These measures or variations on them have been used for over twenty years with considerable success.

Life-3

This measure is a 2-item global "life as a whole" quality of life scale developed by Andrews and Withey (1976). The scale asks the question, "How do you feel about your life as a whole?" and then repeats the same question approximately 15 to 20 minutes later. Responses are given according to a 7-point self rating scale known as the Delighted–Terrible Scale and range from *delighted* to *terrible*. The Delighted–Terrible scale attempts to enhance validity by providing explicit labels for each scale point and by balancing both affect and cognition in the framing of the scale; the Life-3 enhances reliability through the equivalent of a test retest method.

Life-3 was found to be only slightly influenced by demographic variables, accounting for less than 10 percent of the variance. Internal consistency between the two items was calculated to be .81. Validity was examined through a LISREL analysis and was reported to be .77 in one sample and .82 in another. Andrews and Withey (1976) consider the Life-3 to be one of the most sensitive measures of global assessment of the respondent's own current life-as-a-whole situation.

Other scales

A number of other scales created by the researcher were used to assess self-identified religious and political positions (rated from *very conservative* to *very liberal*), frequency of prayer (rated from *never* to *more than once a day*), frequency of religious service attendance (rated from *never or seldom* to *four or more times a week*), lifetime experiences of the presence of God and being punished by God (rated from *I'm sure I have* to *no*), and forgiveness (rated from *disagree strongly* to *agree strongly*).

Analysis

Exploratory and confirmatory factor analyses on the SEI-R were performed to compare results with Genia's (1997) findings. The FFI results were standardized using gender-adjusted norms (Costa and McCrae 1992). Hierarchical multiple regressions were conducted to examine the unique predictive efficacy of the SEI-R over personality in the prediction of both religious/spiritual and nonreligious outcomes.

RESULTS

Initial analysis compared the internal consistency of each scale with the normative values reported by Genia. Coefficient alphas for the SO, SS, and Full scale were .79, .92, and .87, compared to normative values of .79, .95, and .89 respectively. See Table 1.

The SO and SS scales had means of 45 and 68 and standard deviations of 8.2 and 8.8 compared to normative means of 44 and 54 respectively (no normative standard deviations given). Thus the current sample exhibited similar spiritual openness but higher spiritual support scores compared with the initial study participants. The higher score on the SS scale is consistent with the identification of the current sample as persons who are moderately to highly religious, but the failure to detect a higher level of spiritual openness among these highly religious

Table 1. Descriptive Statistics and Alpha Reliabilities

Factor	Males[1]		Females[2]		Normative		Normative
	M	SD	M	SD	M	Alpha	Alpha
Support	68	8.0	69	8.6	54	.92	.95
Openness	44	8.0	45	8.2	44	.79	.79
Total	112	11.0	114	12.3	—	.87	.89

Notes: [1] N = 156; [2] N = 218

Table 2. Factor Congruence Coefficients

SEI item Number	Factor 1	Factor 2	Item Congruence
SS9 SM7	.859	.001	.998
SS23 SM37	.817	.009	.996
SS13 SM8	.811	.063	1.000
SS5 SM4	.805	−.052	.999
SS3 SM3	.792	−.079	.999
SS15 SM28	.780	−.029	.984
SS1 SM1	.668	.094	1.000
SS22 SM33	.654	.079	1.000
SS19 SM30	.655	.025	.994
SS11 SM17	.652	.082	.993
SS21 SM25	.546	−.026	1.000
SS7 SM14	.524	.119	.996
SS17 SM9	.471	.205	.959
SO12 SM31	.462	.449	.993
SO18 SM27	.174	.688	.998
SO4 SM5	.066	.630	.918
SO10 SM13	.244	.563	.999
SO16 SM18	−.014	.529	1.000
SO20 SM35	.179	.536	.932
SO2 SM11	−.220	.502	.962
SO8 SM24	.169	.503	.981
SO14 SM34	−.258	468	.996
SO6 SM6	−.302	.448	1.000
Factor Congruence	.979	.987	.985

persons is noteworthy. The correlation between the SS and the SO factors was .07, which is identical to the normative group.

The second step in evaluating the SEI-R was to determine if the scale revealed a factor structure similar to the original 2-factor solution. The 23 items were subjected to an exploratory factor analysis following Genia's method of

Principal Axis Factoring. Because the correlation between SO and SS was .07 (ns), the constructs were considered to be orthogonal. Selection criteria of eigen values greater than one led to four factors containing 50 percent of the variance, but all items loaded primarily on factors 1 and 2, accounting for 44 percent of the variance. These results were closely similar to Genia's exploratory factor solution using the 23 items.

A forced two factor solution with varimax rotation was performed in order to compare the current data with Genia's results. Factors 1 and 2 had eigenvalues of 7.1 and 2.8 respectively, accounting for 43 percent of the variance, compared to Genia's eigenvalues of 8.6 and 2.9 accounting for 50 percent of the variance. Item loading results paralleled Genia's two factor solution.

Coefficients of congruence (Gorsuch 1983) were calculated to assess the degree of fit determined by using the factor loadings from the two factor solution of the

Table 3. Correlations of SEI-Revised Subscales with Religious and Psychological

Outcome Variable (N = 374)	Spiritual Support	Spiritual Openness
Prayer Frequency	$.57^{**}$	$-.01$
Religious Attendance Frequency	$.49^{**}$	$-.03$
Religious Position	$-.16^{**}$	$.56^{**}$
Forgiveness	$.34^{**}$	$-.08$
Presence of God	$.43^{**}$	$.14^{**}$
Satisfaction with Prayer	$.32^{**}$	$.05$
Satisfaction with God Relationship	$.42^{**}$	$.08$
FMS Vertical	$.76^{**}$	$.12^{*}$
FMS Horizontal	$.55^{**}$	$.25^{**}$
Political Position	$-.08$	$.48^{**}$
Discrimination Against Women	$.05$	$-.52^{**}$
Sexual Attitude Tolerance	$-.33^{**}$	$.60^{**}$
Extramarital Tolerance	$-.13^{**}$	$.23^{**}$
Racism	$-.18^{**}$	$-.37^{**}$
Life Satisfaction: Life-3	$.17^{**}$	$.07$
Whole Life Satisfaction	$.14^{**}$	$.09$
Sexual Life Satisfaction	$.19^{**}$	$.00$
Marriage Satisfaction	$.16^{*}$	$-.01$
Neuroticism	$-.09$	$-.08$
Extraversion	$.10$	$.11^{*}$
Openness to Experience	$-.07$	$.46^{**}$
Agrreableness	$.25^{**}$	$.08$
Conscientiousness	$.10$	$.04$

Notes: N = 212 for Marriage Satisfaction
$^{*}p \le .05$
$^{**}p \le .01$

current data set and comparing them with the original two factor Genia loadings (see Table 2).

Factor congruence was .979 for SS, .987 for SO, and .985 overall. Item congruence coefficients ranged from .918 to 1.000. Thus, the current factor data set provides good congruence with the original set.

The next step in analysis was to examine the outcomes correlating with the Spiritual Support and Spiritual Openness scales, and to assess the additional contribution of each scale above personality in the prediction of the criterion variables. Correlations are shown in Table 3.

It is noted that SS correlated in ways that are expected for a religious variable. It correlated positively with prayer frequency ($r = .57, p \le .01$), religious attendance frequency ($r = .49, p \le .01$), satisfaction in relationship with God ($r = .42, p \le .01$) and prayer satisfaction ($r = .32, p \le .01$), forgiveness ($r = .34, p \le .01$), experience of the presence of God ($r = .43, p \le .01$), and Faith Maturity Vertical ($r = .76, p \le .01$) and Horizontal ($r = .55, p \le .01$). SS had a small negative correlation ($r = .14, p \le .01$) with religious position (a self report measure of broad-minded attitudes toward religion), and it failed to correlate with political position (a similar self report measure of broad-minded political attitudes).

The SS scale correlated with a number of social criterion variables: it showed small but significant positive correlations with both measures of life satisfaction ($rs = .17$ and $.14, p \le .01$), marriage satisfaction ($r = .16, p \le .05$), and satisfaction in one's sexual life ($r = .19, p \le .01$). SS correlated negatively with racism ($r = -.18, p \le .01$), extramarital tolerance ($r = .13, p \le .01$), and tolerance in sexual attitudes ($r = -.33, p \le .01$). It failed to correlate with the measure of discrimination against women. Finally, it exhibited a significant correlation with personality Agreeableness ($r = .25, p \le .01$), which is consistent with other research linking religiousness to personality tender-mindedness (Eysenck 1954; Francis 1992a, 1992b).

The performance of the Spiritual Openness scale was considerably different. SO failed to significantly correlate with prayer frequency, religious attendance, or forgiveness—all variables representing traditional spiritual/religious experience. However, it did evidence small but significant correlations with some spiritual and religious variables, notably experience of the presence of God ($r = .14, p \le .01$), FMS Vertical ($r = .12, p \le .05$), and FMS Horizontal ($r = .25, p \le .05$). Spiritual Openness correlated positively with extramarital tolerance ($r = .23, p \le .01$), which represents behaviors generally at odds with most mainstream religious moral values.

Unlike the SS scale, SO correlated strongly with a broad-minded religious and political position ($rs = .56$ and $.48$ respectively, $p \le .01$) and negatively with the measure of discrimination against women ($r = -.52, p \le .01$). Like SS it correlated negatively with racism ($r = -.37, p \le .01$), but unlike SS, it failed to correlate with any measure of life satisfaction. This last result is contrary to Genia's (1997) finding that SO is associated with feelings of life satisfaction.

SO correlated strongly with personality Openness to Experience ($r = .46$, $p \leq$ .01), and exhibited a small but significant relationship with Extraversion ($r = .11$, $p \leq .05$). These results are consistent with the definition of the variable as representing an expansive and universal viewpoint.

Thus the performance of SO is unlike most other spiritual or religious variables which more strongly correlate with religious activities and experiences such as prayer frequency, church attendance, forgiveness, and with other mainstream religious measures such as the FMS. These results begin to call into question the construct validity of SO as a spiritual variable.

Regression analysis was able to define more clearly the nature of Spiritual Support and Spiritual Openness. For each criterion variable noted above, the personality variables of Neuroticism, Extraversion, Openness to Experience, Agreeableness, and Conscientiousness were entered as a block on step 1, and SS or SO was entered on step 2. The adjusted R^2 resulting from step 1 indicates the amount of variance attributable to the personality model, and the change in adjusted R^2 from step 1 to step 2 indicates the variance attributable to SS or SO after the variance attributable to personality is taken out. This result gives a measure of the uniqueness of each subscale as a predictor apart from personality. Results are summarized in Table 4.

Table 4. Incremental Validity of SO and SS Subscales in Predicting Religious and Psychological Variables[a]

	Spiritual Support			Spiritual Openness		
	Step 1 FFI R^2	Step 2 ΔR^2	B	Step 1 FFI R^2	Step 2 ΔR^2	B
Prayer Frequency	.026	.299***	.56	.026	.000	−.01
Attendance Frequency	.012	.224***	.49	.012	.000	−.01
Religious Position	.128	.026***	−.17	.128	.197***	.50
Forgiveness	.030	.120***	.36	.030	.000	.03
Presence of God	.070	.183***	.44	.070	.000	.03
Satisfaction with Prayer	.110	.066***	.27	.110	.000	.06
Satisfaction with God	.073	.139***	.39	.073	.003	.09
Political Position	.149	.003	−.07	.149	.126***	.40
Women Discrimination	.077	.001	.06	.077	.196***	.50
Sexual Attitude Tolerance	.215	.112***	−.35	.215	.196***	.50
Extramarital Tolerance	.024	.011*	−.12	.024	.034***	.21
Racism	.085	.018**	−.15	.085	.076***	−.32
Life Satisfaction: Life -3	.219	.014**	.13	.219	.002	.07
Whole Life Satisfaction	.180	.005	.09	.180	.011*	.13
Sexual Life Satisfaction	.070	.023**	.17	.070	.000	−.01
Marriage Satisfaction	.060	.016*	−.14	.060	.000	.03

Notes: N is from 367 to 375.
   [a] Adjusted R^2
   $^*p < .05$; $^{**}p < .01$; $^{***}p < .001$

Spiritual Support added significant variance above that of personality with regard to prayer frequency and religious attendance frequency ($\Delta R^2 = .30$ and $.22$ respectively, $p \leq .001$), prayer and God satisfaction ($\Delta R^2 = .07$ and $.14$ respectively, $p \leq .001$), forgiveness ($\Delta R^2 = .12$, $p \leq .001$), and religious position ($\Delta R^2 = .03$, $p \leq .001$). Thus SS is not subsumed by the Five Factor Model of personality, and appears to offer considerable incremental predictive power regarding these criteria of spirituality or religiousness.

Spiritual Support also added small but significant variance above personality to sexual attitude tolerance, extramarital tolerance, racism, life satisfaction, sexual satisfaction, and marriage satisfaction. Except for sexual attitude tolerance, which added a variance of 11 percent ($p \leq .001$), these added variances ranged from 1 percent to 2 percent: small but important for a very limited spiritual variable in comparison with the much broader personality model. Thus, SS is not subsumed by the Five Factor Model of personality in the prediction of these social variables.

Spiritual Openness provided no significant additional variance to prayer frequency and religious attendance frequency, prayer satisfaction and God satisfaction, or forgiveness. Thus SO offers no significant predictive power over personality in the prediction of these spiritual or religious variables.

However, SO offered a sizeable unique contribution to religious position and political position ($\Delta R^2 = .20$ and $.13$, respectively, $p \leq .001$), discrimination against women ($\Delta R^2 = .20$, $p \leq .001$), sexual attitude tolerance ($\Delta R^2 = .20$, $p \leq .001$), and racism ($\Delta R^2 = .08$, $p \leq .001$). Thus SO demonstrates that it is not subsumed by personality Openness to Experience, but offers sizeable incremental predictive power over personality to explain dimensions of these latter variables.

It also is important to note that Spiritual Openness tended to provide additional predictive power toward criteria which involved attitudes, whether religious or secular, as opposed to criteria which were based on behavior or life satisfactions. In contrast, Spiritual Support showed incremental predictive power over personality across behaviors, attitudes, and satisfactions, although some increments were small.

DISCUSSION

This study presented additional information upon which to assess the construct validity of the Spiritual Experience Index–Revised. A sample with much greater diversity in age and geographical distribution but greater specificity of denomination and degree of religiousness was used to expand understanding of the two SEI-R factors of Spiritual Openness and Spiritual Support.

Initial analysis of the performance of the SEI-R showed an internal consistency and factor structure similar to the normative results. The SS factor strongly correlated with a number of spiritual or religious behavioral and satisfaction measures, as well as with the Faith Maturity Scale, a standard measure of spiritual and religious maturity based on Christian criteria. The SS mean score was higher than the normative mean as expected for this highly religious sample.

The SO scale failed to correlate with almost all spiritual or religious behavioral and satisfaction variables, and correlated only weakly with the experience of the presence of God and the Faith Maturity Vertical Scale, but somewhat more strongly with the Faith Maturity Horizontal Scale. The SO mean score in this highly religious group was unexpectedly similar to the normative mean score.

A series of regressions was performed using religious and nonreligious criterion variables and utilizing the Five Factor personality model on the first step and either the SS or SO model on the second step. Results indicated the incremental validity of the SS model in predicting spiritual behavioral and satisfaction outcomes after the variance attributable to the personality model was removed, and somewhat weaker but significant amounts of additional variance with respect to racism, life satisfactions, and sexual attitude tolerance. However, the SO model failed to offer any predictive increment on the religious behavioral and satisfaction measures, while it did offer a wide range of additional variances with respect to the prediction of racism, sexual attitude tolerance, tolerance of extramarital sexuality, discrimination against women, religious position, and political position. SO failed to offer incremental variance to any of the life satisfaction measures except for a small contribution to whole life satisfaction.

These results appear to confirm the validity of the Spiritual Support subscale of the SEI-R for measurement of mainline Christian groups, inasmuch as Roman Catholic Christians tend to situate themselves within the mainstream of United States Christianity (Greeley 1995). SS appears to be a unique and effective predictor not only of spiritual or religious outcomes, but also of a number of important psychosocial outcomes such as racism and life satisfaction. It may prove itself useful both as a research tool and as a short measure for the clinical assessment of a person's level of spiritual meaning and support.

At the same time, results regarding the Spiritual Openness subscale cast doubt on its validity as a spiritual construct. While it provided incremental predictive capability over personality with regard to a number of psychosocial outcomes, it had little correlation with things most persons consider spiritual or religious. Given these results, it seems that SO may be describing some intentional expansiveness or broad-mindedness as a characteristic beyond personality but which does not represent a primarily spiritual construct. These results call for further clarification of the meaning of Spiritual Openness, and most importantly, continuing investigation of the research and clinical utility of the SEI-R.

REFERENCES

Allport, G. W. 1950. *The Individual and His Religion.* New York: Macmillan Publishing Co.
Andrews, F. M., and S. B. Withey. 1976. *Social Indicators of Well-being: Americans' Perceptions of Life Quality.* NY: Plenum Press.

Benson, P. L., M. J. Donahue, and J. A. Erickson. 1993. "The Faith Maturity Scale: Conceptualization, Measurement, and Empirical Validation." *Research in the Social Scientific Study of Religion*, 5, 1–26.

Briggs, S. R. 1992. "Assessing the Five-Factor Model of Personality Description." *Journal of Personality* 60, 253–293.

Campbell, A., P. E. Converse, and W. L. Rodgers. 1976. *The Quality of American Life: Perceptions, Evaluations, and Satisfactions.* NY: Russell Sage.

Costa, P. T., Jr., and R. R. McCrae. 1992. *NEO PI-R: Professional Manual.* Odessa, FL: Psychological Assessment Resources.

Csarny, R. J. 1998. "The Incremental Validity of Religious Constructs in Predicting Quality of Life, Racism, and Sexual Attitudes." UMI Company, No. 9826114. *Dissertation Abstracts International* 59(3b).

Digman, J. M. 1990. "Personality Structure: Emergence of the Five-Factor Model." *Annual Review of Psychology*, 41, 417–440.

Dittes, J. E. 1969. "Psychology of Religion." Pp. 602–659 in *The Handbook of Social Psychology* (2nd ed.) edited by G. Lindzey and E. Aronson. Reading, MA: Addison-Wesley.

Eysenck, H. J. 1954. *The Psychology of Politics.* London: Routledge and Kegan Paul.

Francis, L. J. 1992a. "Religion, Neuroticism, and Psychoticism." Pp. 149–160 in *Religion and Mental Health,* edited by J. F. Schumaker. NY: Oxford University Press.

Francis, L. J. 1992b. "Is Psychoticism Really a Dimension of Personality Fundamental to Religiosity?" *Personality and Individual Differences*, 13,645–652.

Genia, V. 1990. "Religious Development: A Synthesis and Reformulation." *Journal of Religion and Health,* 29, 85–99.

Genia, V. 1991. "The Spiritual Experience Index: A Measure of Spiritual Maturity." *Journal of Religion and Health*, 30, 337–347.

Genia, V. 1997. "The Spiritual Experience Index: Revision and Reformulation." *Review of Religious Research*, 38, 344–361.

Goldberg, L. R. 1981. "Language and Individual Differences: The Search for Universals in Personality Lexicons." *Review of Personality and Social Psychology,* 2, 141–165.

Gorsuch, R. L. 1983. *Factor Analysis.* Hillsdale, NJ: Lawrence Erlbaum Associates.

Gorsuch, R. L. 1984. "Measurement: The Boon and Bane of Investigating Religion." *American Psychologist*, 39, 228–236.

Gorsuch, R. L., and G. D. Venable. 1983. "Development of an 'Age Universal' I-E Scale." *Journal for the Scientific Study of Religion*, 22, 181–187.

Greeley, A. M. 1995. *Religion as Poetry.* New Brunswick, NJ: Transaction Publishers.

King, M. B., and R. A. Hunt. 1971. "The Intrinsic–Extrinsic Concept: A Review and Evaluation." *Journal for the Scientific Study of Religion* 10, 339–356.

Kirkpatrick, L., and R. Hood. 1990. "Intrinsic–extrinsic Religious Orientation: The Boon or Bane of Contemporary Psychology of Religion?" *Journal for the Scientific Study of Religion,* 29, 442–462.

McConahay, J. B. 1986. "Modern Racism, Ambivalence, and the Modern Racism Scale." Pp. 91–125 in *Prejudice, Discrimination, and Racism*, edited by J. F. Dovidio and S. L. Gaertner. Orlando: Academic Press.

McConahay, J. B., B. B. Hardee, and V. Batts. 1981. "Has Racism Declined in America?: It Depends on Who Is Asking and What Is Asked." *Journal of Conflict Resolution,* 25, 563–579.

McCrae, R. R., and P. T. Costa, Jr. 1987. "Validation of the Five-Factor Model of Personality Across Instruments and Observers." *Journal of Personality and Social Psychology* 52: 81–90.

McCrae, R. R., and P. T. Costa, Jr. 1990. *Personality in Adulthood.* NY: The Guilford Press.

Piedmont, R. L., R. R. McCrae, and P. T. Costa, Jr. 1992. "An Assessment of the EPPS from the Perspective of the Five-Factor Model." *Journal of Personality Assessment*, 58, 67–78.

Piedmont, R. L. 1996. "Strategies for Using the Five-Factor Model in Religious Research." Paper presented at the annual meeting of the American Psychological Association, Toronto, Canada.

Saucier, G., and L. R. Goldberg. 1996. "The Language of Personality: Lexical Perspectives on the Five-Factor Model." Pp. 21–50 in *The Five-Factor Model of Personality,* edited by J. S. Wiggins. NY: The Guilford Press.

Valois, R. F. 1980. *The Effects of a Human Sexuality Program on the Attitudes of University Residence Hall Students.* Unpublished master's thesis, University of Illinois, Champaign-Urbana.

Valois, R. F., and J. C. Ory. 1988. "The Valois Sexual Attitude Scale." Pp. 43–44 in *Sexuality-Related Measures: A Compendium*, edited by C. M. Davis, W. L. Yarber, and S. L. Davis. Lake Mills, IA: Graphic Publishing Company.

Van Wicklin, J. F. 1990. "Conceiving and Measuring Ways of Being Religious." *Journal of Psychology and Christianity*, 9, 27–40.

REEXAMINING THE RELATIONSHIP BETWEEN RELIGIOSITY AND LIFE SATISFACTION

Pui-Yan Lam and Thomas Rotolo

ABSTRACT

A large body of literature has attempted to assess the relationship between religiosity and life satisfaction. We use data on 875 individuals from the 1993 General Social Survey to readdress this issue. Unlike previous research, we do not rely on a single, unidimensional measure of life satisfaction. Instead, we use six separate indicators of life satisfaction, each corresponding to a distinct life domain. The life domains include satisfaction with finances, family, friendships, health, city, and nonworking activities. We measure religiosity with three variables: denominational affiliation, strength of affiliation, and frequency of attending religious services. We utilize a series of nested logistic regression models in order to estimate the odds that a respondent is highly satisfied with a particular life domain. The results from these analyses show that these three indicators of religiosity have significant, but differential effects on the six, distinct life satisfaction domains.

Research in the Social Scientific Study of Religion, Volume 11, pages 133-153.
Copyright © 2000 by JAI Press Inc.
All rights of reproduction in any form reserved.
ISBN: 0-7623-0656-4

133

INTRODUCTION

Social scientists interested in studying religious phenomena have long recognized Bohrnstedt's (1983, p. 69) dictum that, "Measurement is a sine qua non of any science." As Gorsuch urges, researchers engaged in the scientific study of religion must occasionally assess measurement procedures in order to better identify "strengths and weaknesses" inherent in any measurement process (1984, p. 228). Researchers interested in religiosity have paid attention to these recommendations, as evidenced in the literature devoted to conceptual and measurement work conducted over the years on exploring the different dimensions of religiosity (see review below). Unfortunately, there has been little agreement on which dimensions of religiosity are the most relevant or how these should be measured (cf. Koenig et al. 1988). Indeed, as we review below, a debate exists in this literature between those who feel that religiosity can be measured as a single, unidimensional concept, and others who argue that religiosity is a multifaceted concept that cannot be measured with a single, simplified scale.

In this paper, we revisit a large body of research that attempts to examine the relationship between religious involvement and life satisfaction. While we do not deny the importance of creating valid and reliable measures of religiosity, in this paper we focus attention on measurement issues with respect to the dependent variable of interest—life satisfaction. Thus unlike previous approaches, we treat both religiosity and life satisfaction as multidimensional concepts; we examine some of the problems in measuring life satisfaction as a unidimensional concept, and propose a new approach to studying the relationship between religious involvement and life satisfaction. Specifically, we explore the relationship between religiosity, represented by three commonly employed indicators, and life satisfaction, as measured by six indicators of satisfaction, each corresponding to a distinct life domain.

CONCEPTUALIZING RELIGIOSITY

The search for objective criteria to evaluate religiosity remains a central issue in the scientific study of religion. Extensive discussions of the literature devoted to this area exist elsewhere; see for example, Gorsuch (1984) or Schumaker (1992). Below, we provide a brief overview of this literature to set the stage for our empirical analyses relating religiosity to life satisfaction.

In early studies, church membership and attendance were often combined to create a single indicator of religiosity. Since the 1950s, however, social scientists have claimed that single-item measures of religiosity are inadequate; unitary measures often faced challenges from researchers who argued that scholars must consider different aspects of religiosity (Steinitz 1980). In one of the earliest studies,

Allport (1950) distinguished between intrinsic and extrinsic religiosity; individuals with an intrinsic orientation see religion as an end in itself, while those with an extrinsic orientations utilize religion for their own, personal benefits. Over the next few decades, researchers, building on typologies proposed by Allport (1950, 1966), Glock (1954), Lenski (1961), and others, developed and tested various multidimensional scales of religiosity.

Allport's research, in particular, paved the way for multidimensional treatments of religiosity. For instance in a series of articles, King and Hunt (1971, 1972, 1975, 1990; Hunt 1968, 1972; King 1967) attempted to identify the most salient dimensions of religiosity by evaluating previously utilized measures with tests from different samples. In one of the earliest studies, King (1967) distinguished nine dimensions of religiosity, encompassing different aspects of religious belief, commitment, and participation. In subsequent research, King and Hunt explored the dimensionality of religiosity in samples of individuals from different denominations, and different geographic areas. They concluded that religiosity consisted of between eight to ten dimensions, with some variations across denominations.

In addition to the research of King and Hunt, Glock and Stark extensively studied the dimensionality of religiosity (Glock and Stark 1965; Stark and Glock 1968). These researchers identified five core dimensions of religiosity: belief, practice (ritual and devotion), experience, knowledge, and consequences. However, Glock and Stark remained critical of Allport's typology of intrinsic and extrinsic religion, arguing instead that Allport equated intrinsic religious motives with authentic religious commitment.

More recently, Gorsuch (1984) suggested that researchers should not treat the dimensionality of religiosity as an "either/or" issue, and proposed that researchers recognize religiosity as both a multidimensional and unidimensional concept. Gorsuch argues that religiosity may be treated as a single, general concept, which in turn can also be divided into various dimensions. In particular, he suggests that in the United States, religious people can be distinguished from nonreligious by a general dimension, and further contends that this general dimension can be "subdivided" into a number of other factors, including church attendance and creedal assent (1984, pp. 232–233).

In sum, while religiosity has been accepted widely as a multidimensional or multifaceted concept, after decades of investigations researchers continue to debate about which aspects of religiosity are the most salient. Further, with secondary data analyses becoming widely accepted and utilized, researchers are forced to rely on measures of religiosity with the items available in the data. While multiple-item scales of religiosity may have higher validity, it appears as if single-item indicators are often adequate if these data limitations are taken into account (cf. Gorsuch and McFarland 1972).

RELIGIOUS INVOLVEMENT AND LIFE SATISFACTION

Studies on the relationship between religion and life satisfaction, or well-being, tend to focus on either physical or mental health issues (see Schumaker 1992). An extensive body of research is devoted to the study of religion and physical well-being (see Koenig et al. 1988 for a review of this literature). Most of this research suggests that religious variables positively influence physical well-being (Frankel and Hewitt 1994; Gorsuch 1988; Ellison 1993). For example, Frankel and Hewitt (1994) report a positive association between faith group involvement and physical health among Canadian university students. However, other studies suggest that the relationship between religion and physical health is spurious, because the relationship between religious attendance and health disappears after controls for other factors such as physical capacity and social support are included in statistical models (see Levin and Markides 1986).

Researchers in the area of religion and mental health have studied the influence of religious factors on mental health indicators such as psychiatric illness and depressive disorders (e.g. Ross 1990) and subjective well-being. While the measurement instruments used to identify psychiatric illness and depression are relatively well-defined, confusion over the measurement of subjective well-being exists. Koenig and colleagues (1988) noted investigators commonly use life-satisfaction, happiness, and other terms interchangeably. Moreover, scholars in this area are far from reaching a consensus on how to validly and reliably measure subjective well being.

Some researchers have utilized a global measure of life satisfaction (i.e., a single scale that attempts to encompass all aspects of life satisfaction) to investigate the impact of religious involvement on general well-being. For instance, Ellison and Gay (1990) find that denominational affiliation and attendance at religious services are both significant predictors of a global life satisfaction measure. Similarly, Poloma and Pendleton (1988) report that religious factors such as satisfaction with and frequency of prayer significantly predict individual's general well being, while St. George and McNamara (1984) find that the effects of church attendance and strength of religious affiliation on global happiness differ by sex and race. While each of these studies presents interesting findings in its own right, they all share the common trait of relying on a very general measure of satisfaction.

Ellison, Gay, and Glass (1989) present a strong argument against using global measures of life satisfaction. Following the lead of others (Campbell, Converse, and Rodgers 1976), Ellison, Gay and Glass convincingly argue that, "a combination of domain-specific indicators of life satisfaction is superior to a global or omnibus measure" (1989, p. 107). Using a composite measure that includes indicators of satisfaction with health, friendships, finances, and family life, Ellison, Gay, and Glass (1989) report that both devotional and participatory aspects of religiosity have relatively small, but persistently positive influences on life satisfaction, while affiliation with certain denominations is positively associated with life satisfaction as well. See Ellison (1991), and Schwab and Petersen (1990) for other examples of research utilizing composite measures.

In summary, as noted by Ellison and Gay (1990), researchers still disagree on how to measure life satisfaction, or personal well-being. Some researchers continue to rely on single global measures of life satisfaction while others utilize composite measures of satisfaction. We argue that studies which rely exclusively on composite or general measures of satisfaction risk oversimplification. Perhaps frequently attending church results in higher levels of satisfaction with friendships, but not satisfaction with finances. People with a strong affiliation to a particular religious denomination may be satisfied with their nonworking activities, such as hobbies, but not with their health and physical condition. Unfortunately, if various aspects of religiosity have different effects on different areas of satisfaction then using a global measure of life satisfaction as a dependent variable essentially masks these differential effects.

Researchers who treat life satisfaction as a multidimensional concept have reported that religiosity and religious participation do have different effects on different areas of satisfaction and well-being. For instance, Steinitz (1980) examines how religious activities (as measured by attendance) and beliefs (as measured by strength of affiliation) relate to various aspects of personal well-being in a population of elderly individuals. Specifically, she considers the relationships of religious factors to six separate dependent variables: self-reported happiness, perceived health, life excitement, and satisfaction with city, family, and health. She reports a positive relationship between religious activities and all six measures of well-being, but strength of affiliation has a significant, positive influence only on satisfaction with city and satisfaction with health.

In addition to using the global measure of happiness discussed earlier, St. George and McNamara (1984) also separately analyzed the effects of religiosity on various aspects of life satisfaction. These researchers examined racial differences in the relationship between religiosity and satisfaction in five specific life domains, including community life, nonwork activities, family life, friendships, and health. They found that various aspects of religiosity, such as church attendance and strength of affiliation, differentially affect the distinct life satisfaction domains. However, since these researchers were primarily interested in exploring racial differences in the influence of religiosity on satisfaction, they did not report details on how religious factors differentially relate to the various dimensions of life satisfaction.

There is another measurement issue that has not been well addressed by scholars interested in the relationship between religiosity and personal well-being. Most of the statistical analyses used by researchers assume that the dependent variable (i.e., life satisfaction) is measured at least at the interval level. However, whether researchers use domain-specific measures or a single, general life satisfaction measure, most of the satisfaction items are Likert-scaled indicators measured at the ordinal level. Many investigators use the raw scores of the items, or the summation of raw scores across a number of items, in order to create the dependent variable. However, the distance in satisfaction between scores of one and two is probably not the same as the distance between three and four in a Likert-scaled item. Thus, treating a sum of ordinal-level variables as if it is were interval or ratio level violates a basic assumption of the most commonly employed statistical technique, ordinary least squares regression analysis.

In this study, we propose a different approach to studying the relationship between religiosity and life satisfaction. First, we conduct separate analyses for six different domains of life satisfaction in order to examine the differential impact of religiosity on each of the various domains. Then, we explicitly recognize that life satisfaction indicators are measured at the ordinal level, rather than the interval or ratio level, and use logistic regression analysis, a more appropriate analytical technique.

A further advantage of logistic regression analysis is freedom from distributional assumptions underlying least squares analysis.

DATA AND METHODS

We utilize data from the 1993 General Social Survey (GSS) in this research. The GSS has been utilized widely by scholars interested in exploring the relationship between religiosity and life satisfaction. The GSS constitutes a probability sample of noninstitutionalized individuals, aged eighteen years or older. In 1993, the questions on the satisfaction items were asked of a representative subsample of 875 respondents, so the sample size used in all of our models is 875.

Dependent Variables

We conduct separate analyses for six different satisfaction items. These domain-specific items of satisfaction correspond to six salient dimensions of social life: (1) Finances; (2) Family Life; (3) Friendships; (4) Health; (5) City; and (6) Nonwork activities . We are interested in exploring how life satisfaction in each of the six domains varies by religious affiliation and participation in religious activities. In order to conduct a critical test of the influence of religiosity on life satisfaction, we treat satisfaction in rather strict terms. For each of the six domains, we separate individuals having high satisfaction within a particular domain from those individuals with moderate to low levels of satisfaction. Thus, if our analyses suggest that religiosity has effects on life satisfaction, we can conclude that these effects are powerful enough to distinguish people with extremely high levels of satisfaction from those with more moderate to low levels.

The General Social Survey asks respondents to report how satisfied they are with: *family life, friendships, health and physical condition, city,* and *nonwork activities.* Responses form a 7-point Likert scale, ranging from "a very great deal" to "none." We code strongly positive responses (a very great deal, a great deal, and quite a bit) as indicating a high level of satisfaction with that particular dimension of social life, and all other responses (a fair amount, some, a little, and none) as indicating moderate to low satisfaction.

With regards to financial satisfaction, GSS respondents were asked, "...So far as you and your family are concerned, would you say that you are pretty well satisfied with your financial situation, more or less satisfied, or not satisfied at all." Respondents claiming that they are "pretty well satisfied" are coded as having a high level of satisfaction with finances, and "more or less satisfied" and "not satisfied" responses are coded as moderate to low satisfaction.

Religious Affiliation and Participation

We examine the impact on life satisfaction of two general aspects of religiosity: the affiliative and the participatory. The affiliative dimension is measured using both denominational membership and self-reported strength of affiliation. We code *Religious affiliation* as a set of nine dummy variables, corresponding to nine major religious groups with "no religious affiliation" as the omitted category. *Strength of Affiliation* is coded as a dummy variable and is included to distinguish between respondents who report a strong affiliation (coded as *one*) with their religious groups and those expressing a weaker affiliation (coded as *zero*). For the participatory dimension of religiosity, we employ a nine-point ordinal scale measuring religious participation that ranges from never to several times a week. Thus, this measure taps an individual's *frequency of attendance* at religious services.

Control Variables

Researchers have suggested that the links between religiosity and psychological well-being found in previous studies may be spurious, because individuals vary in the propensity to participate in social activities and this propensity is related to both religiosity and satisfaction. In an attempt to account for a respondent's core propensity to affiliate, we include as a control variable an indicator of *social affiliation*, measured by the total number of memberships in voluntary associations reported by respondents.

In addition, other variables likely influence religiosity and life satisfaction. Therefore, age (in years) and age-squared, family income, educational attainment (highest year of school completed), trauma (total number of traumatic life events in past year, including family deaths, divorces, periods of unemployment, hospitalizations, and physical disabilities) and three nominal variables representing marital status (married=1), gender (female=1) and race (nonwhite=1) of respondents, are included in the models as control variables.

Analytic Strategy

Nested logistic regression analyses were conducted in order the examine the effects of religious affiliation and participation on the satisfaction on each of the six life-domains. Specifically, for each of the six dependent variables, a series of four nested regression models was estimated: *Model 1*: which includes only the control variables; *Model 2*: with the nine categories for religious affiliation introduced; *Model 3*: which adds the strength of affiliation variable; and lastly, *Model 4*: which adds the frequency of attendance indicator. In each model, the coefficients associated with the independent variables can be used to predict the log odds of being very satisfied with a particular life domain. Exponentiation of a coefficient gives the multiplicative effect of a variable on the odds (i.e., odds ratio) of being very satisfied with a particular life domain, holding all other variables constant (see Agresti 1996, pp. 122–135). In general, the logistic regression model estimates the log odds (or odds after exponentiation) of reporting high satisfaction with a life domain. Odds can be interpreted as a ratio of probabilities. In this case if Y is a dependent variable equaling 1 if respondent reports being high satisfaction with some life domain and equaling 0 if respondent fails to report high satisfaction with some life domain:

(Odds of reporting high satisfaction) =
Prob (Y = High Satisfaction) / Prob (Y = Not High Satisfaction)

As odds increase, the probability of a respondent reporting high satisfaction with some life domain increase (relative to reporting "Not High Satisfaction"), however this probability increase follows a nonlinear, sigmoid-shaped curve, rather than a simple linear increase; estimate from logistic regression models cannot easily be interpreted in terms of changes in probability values. Therefore, we present interpretation of all coefficients in terms of odds, rather than probabilities.

RESULTS

Table 1 presents the results for the four nested logistic regression models for the effects of religious affiliation and participation on satisfaction with finances. As we move from Model 2 to Model 4, we see that respondent reporting affiliation with the Methodist denomination consistently have higher odds of reporting high satisfaction with finances, as compared to those who report no religious affiliation. Interestingly, none of the other affiliation have a significant effect on the odds of satisfaction with finances. Frequency of attendance also has a slight positive effect on satisfaction with finances. With each one-unit increase in attendance the odds of reporting high satisfaction

Table 1. Nested Logistic Regression Models:
Effects of Religious Affiliation and Participation on Satisfaction with Finances
(1993 NORC GSS data; N = 875 for all models)

Independent Variables	Model I Coefficient	Odds	Model II Coefficient	Odds	Model III Coefficient	Odds	Model IV Coefficient	Odds
Intercept	0.985	2.678	0.719	2.053	0.766	2.151	0.833	2.299
	(0.795)		(0.832)		(0.835)		(0.837)	
Age	−0.160***	0.852	−0.160***	0.852	−0.160***	0.852	−0.155***	0.857
	(0.034)		(0.034)		(0.034)		(0.034)	
Age2	0.002***	1.002	0.002***	1.002	0.002***	1.002	0.002***	1.002
	(0.000)		(0.000)		(0.000)		(0.000)	
Married	0.404**	1.497	0.382**	1.466	0.382**	1.465	0.348*	1.416
	(0.187)		(0.190)		(0.190)		(0.192)	
Trauma	−0.495***	0.609	−0.479***	0.620	−0.479***	0.620	−0.485***	0.616
	(0.124)		(0.126)		(0.126)		(0.126)	
Female	0.145	1.155	0.117	1.124	0.105	1.111	0.076	1.079
	(0.173)		(0.178)		(0.179)		(0.180)	
Income	0.144***	1.155	0.146***	1.157	0.147***	1.158	0.145***	1.156
	(0.020)		(0.021)		(0.021)		(0.021)	
Education	0.037	1.038	0.039	1.040	0.038	1.039	0.029	1.029
	(0.037)		(0.039)		(0.035)		(0.036)	
Nonwhite	−0.119	0.888	−0.085	0.918	−0.104	0.901	−0.148	0.863
	(0.227)		(0.238)		(0.240)		(0.242)	
Organization Membership	0.048	1.049	0.039	1.039	0.032	1.033	0.004	1.004
	(0.057)		(0.059)		(0.059)		(0.061)	
Catholic			0.253	1.287	0.208	1.231	0.036	1.037
			(0.300)		(0.305)		(0.320)	
Jewish			−0.119	0.888	−0.179	0.836	−0.224	0.799
			(0.661)		(0.665)		(0.665)	
Southern Baptist			0.364	1.439	0.312	1.366	0.116	1.123
			(0.356)		(0.363)		(0.380)	
Other Baptist			−0.032	0.969	−0.079	0.924	−0.240	0.787
			(0.355)		(0.360)		(0.371)	
Lutheran			0.135	1.145	0.092	1.096	−0.081	0.922
			(0.386)		(0.390)		(0.401)	
Presbyterian			0.856	2.354	0.806	2.239	0.708	2.030
			(0.530)		(0.533)		(0.539)	
Episcopal			0.329	1.389	0.298	1.347	0.228	1.255
			(0.655)		(0.656)		(0.228)	
Methodist			1.295***	3.651	1.254***	3.504	1.108**	3.028
			(0.436)		(0.438)		(0.445)	
Other Protestant			0.270	1.309	0.191	1.211	0.016	1.016
			(0.314)		(0.329)		(0.344)	
Strength of Affiliation					0.152	1.165	−0.033	0.968
					(0.195)		(0.222)	
Frequency of Attendance							0.078*	1.081
							(0.044)	
Deviance	860.8	(df=865)	846.0	(df=856)	845.4	(df=855)	842.2	(df=854)
−2 Log Likelihood Ratio			14.8*	(df=9)	0.6	(df=1)	3.2*	(df=1)

Notes: Numbers in parentheses are standard errors.
*$p < 0.10$ **$p < 0.05$ ***$p < 0.01$.

Table 2. Nested Logistic Regression Models:
Effects of Religious Affiliation and Participation on Satisfaction with Family Life
(1993 NORC GSS data; $N = 875$ for all models)

Indenpendent Variables	Model I Coefficient	Odds	Model II Coefficient	Odds	Model III Coefficient	Odds	Model IV Coefficient	Odds
Intercept	3.178***	23.987	2.415**	11.194	2.554**	12.857	2.577**	13.156
	(0.984)		(1.025)		(1.033)		(1.036)	
Age	−0.088	0.916	−0.102***	0.903	−0.105***	0.900	−0.102***	0.903
	(0.036)		(0.037)		(0.037)		(0.088)	
Age2	0.001**	1.001	0.001**	1.001	0.001**	1.001	0.001**	1.001
	(0.000)		(0.000)		(0.000)		(0.000)	
Married	1.656***	5.239	1.678***	5.353	1.678***	5.356	1.658***	5.248
	(0.261)		(0.270)		(0.270)		(0.271)	
Trauma	−0.382***	0.683	−0.372**	0.689	−0.380**	0.684	−0.380**	0.684
	(0.147)		(0.151)		(0.151)		(0.151)	
Female	0.652***	1.919	0.519**	1.681	0.478**	1.612	0.457**	1.580
	(0.220)		(0.229)		(0.230)		(0.231)	
Income	0.074***	1.077	0.073***	1.075	0.074***	1.077	0.073***	1.076
	(0.023)		(0.024)		(0.024)		(0.024)	
Education	−0.076*	0.927	−0.051	0.950	−0.053	0.959	−0.064	0.938
	(0.042)		(0.043)		(0.044)		(0.075)	
Nonwhite	0.331	1.392	0.239	1.270	0.208	1.231	0.179	1.196
	(0.298)		(0.316)		(0.319)		(0.321)	
Organization Membership	−0.016	0.984	−0.026	0.974	−0.042	0.959	−0.064	0.988
	(0.068)		(0.070)		(0.071)		(0.075)	
Catholic			1.154***	3.172	1.044**	0.579	0.926**	2.525
			(0.355)		(0.363)		(0.383)	
Jewish			−0.433	0.649	−0.547	0.579	−0.574	0.563
			(0.640)		(0.643)		(0.647)	
Southern Baptist			1.274***	3.574	1.119**	3.061	0.995**	2.704
			(0.456)		(0.465)		(0.483)	
Other Baptist			1.284***	3.609	1.163**	3.200	1.054**	2.869
			(0.460)		(0.467)		(0.480)	
Lutheran			1.903***	6.703	1.769***	5.865	1.644***	5.176
			(0.594)		(0.599)		(0.613)	
Presbyterian			0.795	2.214	0.643	1.886	0.539	1.715
			(0.546)		(0.554)		(0.561)	
Episcopal			0.740	2.095	0.688	1.990	0.633	1.883
			(0.733)		(0.740)		(0.738)	
Methodist			1.183***	3.265	1.080**	2.946	0.986**	2.680
			(0.458)		(0.461)		(0.472)	
Other Protestant			0.860**	2.362	0.688*	1.951	0.562	1.755
			(0.358)		(0.378)		(0.394)	
Strength of Affiliation					0.397	1.487	0.276	1.318
					(0.259)		(0.289)	
Frequency of Attendance							0.053	1.054
							(0.056)	
Deviance	592.1	(df=865)	567.9	(df=856)	565.5	(df=855)	564.7	(df=854)
−2 Log Likelihood Ratio			24.2***	(df=9)	2.4	(df=1)	0.9	(df=1)

Notes: Numbers in parentheses are standard errors.
      *$p < 0.10$ **$p < 0.05$ ***$p < 0.01$.

Table 3. Nested Logistic Regression Models: Effects of Religious Affiliation and Participation on Satisfaction with Friendships (1993 NORC GSS data; $N = 875$ for all models)

Independent Variables	Model I		Model II		Model III		Model IV	
	Coefficient	Odds	Coefficient	Odds	Coefficient	Odds	Coefficient	Odds
Intercept	2.229[*]	9.291	1.682[*]	5.378	1.960[**]	7.096	1.995[**]	7.351
	(0.892)		(0.923)		(0.938)		(0.939)	
Age	−0.032	0.969	−0.039	0.962	−0.045	0.956	−0.042	0.959
	(0.035)		(0.035)		(0.036)		(0.036)	
Age2	0.000	1.000	0.000	1.000	0.000	1.000	0.000	1.000
	(0.000)		(0.000)		(0.000)		(0.000)	
Married	−0.131	0.877	−0.149	0.861	−0.156	0.856	−0.173	0.841
	(0.221)		(0.226)		(0.227)		(0.228)	
Trauma	−0.457[***]	0.633	−0.435[***]	0.647	−0.429[***]	0.651	−0.429[***]	0.651
	(0.136)		(0.137)		(0.138)		(0.138)	
Female	0.604[***]	1.829	0.539[***]	1.715	0.482[**]	1.619	0.461[**]	1.585
	(0.197)		(0.203)		(0.205)		(0.138)	
Income	0.054[**]	1.055	0.054[**]	1.056	0.058[**]	1.059	0.057[**]	1.059
	(0.022)		(0.023)		(0.023)		(0.023)	
Education	−0.059	0.943	−0.039	0.961	−0.046	0.955	−0.050	0.951
	(0.038)		(0.039)		(0.040)		(0.040)	
Nonwhite	−0.454[*]	0.635	−0.511[*]	0.600	−0.601[**]	0.548	−0.623[**]	0.536
	(0.252)		(0.266)		(0.272)		(0.273)	
Organization Membership	0.186[***]	1.204	0.173[**]	1.189	0.147[**]	1.158	0.130[*]	1.139
	(0.072)		(0.073)		(0.072)		(0.074)	
Catholic			0.567[*]	1.763	0.392	1.479	0.293	1.341
			(0.330)		(0.336)		(0.353)	
Jewish			−0.828	0.437	−1.035[*]	0.355	−1.063[*]	0.345
			(0.569)		(0.581)		(0.580)	
Southern Baptist			0.705[*]	2.024	0.467	1.595	0.352	1.421
			(0.400)		(0.408)		(0.428)	
Other Baptist			0.540	1.716	0.363	1.438	0.266	1.305
			(0.390)		(0.395)		(0.408)	
Lutheran			0.599	1.821	0.413	1.512	0.313	1.367
			(0.461)		(0.466)		(0.479)	
Presbyterian			0.080	1.083	−0.150	0.861	−0.213	0.808
			(0.488)		(0.495)		(0.500)	
Episcopal			0.829	2.291	0.728	2.072	0.676	1.965
			(0.802)		(0.809)		(0.809)	
Methodist			1.206[**]	3.340	1.043[**]	2.838	0.957[*]	2.605
			(0.480)		(0.482)		(0.491)	
Other Protestant			0.708[**]	2.029	0.369	1.446	0.268	1.307
			(0.354)		(0.370)		(0.386)	
Strength of Affiliation					0.705[***]	2.024	0.596[**]	1.814
					(0.241)		(0.270)	
Frequency of Attendance							0.045	1.046
							(0.050)	
Deviance	706.8	(df=865)	691.0	(df=856)	682.0	(df=855)	681.2	(df=854)
−2 Log Likelihood Ratio			15.8[*]	(df=9)	9.0[***]	(df=1)	0.8	(df=1)

Notes: Numbers in parentheses are standard errors.
[*]$p < 0.10$ [**]$p < 0.05$ [***]$p < 0.01$.

with finances increases by a multiplicative factor of 1.081. Marriage and high income increase the odds of satisfaction with finances, while experiencing traumatic events decreases the odds of satisfaction.

The results for the logistic regression models exploring the relationship between religiosity and satisfaction with family life are presented in Table 2. Model 4 suggests that all of the control variables exhibit significant effects on family life satisfaction, with the exception of education, race, and organization membership. In the full model (Model 4) neither strength of affiliation nor frequency of attendance significantly impacts the odds of reporting high satisfaction with family life. However, five of the nine denominational affiliations (Catholic, Southern Baptist, Other Baptist, Lutheran, and Methodist) significantly increase the odds of reporting high satisfaction with family life, as compared to those who report no religious affiliation. For instance, respondents reporting affiliation with the Lutheran denomination increase the odds of reporting high levels of satisfaction with family life by 5.176 (an increase of over 400 percent) as compared to the odds of a person with no denominational affiliation reporting high satisfaction with family life.

Table 3 presents the results for the logistic regression models predicting the odds of reporting high satisfaction with friendships. In Model 4, only two of the nine denominational affiliations have significant effects on the odds of reporting high satisfaction with friendships, however these effects are in different directions. Respondents reporting affiliation with the Methodist denomination have significantly higher odds (multiplicative factor of 2.605) of reporting high satisfaction with friendships as compared to those with no religious affiliation, while respondents reporting Jewish affiliation have significantly lower odds (multiplicative factor of 0.345) of reporting high satisfaction with friendships as compared to those reporting no affiliation. In addition to the two denominational affiliations having a significant effect, reporting a strong affiliation also significantly increases the odds of reporting high satisfaction with friendships. Lastly, experiencing traumatic events, sex, race, income, and organizational membership all have significant effects on the odds of reporting high satisfaction with friendships.

The logistic regression models predicting high satisfaction with health and physical conditions suggest that only one denominational affiliation and frequency of attendance have significant effects. In Table 4, Model 4, we see that those reporting Jewish affiliation have significantly lower odds of reporting high satisfaction with health and physical conditions as compared to those with no reported religious affiliation. Frequency of attendance has a positive effect on the odds of high satisfaction with health and physical conditions, indicating that those who attend church or religious services more frequently are more likely to report high satisfaction with health and physical conditions. (Editor's note: This apparent relationship may be due to health status; persons with poor health are less likely to go out for any reason.) Additionally, married persons,

Table 4. Nested Logistic Regression Models: Effects of Religious Affiliation and Participation on Satisfaction with Health and Physical Conditions (1993 NORC GSS data; $N = 875$ for all models)

Independent Variables	Model I Coefficient	Odds	Model II Coefficient	Odds	Model III Coefficient	Odds	Model IV Coefficient	Odds
Intercept	−0.519	0.595	−0.763	0.466	−0.731	0.481	−0.670	0.512
	(0.735)		(0.770)		(0.774)		(0.778)	
Age	0.025	1.025	0.023	1.023	0.023	1.023	0.027	1.027
	(0.028)		(0.028)		(0.028)		(0.029)	
Age2	0.000	1.000	0.000	1.000	0.000	1.000	0.000	1.000
	(0.000)		(0.000)		(0.000)		(0.000)	
Married	0.463**	1.589	0.490***	1.632	0.489***	1.630	0.458**	1.581
	(0.183)		(0.187)		(0.187)		(0.188)	
Trauma	−0.329***	0.719	−0.319***	0.727	−0.319***	0.727	−0.322***	0.725
	(0.118)		(0.119)		(0.119)		(0.120)	
Female	−0.148	0.862	−0.196	0.822	−0.203	0.816	−0.239	0.787
	(0.170)		(0.175)		(0.176)		(0.177)	
Income	0.059***	1.061	0.057***	1.058	0.057***	1.059	0.056***	1.057
	(0.018)		(0.019)		(0.019)		(0.019)	
Education	0.018	1.018	0.029	1.030	0.029	1.029	0.022	1.022
	(0.032)		(0.033)		(0.033)		(0.034)	
Nonwhite	0.195	1.215	0.224	1.251	0.214	1.238	0.166	1.180
	(0.233)		(0.243)		(0.244)		(0.245)	
Organization Membership	0.104*	1.110	0.106*	1.112	0.102**	1.107	0.065	1.067
	(0.057)		(0.058)		(0.058)		(0.061)	
Catholic			0.161	1.174	0.137	1.146	−0.065	0.937
			(0.302)		(0.307)		(0.321)	
Jewish			−1.173**	0.309	−1.199**	0.301	−1.250**	0.286
			(0.557)		(0.560)		(0.563)	
Southern Baptist			0.646*	1.907	0.613	1.846	0.380	1.462
			(0.375)		(0.382)		(0.396)	
Other Baptist			0.086	1.090	0.061	1.062	−0.121	0.886
			(0.351)		(0.356)		(0.366)	
Lutheran			0.540	1.717	0.515	1.674	0.317	1.373
			(0.411)		(0.415)		(0.425)	
Presbyterian			−0.028	0.972	−0.056	0.945	−0.195	0.823
			(0.448)		(0.452)		(0.456)	
Episcopal			1.089	2.970	1.070	2.915	0.972	2.644
			(0.807)		(0.809)		(0.808)	
Methodist			0.168	1.183	0.148	1.159	−0.007	0.993
			(0.363)		(0.366)		(0.373)	
Other Protestant			0.025	1.025	−0.017	0.983	−0.212	0.809
			(0.312)		(0.327)		(0.339)	
Strength of Affiliation					0.082	1.086	−0.127	0.880
					(0.188)		(0.212)	
Frequency of Attendance							0.089**	1.093
							(0.041)	
Deviance	909.6	(df=865)	895.2	(df=856)	895.0	(df=855)	890.2	(df=854)
−2 Log Likelihood Ratio			14.5	(df=9)	0.2	(df=1)	4.7**	(df=1)

Notes: Numbers in parentheses are standard errors.
 *$p < 0.10$ **$p < 0.05$ ***$p < 0.01$.

Table 5. Nested Logistic Regression Models: Effects of Religious Affiliation and Participation on Satisfaction with City
(1993 NORC GSS data; $N = 875$ for all models)

Indenpendent Variables	Model I Coefficient	Odds	Model II Coefficient	Odds	Model III Coefficient	Odds	Model IV Coefficient	Odds
Intercept	−2.194***	0.112	−2.287***	0.102	−2.210***	0.110	−2.215***	0.109
	(0.678)		(0.709)		(0.711)		(0.712)	
Age	0.025	1.025	0.023	1.023	0.022	1.022	0.021	1.022
	(0.027)		(0.027)		(0.027)		(0.027)	
Age2	0.000	1.000	0.000	1.000	0.000	1.000	0.000	1.000
	(0.000)		(0.000)		(0.000)		(0.000)	
Married	0.352**	1.422	0.388**	1.402	0.388***	1.402	0.341***	1.406
	(0.168)		(0.170)		(0.170)		(0.171)	
Trauma	−0.293***	0.746	−0.291**	0.747	−0.291**	0.747	−0.291**	0.748
	(0.113)		(0.114)		(0.114)		(0.114)	
Female	0.421***	1.524	0.417***	1.518	0.398**	1.489	0.401**	1.494
	(0.152)		(0.156)		(0.157)		(0.158)	
Income	0.014	1.014	0.012	1.012	0.014	1.014	0.014	1.014
	(0.017)		(0.017)		(0.018)		(0.018)	
Education	0.086***	1.090	0.087***	1.091	0.085***	1.088	0.085***	1.089
	(0.030)		(0.030)		(0.030)		(0.031)	
Nonwhite	−0.228	0.796	−0.272	0.762	−0.314	0.730	−0.310	0.734
	(0.206)		(0.215)		(0.217)		(0.218)	
Organization Membership	0.084*	1.088	0.081	1.084	0.067	1.070	0.070	1.073
	(0.051)		(0.051)		(0.051)		(0.053)	
Catholic			0.155	1.167	0.062	1.064	0.079	1.082
			(0.272)		(0.276)		(0.289)	
Jewish			0.450	1.569	0.348	1.416	0.353	1.423
			(0.630)		(0.632)		(0.633)	
Southern Baptist			0.258	1.294	0.142	1.152	0.162	1.176
			(0.319)		(0.325)		(0.341)	
Other Baptist			0.235	1.265	0.142	1.153	0.158	1.172
			(0.325)		(0.329)		(0.339)	
Lutheran			−0.026	0.975	−0.119	0.888	−0.102	0.903
			(0.344)		(0.348)		(0.358)	
Presbyterian			−0.198	0.821	−0.299	0.741	−0.288	0.749
			(0.413)		(0.418)		(0.421)	
Episcopal			1.418*	4.127	1.356*	3.879	1.363*	3.906
			(0.786)		(0.787)		(0.788)	
Methodist			0.601*	1.824	0.529	1.698	0.543	1.720
			(0.347)		(0.348)		(0.354)	
Other Protestant			0.269	1.309	0.108	1.114	0.126	1.134
			(0.285)		(0.298)		(0.312)	
Strength of Affiliation					0.310*	1.364	0.328*	1.388
					(0.171)		(0.194)	
Frequency of Attendance							−0.008	0.993
							(0.038)	
Deviance	1050.8	(df=865)	1041.5	(df=856)	1038.1	(df=855)	1038.1	(df=854)
−2 Log Likelihood Ratio			9.3	(df=9)	3.3*	(df=1)	0.0	(df=1)

Notes: Numbers in parentheses are standard errors.
*$p < 0.10$ **$p < 0.05$ ***$p < 0.01$.

Table 6.   Nested Logistic Regression Models: Effects of Religious Affiliation and Participation on Satisfaction with Non-Working Activities (1993 NORC GSS data; N = 875 for all models)

Independent Variables	Model I Coefficient	Odds	Model II Coefficient	Odds	Model III Coefficient	Odds	Model IV Coefficient	Odds
Intercept	−0.395	0.674	−0.035	0.966	−0.057	0.945	−0.085	0.919
	(0.747)		(0.788)		(0.791)		(0.792)	
Age	0.010	1.010	0.009	1.009	0.009	1.009	0.008	1.008
	(0.029)		(0.030)		(0.030)		(0.030)	
Age2	0.000	1.000	0.000	1.000	0.000	1.000	0.000	1.000
	(0.000)		(0.000)		(0.000)		(0.000)	
Married	−0.144	0.866	−0.097	0.908	−0.097	0.908	−0.087	0.916
	(0.189)		(0.192)		(0.192)		(0.193)	
Trauma	−0.288**	0.750	−0.285**	0.752	−0.286**	0.752	−0.286**	0.751
	(0.120)		(0.122)		(0.122)		(0.122)	
Female	−0.096	0.909	−0.033	0.968	−0.029	0.972	−0.018	0.983
	(0.171)		(0.175)		(0.176)		(0.177)	
Income	0.058***	1.060	0.059***	1.061	0.059***	1.060	0.059***	1.061
	(0.019)		(0.019)		(0.019)		(0.019)	
Education	0.027	1.027	0.023	1.023	0.024	1.024	0.026	1.027
	(0.033)		(0.034)		(0.034)		(0.034)	
Nonwhite	−0.271	0.763	−0.155	0.856	−0.148	0.863	−0.133	0.875
	(0.222)		(0.234)		(0.235)		(0.236)	
Organization Membership	0.190***	1.209	0.184***	1.202	0.187***	1.206	0.197***	1.218
	(0.061)		(0.062)		(0.063)		(0.065)	
Catholic			−0.603*	0.547	−0.586*	0.557	−0.531	0.588
			(0.322)		(0.327)		(0.341)	
Jewish			−0.685	0.504	−0.666	0.514	−0.652	0.521
			(0.647)		(0.650)		(0.651)	
Southern Baptist			−0.251	0.778	−0.228	0.796	−0.162	0.850
			(0.376)		(0.383)		(0.399)	
Other Baptist			−0.815**	0.443	−0.796**	0.451	−0.745**	0.475
			(0.361)		(0.365)		(0.376)	
Lutheran			−0.510	0.601	−0.492	0.612	−0.438	0.645
			(0.404)		(0.408)		(0.419)	
Presbyterian			−0.356	0.701	−0.337	0.714	−0.300	0.741
			(0.486)		(0.489)		(0.493)	
Episcopal			1.115	3.050	1.128	3.090	1.156	3.178
			(1.072)		(1.073)		(1.075)	
Methodist			0.057	1.059	0.073	1.076	0.116	1.123
			(0.411)		(0.415)		(0.422)	
Other Protestant			−0.138	0.875	−0.102	0.903	−0.044	0.957
			(0.346)		(0.360)		(0.374)	
Strength of Affiliation					−0.060	0.942	−0.003	0.997
					(0.188)		(0.212)	
Frequency of Attendance							−0.025	0.976
							(0.042)	
Deviance	893.6	(df=865)	878.8	(df=856)	878.7	(df=855)	878.3	(df=854)
−2 Log Likelihood Ratio			14.9*	(df=9)	0.1	(df=1)	0.3	(df=1)

Notes: Numbers in parentheses are standard errors.
        $*p < 0.10$ $**p < 0.05$ $***p < 0.01$.

Table 7.   Summary of Relationship between Religiosity Indicators and
Six Life Satisfaction Domains are presented in Logistic Regression Models,
Tables 1-6. Denomination Column Reports which Specific Denominations
Display Significant Effect on Life Satisfaction Domain in Parentheses

	Denomination	*Strength of Affiliation*	*Attendance*
Finances	Positive effect- (Methodist)	No effect	Positive effect
Family	Positive effect- (Catholic, Lutheran, S. Baptist, Other Baptist, Methodist)	No effect	No effect
Friendships	Negative effect- (Jewish) Positive effect- (Methodist)	Positive effect	No effect
Health	Negative effect- (Jewish)	No effect	Positive effect
City	Positive effect- (Episcopal)	Positive effect	No effect
Non-working	Negative effect- (Other Baptist)	No effect	No effect

and those with higher family incomes have higher odds of reporting high satisfaction with health and physical conditions, while not surprisingly, respondents reporting traumatic life events have lower odds of satisfaction with health
and physical conditions.

Table 5 presents the results from the models predicting the odds of high satisfaction with city. In Models 2 through 4, respondents reporting affiliation with the
Episcopal denomination have significantly increased odds of high satisfaction
with city as compared to those not reporting a religious affiliation. Those who
reported a strong affiliation have an increased odds of reporting high satisfaction
with city life, however respondents who attend church or religious services more
frequently have the same odds of reporting high satisfaction with city life, as those
who attend less frequently. The effects of the control variables are similar to those
reported in previous tables, however education now has a significant effect; people with higher levels of education have increased odds of reporting satisfaction
with city life.

Table 6 displays the logistic regression model results for the odds of high satisfaction with non working activities, such as hobbies. Only one religiosity variable, affiliation with Southern Baptist as compared to no affiliation, is significant
in all three models including religiosity variables. In all models, affiliation with an
Other Baptist denomination decreases the odds of high satisfaction with nonworking activities. Strength of affiliation and frequency of attendance fail to significantly increase or decrease the odds of satisfaction with nonworking activities.
Organizational membership and high income significantly increase the odds of
satisfaction with nonworking activities, while traumatic experiences decrease the
odds of satisfaction.

DISCUSSION

At this point, it may not be entirely clear to readers how the various religiosity indicators relate to the domains of life satisfaction. Table 7 presents a summary of the relationships of the three broad religiosity variables (Denomination, Strength of Affiliation, Attendance) on each domain. This table clearly illustrates that the predictive power of the various religiosity indicators differ by life satisfaction domain.

At least one of the nine possible effects of denominational affiliation is significantly related to each life satisfaction domain, however these relationships differ by type of satisfaction. In some cases, affiliation with a particular religious denomination increases the odds of reporting high satisfaction—satisfaction with family, friendships, city, and finances—while in other cases affiliation decreases the odds of high satisfaction—health and physical condition, friendships, and nonworking activities.

The most consistent relationships, however, are found in the model predicting the odds of high satisfaction with family life. In this case, respondents reporting membership in over half of the denominations have increased odds of high satisfaction as compared to respondents with no affiliation. None of the denominational variables has a significant negative relationship to satisfaction with family life; only the coefficient associated with the Jewish denomination is negative, but this effect is not statistically significant. Furthermore, the other two religiosity indicators, strength of affiliation and frequency of attendance, fail to have significant relationships to high satisfaction with family life.

Strength of affiliation has positive and significant relationships to two of the life satisfaction domains: friendships and city. Strength of affiliation is not significantly related to the odds of high satisfaction in any of the other four life satisfaction domains. Frequency of attendance does not significantly relate to satisfaction with friendships or city, while only one or two of the denominations display significant relationships to satisfaction in these domains.

Frequency of attendance has a significant and positive relationship to satisfaction in two life domains: health/physical condition and finances. The frequency of attendance variable, however, fails to have a significant effect on any of the other four life domains. As can be inferred from the discussion above, neither strength of attendance, nor the denominational variables, significantly relate to satisfaction with health/physical condition or finances.

In sum, it is interesting to note that the three religiosity indicators seem to have mutually exclusive relationships to the six life satisfaction domains. By and large, the denominational affiliation variables have a consistent relationship only to satisfaction with family, the strength of affiliation variable has a positive relationship to satisfaction with city and friendships, and the frequency of attendance variable has a positive effect on the remaining two life satisfaction domains: finances and health.

What do these results suggest? First, while most studies rely on factor analytic strategies to assess the dimensionality of religious indicators, these findings provide another (negative) means by which to assess the construct validity of treating religiosity as a single, global concept. According to Carmines and Zeller, construct validation requires that researchers "compare the correlations of each empirical dimension [of an underlying concept] with a set of theoretically relevant variables" (1979, p. 67).

As Cronbach and Meehl suggest, "Construct validity must be investigated whenever no criterion or universe of content is accepted as entirely adequate to define the quality to be measured" (1955, p. 282, cited in Carmines and Zeller 1979). Thus, given the long history of debates over the possible dimensionality of religiosity, a variety of assessments of construct validity seem particularly appropriate, yet remain notably lacking in the literature.

If our three commonly employed indicators of religious involvement did represent a single global dimension of religiosity, then the three factors should relate to the various satisfaction measures in a parallel fashion. The summary of the findings presented in Table 7 demonstrate that the three religiosity indicators fail to relate similarly to the six satisfaction domains. Thus, one might conclude that global indicators of religiosity are inappropriate in most research settings, and researchers exploring the influence of religiosity on satisfaction may report different or even contradictory results, depending on the measure of religiosity utilized.

On the other hand, the presence of negative evidence in a test of construct validation does not necessarily imply that a global indicator lacks construct validity. As Carmines and Zeller (1979) explain, tests of construct validity for one concept imply tests of construct validity for measures of the other theoretical concepts. In our case, the differential results may due to the multidimensionality of life satisfaction; individuals can express satisfaction with one life domain, and still be quite unsatisfied with other domains. Indeed, one interesting way to view these results is by considering whether a respondent is assessing a life satisfaction domain that must be assessed with respect to personal concerns or individual-level properties or traits, or external concerns conceptualized more often in terms of social phenomena.

Two of the measures of religiosity, denominational affiliation, and strength of affiliation, relate to three, primarily social, life satisfaction domains. Satisfaction with family, friends, and city are assessed with respect to situations that remain largely external to the individual. Consider satisfaction with family life; to put it simply, with the exception of marriage in more recent times, individuals don't choose their relatives. Individual satisfaction with family is highly dependent upon the actions of others, and an individual's interactions with those others. We do of course, exert an influence on the development and behavior of certain family members, but we assess our satisfaction with family based on external, social situations.

Similarly, satisfaction with friends remains a social concern. For instance, if a close friend loses his or her job and moves to another neighborhood, an individual must assess this as an action external to the individual. Finally, an individual's satisfaction with city of residence also is assessed in relation to conditions that are most often considered social phenomena. Of course, individuals may choose which city they live in, but if the city suddenly decides to cut back on garbage collection or faces high crime rates, then individuals cannot simply solve these issues on their own.

In contrast, the frequency of attendance variable has a small, but significant (p<.05) relationship to satisfaction with the health/physical condition of the respondent. Health, both mental and physical, is obviously a personal characteristic, assessed in terms of how well (or ill) an individual is at any point in time. Is the *respondent* sick or well? This determination is made by reference to the health status of the self, rather than to some external condition (e.g. the health of one's family members or friends).

Frequency of attendance also has a significant relationship to satisfaction with finances, a domain which many might evaluate with respect to an individual concern. That is, respondents evaluate the financial health of the self—Is the *respondent* financially secure?—not the financial health of friends or family. However, the GSS asked respondents to assess the financial situation of both the individual and his or her *family*, so this domain might be more appropriately labeled as a hybrid—evaluated with respect to both individual and social concerns. Of course, conclusions about the relationship of frequency of attendance to satisfaction with finances should be tempered, recognizing that magnitude of the effect is very small (i.e., the multiplicative effect on the odds is only slightly greater than 1.0). Regardless, the set of results summarized in Table 7 suggest that researchers interested in life satisfaction would do well to explore dimensionality of the concept.

In conclusion, this research has demonstrated how different facets of religiosity have different relationships to various life satisfaction domains. We utilized logistic regression models to explore the relationship of three measures of religiosity: denominational affiliation, strength of affiliation, and frequency of attending church or religious services to six domains of life satisfaction. Our results indicate that the three measures of religiosity have differential effects on life satisfaction and suggest that religious scholars interested in life satisfaction should continue to pay close attention to measurement issues in the future.

ACKNOWLEDGMENT

Armand Mauss provided helpful comments on earlier drafts of this manuscript.

REFERENCES

Allport, G. W. 1950. *The Individual and His Religion*. New York: Macmillan.
_____. 1966. "The Religious Context of Prejudice." *Journal for the Scientific Study of Religion*, 5, 447–457.
Bohrnstedt, G. W. 1983. "Measurement." Pp.69–121 in *Handbook of Survey Research* edited by P. H. Rossi, J. D. Wright, and A. B. Anderson. San Diego, CA: Academic Press.
Campbell, A., P. Converse, and W. Rodgers. 1976. *The Quality of American Life: Perceptions, Evaluations, and Satisfactions*. New York: Russell Sage Foundation.
Carmines, E. G. and R. A. Zeller. 1979. *Reliability and Validity Assessment*. Newbury Park, CA: Sage University Press.
Ellison, C. G. 1991. "Religious Involvement and Subjective Well-Being." *Journal of Health and Social Behavior*. 32 (March), 80–90.
_____. 1993. "Religion, the Life Stress Paradigm and the Study of Depression." Pp. 78–121 in *Religion in Aging and Health* edited by J. S. Levin. Newbury Park, CA: Sage.
Ellison, C. G. and D. A. Gay. 1990. "Region, Religious Commitment, and Life Satisfaction among Black Americans." *The Sociological Quarterly*. 31(1), 123–147.
Ellison, C. G., D. A. Gay and T. A. Glass. 1989. "Does Religious Commitment Contribute to Individual Life Satisfaction." *Social Forces*. 68(1), 100–123.
Frankel, B. G. and W. E. Hewitt. 1994. "Religion and Well-Being among Canadian University sStudents: The Role of Faith Groups on Campus." *Journal for the Scientific Study of Religion*. 33(1), 62–73.
Glock, C. Y. 1954. *Toward a Typology of Religious Orientation*. New York: Bureau of Applied Social Science, Columbia University.
Glock, C. Y. and R. Stark. 1965. *Religion and Society in Tension*. Chicago, IL: Rand McNally.
Gorsuch, R. L. 1984. "Measurement: The Boon and Bane of Investigating Religion." *American Psychologist*. 39(3),228–236.
_____. 1988. "Psychology of Religion." *Annual Review of Psychology*, 39, 201–221.
Gorsuch, R. L. and S. McFarland. 1972. "Single vs. Multiple-Item Scales for Measuring Religious Values." *Journal for the Scientific Study of Religion*, 11(1), 53–64.
Hunt, R. A. 1968. "The Interpretation of the Religious Scale of the Allport-Vernon-Lindzey Study of Values." *Journal for the Scientific Study of Religion*, 7(1), 65-77.
_____.1972. "Mythological-Symbolic Religious Commitment: The LAM Scale." *Journal for the Scientific Study of Religion*, 11(1), 42–52.
Hunt, R. A. and M. King. 1971. "The Intrinsic-Extrinsic Concept: A Review and Evaluation." *Journal for the Scientific Study of Religion*, 10(4), 339–356.
King, M. B. 1967. "Measuring the Religious Variable: Nine Proposed Dimensions." *Journal for the Scientific Study of Religion*, 6(2),173–190.
King, M. B. and R. Hunt. 1969. "Measuring the Religious Variable: Amended Findings." *Journal for the Scientific Study of Religion*, 8(2), 321–323.
_____. 1972. "Measuring the Religious Variable: Replication." *Journal for the Scientific Study of Religion*, 11(3), 240–251.
_____. 1975. "Measuring the Religious Variable: National Replication." *Journal for the Scientific Study of Religion*, 14(1), 13–22.
_____. 1990. "Measuring the Religious Variable: Final Comment." *Journal for the Scientific Study of Religion*, 29(4), 531–535.
Koenig, H. G., M. Smiley, and J. A. P. Gonzales. 1988. *Religion, Health, and Aging*. Westport, CT: Greenwood Press.
Lenski, G. 1961. *The Religious Factor*. Garden City, NY: Doubleday.
Levin, J. S. and K. S. Markides. 1986. "Religious Attendance and Subjective Health." *Journal for the Scientific Study of Religion*. 25(1), 31–39.

Poloma, M. M. and B. F. Pendleton. 1990. "Religious Domains and General Well-Being." *Social Indicator Research*, 22, 255–276.

Ross, C. E. 1990. "Religion and Psychological Distress." *Journal for the Scientific Study of Religion*, 19(2), 236–245.

Schumaker, J. F. 1992. *Religion and Mental Health*. New York: Oxford University Press.

Schwab, R. and K. U. Petersen. 1990. "Religiousness: Its Relation to Loneliness, Neuroticism, and Subjective Well-Being." *Journal for the Scientific Study of Religion*, 29(3), 335–345.

Stark, R. and C. Glock. 1968. *American Piety: The Nature of Religious Commitment*. Berkeley, CA: University of California Press.

St. George, A. and P. H. McNamara. 1984. "Religion, Race, and Psychological Well-Being." *Journal for the Scientific Study of Religion*, 23(4), 351–363.

Steinitz, L. Y. 1980. "Religiosity, Well-Being and Weltanschauung Among the Elderly." *Journal for the Scientific Study of Religion*, 19(1), 60–67.

MORAL BOUNDARIES IN CHRISTIAN DISCOURSE ON POPULAR MUSIC

Andreas Häger

ABSTRACT

This paper is part of a larger study of the Christian discourse on popular music. The object of study is the discourse *about* popular music, not the music or the culture itself. The study examines examples of how the issue of popular music has been debated in churches both in the United States and Europe since the 1950s. The study is concerned with what function this discourse, that is, the Christian rock debate, performs within the religious institutions, and not primarily what it means to the fans or the musicians. This debate is presented here as an example of how institutional religion relates to modern society.

What is presented in this paper is part of a larger study of the Christian discourse on popular music. The study examines examples of how the issue of popular music has been debated in churches both in the United States and Europe since the 1950s. This debate is presented here as an example of how institutional religion relates to modern society. As a starting point for the main theme of this article, I will briefly present the central ideas in the larger study.

Research in the Social Scientific Study of Religion, Volume 11, pages 155-171.

The object of study is the discourse *about* popular music, not the music or the culture itself, to the extent that such a distinction can be made. The study focuses on the question of what function this discourse, that is, the Christian rock debate, performs within the religious institutions, and not primarily what it means to the fans or the musicians. The main point of departure is the assumption that Christianity as a religion, and—to a varying degree—the institutions that uphold this religion, make claims to unique legitimacy, and attempt to monopolize the right and capacity to explain individual and social existence. In a modern pluralistic society, this monopoly is constantly threatened by the "secular" culture, and not the least by popular music. The Christian rock discourse can be seen as a defense of the monopoly claims against this threat.

Two basic strategies of defense can be observed, depending on what type of institution is wielding the defense. The strategy characteristic of sect-type organizations is the maintaining of sharp boundaries between "us" and "them," defining what is outside as evil and worthless. The strategy ideally used within church-type religious organizations is an attempt to convince oneself and others that the whole of existence is included in one's own "symbolic universe," to incorporate everything into one's own sphere. In this text the focus is on the first of these strategies, but it must be recognized that this represents only part of the picture.[1]

MAIN CONCEPTS

The strategy of drawing a sharp line between one's own group and modern society, in the Christian rock discourse represented as the demarcation of rock, is based on a distinctively dualistic world view. This world view is expressed in a series of dichotomies of which the most fundamental are we/them and good/evil. The strategy of demarcation is carried out through various means of defining rock as something "other," as strange and foreign, belonging to another group, another world—a world as evil as ours is good. This evil should of course be avoided by a good person; the definition of rock as strange and evil can thus be understood as a religiously legitimated social control.

The boundary between one's own group and the evil rock music is drawn on the one hand on a metaphysical level: rock is defined as demonic; on the other hand on a cultural level: rock originates from and belongs in cultures that are strange to us, distant—geographically, or in terms of generation, or class—and perhaps "primitive." Rock is also defined as a vehicle of foreign religions. Although the world of rock music is quite male dominated, rock is also defined as "other" on the basis of gender; rock culture is placed in a female sphere as male rock artists are criticized for traditionally feminine attributes such as long hair or make up (see below for examples).

Perhaps particularly the case of the gender boundary causes a consideration of a slight change of perspective. In addition to working hard on maintaining the boundaries between "us" and "them," the antirock discourse is focused on maintaining ordering boundaries, on organizing the world that is about to be thrown into complete chaos by rock music. Rock is seen as both a sign of and a reason for much of what is evil and chaotic.

Here I follow the British anthropologist Mary Douglas, who defines dirt, sin, as that which is perceived as being in the wrong place, on the wrong side of the border; or that which does not fit into any category, thus questioning the very existence of boundaries. Douglas (1966, pp. 35–36) writes

> Shoes are not dirty in themselves, but it is dirty to place them on the dining table; food is not dirty in itself, but it is dirty to leave cooking utensils in the bedroom, or food bespattered on clothing; similarly, bathroom equipment in the drawing room; clothing lying on chairs; outdoor things indoors; upstairs things downstairs; under-clothing where over-clothing should be; and so on.

In her classic study, Douglas (1966) shows how the social construction of "dirt" works not only in Anglo-Saxon bourgeoisie—no "upstairs things downstairs"—but also in the Jewish system of classification of animals. Defining shellfish as impure by being neither land nor sea animal, is, I argue, paralleled in the definition of a hard rocker as "impure" by being neither—due, for example, to long hair—"traditionally" male, nor female.

Bernice Martin (1979;1981) shows in her discussion of "counter culture," including rock music, how the approach of Mary Douglas is relevant in this field. Martin claims that the questioning of boundaries, what she calls "the sacralisation of disorder," is at the very core of rock culture. Following Victor Turner (cf. e.g. Turner 1982), Martin (1979) understands contemporary youth culture as "liminoid," as an attempt to live in a constant state of the taboo-breaking and ambiguous role-play that according to Turner characterizes a ritual. This "antistructure" character of the liminoid rock culture is what the antirock discourse reacts against.[2]

The focus on boundaries in Christian antirock discourse is partly on the boundary between "us" and "them," and partly on the ordering boundaries—for example, between male and female—that hold chaos at bay. These two aspects can be understood to relate to each other in two ways. First, the defense of order against chaos is also a defense of one's own group against the chaotic surroundings. One's own group is characterized by sacred order, *nomos*, while everything around it is *chaos* (Berger and Luckmann 1987/1966, p. 132; Eliade 1959, pp. 62–64). By emphasizing the order identified with "us," the boundaries against the world are strengthened. Second, the line between one's own group and the surrounding world is identified with at least some of the discussed ordering boundaries. By strengthening the line between, for example, ethnic categories, and identifying oneself with one particular category and the others with another, the line between "us" and "them" is simultaneously drawn sharper. The other category is furthermore often described as more "chaotic," (closer to a presumed natural state) as in a slightly different fashion has been the case in discourses on the "other" with respect to both ethnicity and gender. There are "multiple layers" of boundaries, and the definition of, for example, a cultural boundary can simultaneously be the definition of the boundary between rock and religion, between us and them, and between good and evil.

The importance of the identification of group boundary with ordering boundaries probably depends on the subdiscourse as well as on which ordering boundary is defended. In the American rock resistance of the 1950s, the ethnic boundary was more clearly identified with the border around the own group than it is in contemporary antirock discourse, and the boundary between male and female should in most cases be more difficult to apply than, for example, ethnic boundaries.

From a Durkheimian point of view—which is the one largely taken by Douglas (1966)—it is in the root of religion to draw a line between the sacred and the profane. Therefore it should not be a great surprise that this can be seen also in Christian discourse on popular music. Apart from this discovery, the main point here will be to see how rock is placed on the profane(st) end of the spectrum and how the line between sacred and profane is identified with the line between one's own group of faithful and the surrounding modern society.

In the remainder of this text the focus will be on a discussion of empirical examples from contemporary American antirock discourse. These examples will be used as illustrations of the main points in the previous outline.

The first example discussed is an excerpt dealing with the singer Little Richard, and this text is chosen in order to attempt to demonstrate how the concept of ordering boundaries generally can contribute to an understanding of Christian discourse on popular music.

Two particular boundaries are then inspected more closely: the gender dichotomy as a prime case of ordering boundary; and the line between rock and religion, in the Christian antirock discourse most clearly identified with the boundary between "us" and "them."

The examples are from American (and some Scandinavian) books debating rock music. The chosen quotes are to be seen primarily as illuminating instances. They are not attempts to test a hypothesis, but serve to illustrate a model of understanding of Christian rock discourse. This should be kept in mind perhaps especially when viewing the collection of the examined writers. They all present rather extreme negative views on rock music and the world it comes from. Several of them represent a strident brand of fundamentalist Christianity and their arguments are based on their religious views. It should also be kept in mind that my discussion of these arguments is not a questioning of their base, of the particular perspective of the debaters, but it is rather an analysis from another particular perspective, the one outlined above. The fact that my analysis from this perspective sometimes can sound like harsh criticism does not imply that I entirely doubt the rock debaters' "good intentions," to protect their readers and readers' children from a great evil.

Many of the examples are taken from the books of one single author by the name of Jeff Godwin. His work is however understood here not as the representations of one single person but of a discourse. There are several reasons for this. First, Godwin is far from alone in expressing these views, even if he seems to be the American antirock writer the most widely spread in Scandinavia. Second, he is not alone in producing and distributing "his" books. Rather, he is backed by a publishing company and an international chain of distributors—from the companies in Canada, Europe, and Australia listed in the books (e.g. Godwin 1990, p. 4) to the saleswoman who strongly recommended his work to me in a small basement book shop in Stockholm, Sweden. Some of his work can also be found on the Internet on sites put up by Christian organizations.[3] Thirdly, he is received by an audience of readers who are not all as critical as I try to be. The Swedish antirock debater Ann Ekeberg (1991) is, for example, apparently greatly influenced by parts of Godwin's books, although without referring to him.[4]

A CASE

In the following I will bring up as examples some quotes from Jeff Godwin's discussion of one of the legends of rock, Little Richard (Godwin 1988, pp. 37–41). The passage contains several remarks on what is perceived as Little Richard's breaking of gender, ethnic, and other boundaries. The passage on Little Richard may not contain the most strident evocations of ordering boundaries, but may all the more clearly show the possible use of the boundary concept in understanding Christian antirock discourse.

Godwin (1988, p. 38) describes Little Richard's childhood and his rise to fame. Of Little Richard's father, he writes:

> Free with the belt and disgusted with his son's feminine attitudes, Bud Penniman whaled the tar out of his boy often. (Godwin 1988, p. 38)

It is well known that several other successful artists, for example, Michael Jackson and Sinéad O'Connor, had suffered severe abuse as children, and have tried to come to terms with this in their work. By his choice of expressions, Godwin hardly shows any compassion for the battered child but rather seems to sympathize with the father's "disgust" with Richard's "feminine attitudes." This understanding of the sentence is confirmed when Godwin (1988, p. 38) continues:

> Wickedly rebellious, Richard soon crossed the line into true homo and bi-sexuality. His perversion began with sneaking into his mother's bedroom to secretly apply makeup and perfume. This quickly led to sexual contacts with loose women in the neighborhood. Soon, while barely into his teens, he had his first homosexual encounter.[5]

As in many other similar reports, one of which (Larson 1987, pp. 29–33) is discussed further below, what is presented as the apparently greatest offence is the questioning of the boundary between male and female. This transgression is here represented by Little Richard's use of makeup, his (reported) homosexuality—arguably the strongest questioning of the gender dichotomy—and perhaps also the "sneaking" into the female realm of his mother's room. The causal chain from "makeup and perfume," over "loose women," to "true homo and bi-sexuality" is presented as self-evident. Similar argumentation, seeing "traditionally" female attire—makeup, clothing as well as long hair—when used by men as a sign (and here even a cause) of homosexuality, is common in fundamentalist discourse and further examples are discussed below.

Godwin (1988, p. 39) writes:

> In 1955 his first big hit ("Tutti Frutti") smashed into both white and segregated black radio stations, something unheard of at the time. The words to the song were so filthy they had to be rewritten. In concert, Little Richard half howled, while pounding the piano with his feet. Fans, both black and white, flocked to his musical altar as their parents looked on in shock. Preachers denounced him from their pulpits and were promptly labeled as racists. Rock & Roll was born.

Apart from blurring the line between male and female, the music and performance of Little Richard—and a significant portion of the popular music following him—crossed ethnic boundaries. Godwin emphasizes this in his description of the "unheard of" radio play, and in the categorization of the fans as "both black and white." In a generally very negative account of Little Richard, Godwin presents the artist's appeal to white fans as a significant fact worth mentioning, but this fact appears not to be understood as vindicating Little Richard from the (other) transgressions.

The second sentence in the previous quote refers back to the first: the rewriting of the lyrics was a consequence of—or a prerequisite for—playing on "white" radio stations. The view that the white audience had higher standards when it came to song lyrics is presented as more or less self evident—as it was to the white "moral crusaders" of the 1950s and apparently is to Godwin 30 years later. This is affirmed by the choice of words: the lyrics "had to" be rewritten, not merely "were" rewritten, and they were "filthy," a stronger word than for example "dirty" or "explicit." The lyrics are presented as an example of why the boundary between black and white in Godwin's view should be kept intact: the white Americans, and particularly the young, are threatened by black "filth."[6]

The opening up of the border between black and white was one of the main lines of criticism against rock in the beginning of its era (Martin and Seagrave 1988). Godwin clearly does not resist this criticism. He rather sides with the preachers who "denounced [Little Richard] from the pulpit," and he questions the denunciation as racist. The last sentence of the quote can be understood as a summing up, and shows the significance Godwin attributes to the blurring of racial boundaries in the rock culture he so strongly abhors.[7]

Godwin also comments on Little Richard's church background:

> Leading a bizarre, schizophrenic lifestyle, Little Richard divided his time between sexual devi-
> ance and old-time religion. He haunted the local Baptist churches of Macon, Georgia where he
> bellowed and screamed the hymns like a maniac until the congregation booted him out the door.
> Religion to Richard was a stage, an audience and a chance to perform. (Godwin 1988, p. 38)

Mentioning Little Richard's becoming an evangelist Godwin (1988, p. 40) talks
of his "conversion," using quotation marks to express disbelief. After a quote of
Little Richard's denouncing rock, calling it "demonic" and "driving people from
Christ" (Godwin 1988, p. 41), Godwin finishes the passage on Little Richard
describing how the artist "ignored his own advice" and made a record as well as a

> video show[ing] him seated at the piano with a big grin on his face as his hands pounded out
> the piston-pumping rhythm. With a new album in the stores, Little Richard was once again in
> his well-worn driver's seat, stoking the fires of Satan's Rock & Roll. Some people never learn.
> (Godwin 1988, p. 41)

Many of the pioneers of rock had a background in United States Southern evangelical religiosity, and to many the forced choice between rock'n'roll and the
church was very difficult. Jerry Lee Lewis expresses the conviction that a choice
had to be made, and the guilt that this caused:

> I'm lost and undone....I should've been a Christian, but I was too weak for the gospel. I'm a
> rock'n'roll cat. We all have to answer to God on Judgement Day. (Turner 1988, p. 18)

The same emotional conflict—fueled by the antirock crusaders—has worried Little Richard (Turner 1988, pp. 20–21). To Godwin it is not much of a dilemma:
there is a sharp line between the church and the world, and trying to be both a rock
star and a Christian is impossible. He expresses this by calling Little Richard's life
"bizarre, schizophrenic" and even questions the attempts by Little Richard to stay,
so to speak, on Godwin's side of the boundary by putting the conversion in
quotation marks and claiming that "some people never learn."

Steve Turner also quotes Little Richard's one-time views on "demonic" rock
music, in his book on "rock'n'roll and the search for redemption" (as the subtitle
puts it), but then continues (Turner 1988, p. 21):

> Yet the gap between rock'n'roll and the Rock of Ages is not as great as Richard now believes.
> He himself took his style almost wholesale from the Church. Indeed, his first recordings were
> for a gospel label.

Godwin does not refer to this connection, but instead says that Little Richard

> drew on the styles and influences of the blues and R&B artists of the day. (Godwin 1988, p. 39)

and talks of Little Richard being "booted" from his church for "bellowing" and "screaming." Godwin and Turner apparently have different views both on the historical relation between the African-American church(es) and rock music, and on the spirituality and style of worship in these churches. Godwin denies a clear connection—though perhaps clearer in many other cases than Little Richard—in order to emphasize the line he wants to draw the sharpest of all, the one between institutional Christianity and rock music.

All the boundaries that are emphasized in the discussed passage on Little Richard are commonly defended throughout the antirock discourse. Other examples of such boundaries are the lines between "elite" and "popular" culture, between sexuality and religion, as well as between generations.

Here I will just briefly cite some examples of these. The difference between high and low culture is expressed, for example, by Godwin (1990, p. 40) who argues that "rock music is not even music," and by Myers (1989, p. xiv) who claims that

one need not take classes in music appreciation to listen to the latest release from Madonna.

or by Ekeberg (1991, p. 63; my translation from Swedish):

I think it is important that small children can hear music by Bach, Beethoven and other musical masters. Then they can grow up with the discipline, geometry and mathematical order of that music instead of with the chaotic rock music.

Strong emphasis on the generation gap is achieved already by the clear tendency in many books, such as Larson (1987) or Ekeberg (1991), to direct comments explicitly to the parents of the rock consuming youth. The above quote from Godwin (1988, p. 39) on Little Richard's concert going fans and their "shocked" parents also evokes the generation gap.

The antirock discourse perceives a transgression of the boundary between sexuality and religion—or perhaps the physical and the spiritual—for example, in criticising Christian rap, since

Without the words, what exactly is Rap MUSIC saying? The answer is found in one word: ...*SEX*! (Godwin 1990, p. 160)

or in the criticism of artists who, like Madonna or Prince (as he was formerly known), combine religious and sexual references in their work (Larson 1987, pp. 177–178). The sexuality/religion boundary may be understood as the boundary between flesh and spirit, briefly discussed below.

The ethnic or cultural boundary that is defined in the Little Richard example is evoked in many other instances of antirock discourse. There is on the one hand a recurring definition of rock as something other, as culturally foreign—as "heathen jungle boogie" as Godwin (1990, p. 76) puts it, or as belonging to the opposite side in the cold war, being defined as Western decadence or part of the

Communist plot respectively (cf. Martin and Seagrave 1988). Larson (1987, pp. 41–47) in his turn discusses the influence from Eastern religion on Western rock, and mourns

> Kipling's dictum, 'East is East and West is West, and never the twain shall meet' being proved wrong. (Larson 1987, p. 42)

SEX, GENDER & ROCK'N'ROLL

In the following I will focus on one of the boundaries mentioned in the discussion on Jeff Godwin and Little Richard, the boundary between male and female. It is here used as an example of an organizing, ordering boundary, the transgression of which seems to be particularly threatening. It is of special interest due to the importance of the gender dichotomy in the history of Christianity as well as of other (world) religions.[8] The way this boundary is used in the antirock discourse also shows its significance, since the basis for its use and its expected function is that a very sharp line between male and female—and masculine and feminine—is completely taken for granted.

The gender dichotomy is here understood as socially constructed. The examples used show how the gender dichotomy is upheld also in the Christian antirock discourse. In this section, the paper touches upon the discipline of gender studies, a part of which is concerned with the social construction of gender.[9]

Godwin (1988, p. 275) writes about the successful Christian heavy metal group Stryper:

> The members of Stryper wear their hair long and womanish by anyone's definition, and so do the angels on their album cover. This is a perversion of nature, according to the Bible.

The angels he mentions can be found on the cover of the Stryper album "To Hell with the Devil." The cover—reproduced in Godwin (1988, p. 249)—shows four angels, the same number as the members of Stryper, and since one angel furthermore is holding a guitar I am led to understand these angels as a kind of ideal self-image of the group. Of these angels Godwin (1988, p. 275) continues:

> Do angels really wear mascara and jewel[le]ry? [...] Do angels really have pierced ears? What about all that hair? One word describes this picture perfectly: Blasphemy.

One trait that Godwin neglects to mention, although at least on the black-and-white reproduction included in his book it is much more striking than the "pierced ears"—no sign of earrings are visible—is the angels' very well developed muscles, which are represented in an almost surrealistically detailed fashion. These muscles apparently go well with Godwin's—and the members' of Stryper—image of how a man, or perhaps a male angel, should look, and the muscles also quite clearly denote that the characters in the picture are considered male. This in its turn causes Godwin to grieve all the more over the mascara, the pierced ears, and the long hair, which would not have been quite as problematic had the angels been female.

In a discussion on "what is wrong" with the appearance of Christian artists, Godwin (1990, p. 171) states two things:

1. *The outward appearance is a real key to the inner person.*
2. *Wickedness cannot be hid.* [boldface in original]

And one type of outward sign Godwin sees of this wicked inner state should be evident: "feminine" traits. Whether the wickedness in itself also is perceived as "female" is another question. One answer is given by Godwin (1988, p. 112) in a comment on the appearance of the symbol for yin and yang on the cover of an album by the singer Stevie Nicks:

'Yin and yang' is more occult jargon for the delicate balance between male and female and good and evil. (Godwin 1988, p. 112)

Here Godwin places the dichotomies male/female and good/evil next to each other in a manner that very well can be interpreted as showing that he perceives them as parallel, and the order in which the respective poles of the dichotomies are represented is not necessarily a coincidence.[10] If not, then male rock musicians, questioning the boundary between male and female by wearing long hair and ear rings, also blur the boundary between good and evil, and are therefore subject to Godwin's condemnation.

Bob Larson is the most legendary American Christian antirock crusader and, according to the back cover of one of his books (Larson 1987), he has lectured on "contemporary culture" in more than 70 countries. Like many of his cocrusaders, he addresses himself explicitly to parents, warning them of rock music and advocating "Christ-honoring musical norms for your family" (Larson 1987, p. 11). One of the things that apparently does not fit well with these norms is the rock music that according to Larson promotes homosexuality—a major threat to the gender dichotomy. This theme is treated in a chapter called "A chip off the old block" which begins:

'Your son acts just like you,' Mom says. Whether the mother is frustrated or admiring, the result is usually the same: Dad flushes with pride. He wants his son to be like him. But for some parents, the flush turns to a blush. The Gay Revolution is upon us, and the sons we wanted to be football heroes discover they would rather frequent gay bars. (Larson 1987, p. 29)

Larson talks to parents and warns them what can happen if their children listen to rock music. In the "flush/blush" contrast in the above quote, as well as in the assertion that

> Your reputation is affected by your child's behaviour. (Larson 1987, p. 29)

is clearly stated that parents should watch out: they can lose their prestige in a society where the ideal for a young man is "the football hero." Larson (1987, p. 29) further writes that:

> ...the real influences on style and morality are entertainment stars, who have a profound impact upon youthful sexual identity.

and continues by listing which rock stars should be avoided by parents defending their reputation against "the Gay Revolution:"

> Various artists have reflected homosexuality in their appearance. Before his death, Keith Moon of The Who appeared in public wearing women's clothing. (Larson 1987, p. 30)

That is all Larson says about Keith Moon. The fact that he has been seen "in public," without specification whether on or off stage, dressed in "women's clothing"—another rather imprecise remark—should in Larson's opinion, and in the opinion he expects from his readers, be taken as a guarantee that Moon was a homosexual. Could the aside "before his death" in addition be interpreted as a reminder that "the wages of sin are death?" Remarks such as:

> For years, Mick Jagger of the Rolling Stones has worn mascara to further flaunt his reported bisexuality. (Larson 1987, p. 30)

and

> Todd Rundgren leaped on the bandwagon by adding varicolored hues to his shoulder-length locks. (Larson 1987, p. 32)

continues in the same vein: a "feminine" attribute—mascara or long, curled, *and* colored hair—is described as a way of showing homosexuality, or, in the case of Mick Jagger, apparently bisexuality.

All forms of crossing the border between what by "traditional"—not to say petit bourgeois—standards is perceived as male and female, are by Larson and others taken as a deviance from the heterosexual norm. Larson presumes identity between androgyny—however defined—and homosexuality, and makes this presumption the basis of his whole argument. He further assumes that a young person's contact with such border-crossing artists in itself can "have a profound impact upon youthful sexual identity," or put in other words:

> Your child may know homosexuality is wrong, but how long can *he* fend off *his* rock idol's insistence that gay is good? (Larson 1987, p. 33; italics added)

Larson (1987, p. 33) proposes a "worst possible scenario":

> Sadly, in some homes, the son isn't a chip off his dad's block. Rather, he's been rewhittled to
> more closely resemble the likes of David Bowie.

whom Larson (1987, p. 32) describes as

> ...sporting orange hair and laced high-heeled boots, moving effeminately to a rock beat.

It is apparent that whether Larson talks of "your child" or "the son," the young
men are the ones he worries about, they are the ones in danger of becoming
"effeminate," being convinced by rock artists that "gay is good"—instead of
becoming like their fathers, real men. Rock is explicitly described as a threat to
the communication of "traditional" values of what a man should be, and a man
should not have colored hair or high heels—that is for women, or queers.

"COAL OFF SATAN'S ALTARS"—DRAWING
THE LINE BETWEEN ROCK AND RELIGION[11]

In his discussion of Little Richard, Jeff Godwin shows great disbelief in this artist's ability to be both rock musician and Christian, and even doubts the possibility of Little Richard's conversion to Christianity. Godwin's Swedish counterpart,
Thomas Arnroth (1991, p. 141) writes, in a similar vein, of some Christians being
"wrongfully hungry to see artists become believers." Both of these authors represent parts of Christianity where conversion is greatly stressed; therefore implicitly
or explicitly denying this conversion to some people is a very strong statement. It
draws a very sharp line between Christianity and rock music.[12]

It is rather self evident—in comparison with for example the defense of the
gender dichotomy—that the Christian antirock discourse should be concerned
with drawing a line between Christianity and rock. This is an explicit purpose
of the discourse, and this is the purpose served also when the line between
male and female is emphasized as an attempt to preserve "order" in a chaotic
world. A strong but still indirect mode of promoting the same argument is the
definition of rock as a vehicle for nonChristian world views, including
satanism.

In the last part of this article I will discuss some examples of how the boundary
between rock and Christianity is drawn more explicitly, how these two domains
are defined as completely incompatible. Christianity is described as unsuitable in
rock, and—which is the theme of the rest of this paper—rock music is described
as unsuitable in church and for Christians.[13]

In the beginning of this paper I refer to two—at least in some sense—opposing
streams within the Christian rock discourse: the antirock discourse discussed in
this paper and the "incorporating" Christian rock discourse. There is also a Christian rock discourse attempting to discriminate between "good" and "bad" rock,

devoting itself mostly to "contemporary Christian music", and to a great extent ignoring the rest.[14][15]

Larson (1987, pp. 109–113) suggests "contemporary Christian music" as an alternative to "secular" rock, "filling the vacuum" after the suggested smashing of secular rock albums, and says that:

...even the worst modern attempts at expressing Christian faith are better than the secular sex-drenched paeans to hedonism.

There is, however, a great deal of strong resistance also to Christian rock among the antirock crusaders—there is far from a consensus behind the strategy of sorting into (comparatively) good "Christian" and evil "secular" rock. Stryper and Petra are two of the most successful groups in Christian rock history. Of these Godwin (1988) writes:

Unless [Stryper] repent, they will continue to be servants of antichrist...and the enemies of God. (Godwin 1988, p. 298)

and

...Satan is the true master behind [Petra's] music (Godwin 1988, p. 312).

Godwin devotes one whole book to opposing the sorting strategy, asking "What's wrong with Christian rock?" (Godwin 1990), and finding several answers, for example the outward appearance, as discussed above. In a passage headlined "Are you sucked in?" Godwin (1990, p. 23) writes:

Are the grand old hymns of the faith a moldy slice of boring drivel to you? If so, you can be sure of two things:

1. Carnal C[hristian]-Rock propaganda has totally brainwashed your mind, and
2. You're showing utter contempt for the richest wealth of scriptural music ever created.

As an example of "scriptural music," Godwin (1990, p. 24) quotes two verses—giving no title, crediting neither author nor source—of the hymn "Holy, holy, holy" by Reginald Heber (1783–1826) (*Hymns...*, pp. 200–201), containing lyrics such as "Cherubim and seraphim falling down before Thee/Who wert, and art, and evermore shalt be." Of the reaction to this hymn Godwin (1990, p. 24) presupposes:

A generation raised on T.V., videos, rock/pop and other musical muck will look at those hymn stanzas and want to throw up. 'But I just don't understand that stuff,' they'll complain. No wonder, it's all from the Bible.

The text does contain biblical paraphrase (e.g. of Rev. 4:8), but there are of course more recent English translations—"no wonder, it's all 17th century English" would be a possibly fairer comment. Implicit in Godwin's reasoning—and in virtually all of the Christian antirock discourse—is a markedly dualistic world view: the bible, and Christianity, is governed by the spirit of God, and not understanding the (King James) bible is a sign of not being influenced by this spirit. Rock is claimed to influence its listeners not to understand Christianity and even to "throw up" at the sight of it, since, as Godwin (1990, p. 6; boldface in original) puts it:

'Christian' rock is the music of: ANTICHRIST!

In another evocation of a dualistic world view, Godwin (1988, p. 228) writes:

The flesh and the spirit are in constant opposition to each other and produce only warring and confusion...At the bedrock of its foundation, 'Christian' rock and the Bible are in direct opposition to each other. Why? Because C-Rock says that the flesh (worldly musical styles) when combined with the spirit (godly words of praise) will produce more spirit. Unfortunately, Galatians 5:16,17 says just the opposite.

The bible passage referred to talks of the opposition between flesh—in other translations "human nature" or "self-indulgence"—and spirit, in the context of Paul's warning the Galatians against quarreling with each other. It is clear that this opposition, interpreted in variable ways, has been of great importance within Protestant Christianity, and the dichotomy is defended in many instances also in the Christian antirock discourse. Here it is evoked to quite explicitly define the line between rock and Christianity, the incompatibility of one with the other.

Describing a visit to a concert with the Christian hard rock group Stryper, Godwin (1988, pp. 286–287) reports that a concert goer's "[...] shirt had this blasphemous message on the back: "JESUS CHRIST ROCKS.""

He explains that this text is blasphemous because when used as a verb the word "rocks" means "to move back and forth, to sway from side to side," thus the sentence on the shirt "...indicates that Christ is not the dependable and unchanging cornerstone all true disciples depend on" (Godwin 1988, p. 286). He continues:

Maybe these C-Rock fans think our Lord tunes in to the top 40 on His Heavenly transistor radio and boogies on over to the four and twenty elders for a jam session. Jesus on drums? Blasphemy! (Godwin 1988, p. 287)

Interesting though the semantic examination might be, I believe it is rather obvious that the music–oriented interpretation of the word "rocks" is the one central to both Godwin and the shirt's wearer. To my mind, the description of the celestial jam session is quite humorous, which somehow takes the edge off Godwin's argumentation. I cannot however see that this is intended, but rather assume that Godwin is quite serious in his attempt to demonstrate the absolutely irreconcilable natures of rock and Christianity, summed up in the emphatic negative answer to the question of "Jesus on drums?" Or as Wilkerson (1985, pp. 156–157) puts it, also discussing the heavenly sounds:

> You will see and hear instruments never seen before, and players who are seraphims. Cherubs will add their voices. What kind of music will it be? Will it be rock? Will you suddenly have to change your style? Maybe you've been flooding your soul with the wrong music! As for me, I am singing right now the songs I'll sing then, to a music that will not be strange over there.

As was seen earlier, Godwin is reluctant to see any historical connection between the traditional styles of African American worship and rock music. In his earliest book he presents a lengthy discussion on the vocal expression, the "screaming," of rock singers and their audiences (Godwin 1985, pp. 204–208). Influence from the vocal styles of African-American Christianity—the "shouting"—can be traced to rock vocalists of this day. Godwin, however, traces the vocal style to sounds produced during male homosexual intercourse, or to something he refers to as "a Gay mating call" (Godwin 1985, p. 204). He states that this "screaming...started Satan's Sexual Revolution" (Godwin 1985, p. 208).

Seeing the two alternative suggestions of the historical roots of vocal styles in rock music, it seems rather clear that Godwin's version to a great extent serves the purpose of denying any historical connection between (African) American Christianity and rock music, in order to draw a stronger boundary between the two.

In the beginning of this paper I referred to my understanding of the Christian rock discourse as an example of the relation of institutional Christianity to modern society and particularly contemporary culture. Godwin (1990, pp. 112–113) quotes a producer of contemporary Christian music, Brown Bannister, who objects to the "separatist mentality of most churches...and their opinions on culture." Godwin (1990, p. 113) retorts:

> I've got news for Brown. America's churches need MORE separation, not less!...see what happened when the Israelites mixed with the pagans around them. Did those pagans get saved? No way! The Israelites fell into their neighbour's sins!

This is then a quite explicit declaration of Godwin's program, and the program of similar sect-oriented individuals and groups, American "fundamentalists" or others: the world around us is evil, and we who are the chosen—as the people of Israel—should be as separate from it as possible.

> The Bible says: "Abstain from all appearances of evil" (I Thessalonians 5:22) The Lord calls us to maintain holiness (separation) from the world. When C-rock groups have the same hairstyles, outfits, jewel[le]ry, concerts, light shows, fog machines and musical noise as their secular doubles, they are presenting an APPEARANCE of evil. God will NOT bless that. ...Rock music is of the world. If you love rock music, you love the world. If you love the world, you are the enemy of God, says James 4:4 (Godwin 1988, pp. 242–243).

The quote sums up the motivation of the Christian antirock discourse: rock is part of modern society, and the strategy used by sect-type religious organizations to cope with this society is to separate from the world, to maintain sharp boundaries.

NOTES

1. The thoughts on the two strategies are developed on the basis of the discussion on legitimation in Berger and Luckmann (1987, particularly pages 130–134).

2. It is possible to argue—and will possibly be argued by me in a subsequent paper—that the incorporating Christian rock discourse relates to the other aspect ascribed to contemporary popular culture by Martin and Turner, the "communitas."

3. For example at www.av1611.org/crock, "Dial-the-truth-ministeries" present several texts by Godwin (or did October 16th 1998).

4. One example of this is a passage discussing the presumed foretelling of the Beatles in the Bible, more precisely in Revelations chapter 9 (Godwin 1985, p. 91; Ekeberg 1991, pp. 106–113).

5. Concerning the father–son relation Godwin (1988, p. 38) also states, about Little Richard's running away at fourteen: "Richard's dad wasn't sorry to see him go. Deep inside, no dad wants a homosexual son. Bud Penniman was no exception."

6. I have no knowledge of Godwin's views on racial integration in general, and they may well clash with my analysis here, but that would not remove the possibility of reading the quoted passage in this particular way.

7. One further comment on this quote: the use of the term "howl" to describe Little Richard's vocal style can be seen as an indication that the artist is understood as transgressing one further boundary, between human and animal—an indication present also in the self-understanding of some artists, and even in the same tradition as in the pseudonym of the blues legend Howlin' Wolf.

8. To merely touch upon the importance attributed to the gender dichotomy by the same "fundamentalist" groups active also in the rock resistance, two well-known major issues in conservative Christianity can be mentioned: the ordination of women and homosexuality.

9. More specifically, the matter of how the gender dichotomy is threatened by homosexuality, and defended, is discussed, for example, by Butler (1990).

10. Even if some traditional interpretations (cf. Nielsen *et al.* 1990, p. 270) of the yin-yang symbol support Godwin, the distinct difference is that in Chinese tradition, the symbol expresses unity, while Godwin emphasizes incompatibility and opposition. The key phrase is "occult jargon."

11. The quote in the subheading refers to a passage in a book by one of the most famous contemporary evangelical preachers, David Wilkerson. Wilkerson (1985, p. 126) describes Christian rock as to "take coals off Satan's personal altars and bring them into God's presence, to lay them on his altar," and so presents a very striking metaphor for the incompatibility of Christianity and rock music.

12. The possibility of conversion is not completely denied, and in some cases the "former rock artist, now Christian" may be given a great deal of publicity. The "now–then" perspective, as opposed to "both rock artist and Christian," however retains the boundary. And the focus on such cases emphasizes the uniqueness, and defines the conversion as rather an anomaly. The unique transgression thus only calls attention to the boundary. A parallel could perhaps be made to the discussion by Douglas (1966, p. 169–174) on the position of the pangolin among the Lele.

13. In the incorporating Christian "pro" rock discourse, the argumentation is for a strong compatibility and sometimes almost the identity of rock and Christianity (cf. Häger 1996).

14. A parallel could be seen to Grossberg's (1993) discussion on the discourse on popular music in the American political right, where he talks of three different strategies: rejecting, discriminating, and appropriating.

15. The mechanisms for the "middle-way" sorting strategy are the same as in the "extreme" strategies: sorting is done by devaluating some—for example, "secular" rock, and incorporating some—for example, the musical sound. Cf. Miller (1993) for a very explicit use of this strategy.

REFERENCES

Arnroth, T. 1991. *Dina harpors buller.* Uppsala: Trons Värld Ordbild.

Berger, P. and T. Luckmann. 1987/1966. *The Social Construction of Reality: A Treatise in the Sociology of Knowledge.* Harmondsworth: Penguin.

Butler, J.1990. *Gender Trouble: Feminism and the Subversion of Identity.* NY: Routledge.

Douglas, M. 1966. *Purity and Danger: An analysis of concepts of pollution and taboo.* London: Routledge & Kegan, Paul.

Ekeberg, A. 1991. *För Sverige - på tiden: En exposé över ungdomskulturen* [For Sweden-these times: An exposé of the culture of youth]. Stockholm: Ann Ekeberg.

Eliade, M. 1959. *The Sacred and the Profane. The Nature of Religion.* San Diego, CA: Harcourt Brace.

Godwin, J. 1985. *The Devil's Disciples: The Truth About Rock.* Chino, CA: Chick Publications.

_____. 1988. *Dancing With Demons: The Musics Real Master.* Chino, CA: Chick Publications.

_____.1990. *What's Wring with Christian Rock?* Chino, CA: Chick Publications.

Grossberg, L. 1993. "The Framing of Rock: Rock and the New Conservatism." T. Bennett et al. (eds), *Rock and Popular Music: Politics, Policies, Institutions,* pp. 193–209. NY: Routledge.

Häger, A. 1996. "Like a Prophet: On Christian Interpretations in a Madonna Video." In T. Ahlbäck (ed.), *Dance, Music, Art and Religion,* pp. ; 151–174. bo: The Donner Institute for Research in Religious and Cultural History.

Hymns Ancient & Modern, New Standard, 1995. Beccles: Hymns Ancient & Modern.

Larson, B. 1987. *Larson's Book of Rock.* Wheaton IL: Tyndale House.

Martin, B. 1979. "The Sacralization of Disorder: Symbolism in Rock Music." *Sociological Analysis* 40, 87–124.

Martin, B. 1981. *A Sociology of Contemporary Cultural Change.* NY: St Martins.

Martin, L. and K. Seagrave. 1988. *Anti-Rock: The Opposition to Rock'n'roll.* Hamden CN: Archon.

Miller, S. 1993. *The Contemporary Christian Music Debate: Worldly Compromise or Agent of Renewal?* Wheaton IL: Tyndale House.

Myers, K. 1989. *All God's Children and Blue Suede Shoes: Christians & Popular Culture.* Wheaton IL: Crossway.

Nielsen, C. N. Jr. et al. 1990. *Religions of the World.* NY: St. Martin's Press.

Turner, S. 1988. *Hungry for Heaven: Rock'n'roll and the search for redemption.* London: Hodder & Stoughton.

Turner, V. 1982. *From Ritual to Theatre: The Human Seriousness of Play.* NY: Performing Arts Journal Publications.

Wilkerson, D. 1985. *Set the Trumpet to Thy Mouth.* New Kensington PA: Whitaker House.

ARE RURAL CLERGY IN THE CHURCH OF ENGLAND UNDER GREATER STRESS?
A STUDY IN EMPIRICAL THEOLOGY

Leslie J. Francis and Christopher J. F. Rutledge

ABSTRACT

This study begins by examining the concept of clergy stress and the theory that rural clergy may be under greater stress than other clergy. Then it reviews available empirical evidence concerned with the distinctiveness of the rural church, the assessment of clergy stress and burnout, and the role of personality in clergy research. Against this background new data are presented on Maslach's three component model of burnout (emotional exhaustion, depersonalization, and personal accomplishment) among a random sample of over one thousand full-time stipendiary male parochial Anglican clergy. The evidence suggests that rural clergy have a lower sense of personal accomplishment than comparable clergy working in other types of parishes, but that they suffer neither from higher levels of emotional exhaustion nor from higher levels of depersonalization.

Research in the Social Scientific Study of Religion, Volume 11, pages 173-191.

173

INTRODUCTION

Clergy Stress

In an early and classic empirical study in the psychology of religion, Sir Francis Galton (1872) accounted for the comparative longevity of the clergy in England, not in terms of the effectiveness of their daily prayers to be protected from trouble and disease, but in terms of their "easy country life and family repose." For Galton, the clergy of the late nineteenth century were not noted as a class under undue stress. Towards the end of the twentieth century, however, a very different assumption has come to the fore. Books on clergy stress and clergy burnout are beginning to project the issue into greater prominence, although as yet no consensus of definition, method, or diagnosis has emerged. The range of perspectives from which the issue is now discussed is illustrated by reference to five specific texts written during the 1980s and 1990s.

First, in *Ministry Burnout*, John A. Sanford (1982) considered the matter from the dual perspective of Jungian analyst and Anglican priest. He argued that religious ministers are particularly susceptible in their work to that feeling of joyless exhaustion popularly known as burnout and identified eight characteristics of ministry which could generate such feeling. The job of ministry is never finished. Ministers cannot easily tell if their work is having any results. The work of ministry can be repetitive. Ministers are dealing constantly with people's expectations. Ministers must work with the same people year in and year out. Because ministers work with people in need there is a particularly great drain on their energy. Ministers deal with many people who come to their church not for solid spiritual food but for egocentric temporary palliatives. Ministers must function a great deal of the time through a *persona*, while the effort of maintaining an effective *persona* can place a considerable drain on energy. Ministers may become exhausted by failure.

Second, Mary Anne Coate's (1989) study, *Clergy Stress: the hidden conflicts in ministry*, adopted a psychotherapeutic perspective, shaped by first-hand experience as a member of a religious community and then as part of a diocesan team. She argued that, although everyone is subject to stress at times, ministers often find it especially difficult to admit to the pressures of their work, feeling perhaps that they should somehow be "better" than their secular counterparts. She discussed the roots of clergy stress within four main areas, as the strain of caring, the strain of relating to God, the strain of proclaiming, and the strain of being.

Third, John Davey's (1995) study, *Burnout: stress in the ministry*, was written from the perspective of a chartered (licensed) psychologist and Anglican priest. Davey argued that ministry is a particularly stressful occupation and identified four main sources of stress for the clergy. The first area concerns the ministerial role, balancing role expectations with role performance, and confronting role conflict, role ambiguity, and role overload. The second area concerns career development. The third area concerns appropriate support and recognition. Clergy perceive themselves to be overworked, underappreciated, and lack confidence that their particular skills and aptitudes will be recognized and utilized by those in authority. The fourth area concerns the interface between home and work and the problems of balancing the use of the parsonage as the centre for both domestic and professional life.

Fourth, in a study concerned specifically with clergy marriages, Kirk and Leary (1994) devote a chapter to identifying the sources of clergy stress in contemporary society. In particular they draw attention to five factors. First, they point to the problems of marginality. Contemporary clergy, they argue, "will inevitably at some point experience their ministry, and, because role and person are intimately linked, themselves as marginal to the society of the late-twentieth century." Second, they point to the problem of alienation. A sense of alienation, they argue, "may be induced by the fact that a parish priest must to a certain extent consider himself rootless, free to go where he is sent in God's name, but at the same time tied by the nesting instincts of a wife and family.". Third, they point to social isolation. Clergy, they argue, "have the same social and emotional needs for friendship, enjoyment, fun, and support as most other people, but it can be difficult for these to be met within the parish." Fourth, they point to a lack of leisure time and financial constraints. Isolation will be increased, they argue, by "a constant shortage of money and the leisure to visit friends and family." Fifth they point to the problem of illness.

A job which is often seven days a week, lack of leisure time and holidays, constant nagging worries about money, frequent moves, the inescapability of living "over the shop," the pressures of bearing so many expectations, so much pain, the new skills to be learned, the new role to be discerned, the upheaval and change in the church, the feeling of being at worst a failure, at best an irrelevance—these factors can take a huge toll on the physical, mental, emotional, and spiritual health of the clergy household.

Fifth, unlike the previous studies, Ben Fletcher (1990) based his study, *Clergy under Stress*, on a questionnaire survey, attracting 216 usable responses from mailing 372 full-time parochial clergy in the Church of England. For the first time this study promised an objective assessment of stress levels among the Anglican clergy. Fletcher drew the following main conclusions from his survey. Overall the clergy were satisfied with their jobs, and only 3 percent expressed a desire to get out of ministry if they could. On the other hand, many of the clergy were disillusioned with aspects of their job, such as poor attendance by parishioners. Self-esteem was not particularly high. Having to satisfy the expectations of others was a major demand, as was the feeling of being constantly on call. A significant proportion of the clergy were struggling to manage financially. Many aspects of work were associated with strain. Certain job demands and job disillusionment played a role in depression and anxiety, including having to put on a public face, lack of tangible results, and being in conflict situations. However, the objective measures of strain showed the clergy to be under less stress than Fletcher had anticipated. The percentages of clergy who scored at significantly elevated levels on the depression, free-floating anxiety, and somatic anxiety scales were very low indeed. Moreover, despite their obvious concerns about various aspects of their work, only 5 percent of the clergy who responded to the survey found their job to be so pressured as to be a constant source of stress. Although Fletcher's study made some contribution to knowledge about stress among the Anglican clergy, the usefulness of that research is limited by the relatively small size of the sample and by the restricted indices of stress employed.

In summary, the literature suggests that the issues of stress and burnout among the clergy are of contemporary significance, but underresearched.

Stress Among Rural Clergy

Although there is a growing view that stress may be a particular problem among clergy serving in rural areas, clear comment and precise research on the issue remain scarce. Rather than commenting on stress among the rural clergy, the Rural Church Project reported by Davies, Watkins and Winter (1991) focussed on the more positive perspective of job satisfaction. They found that, when clergy were asked in their postal survey to indicate the areas of work which gave them the most satisfaction, an overwhelming response was received. Only 2 percent of the rural clergy commented that no part of their ministry was particularly reward-ing. While the majority of the clergy also listed specific areas of problems associ-ated with their work, these problems tended to be ones associated with ministry in any geographical environment. Problems associated with specifically rural circumstances, including the difficulties of multiparish work and small congregations, accounted for just 5 percent of the responses.

In his book, *The Country Parson*, Anthony Russell (1993) argued that:

> today the complaints of the clergy tend to be not about secularity or about terms and conditions of their employment, but centre upon the perception of the clergy as being an occupational group under stress.

For Russell stress is rooted in an overbusy job which has no easily defined bound-aries. The demands, he argues, made upon the modern rural clergy, looking after multiparish benefices, may be extensive. The lack of clarity about the role of the clergy in a rapidly changing society and a rapidly changing church adds to this stress. Increasingly clergy perceive themselves as unsupported by bishops and archdeacons.

The Archbishops' Commission on Rural Areas (1990), *Faith in the Country-side*, identified the additional pressures which a rural living may place on the fam-ily life of clergy, in comparison with their urban and suburban colleagues. Life in a country parish may restrict employment opportunities for clergy spouses, generate more demands from growing children to be transported to school and to leisure activities, increase the cost of living, and necessitate a second car.

Andrew Bowden's (1994) analysis, *Ministry in the Countryside*, catalogued the additional pressures which a rural living may place on the work life of clergy, in comparison with their urban and suburban colleagues. Work in a country benefice may involve a weight of administration relating to each parish. Each community supports a church building and faces recurrent financial pressures. The Sunday pattern of services involves moving from church to church, often for small congregations. Each rural community has its own expectations of the parish priest, often supported by a recent history of being a sole cure. Work with children, youth, and young families is often accompanied by a sense of failure. Many rural clergy feel that those who run the diocese do not appreciate how different and demanding the rural job really is.

The report of the Church in Wales Board of Mission Rural Commission (Church in Wales, 1992), *The Church in the Welsh Countryside*, argued that inadequate time off is a substantial cause of stress among rural clergy and that overwork is made worse in multiparish benefices where each parish lacks awareness of the overall workload of the cleric.

In summary, the literature clearly hints that stress and burnout may be particularly pressing issues among rural clergy, but there remains a clear lack of empirical evidence to test the truth of this assertion.

Is the Rural Church Really That Different?

Concern that levels of experienced stress may be different among rural clergy in comparison with clergy working in other geographical areas is really part of a wider question concerned with the distinctive characteristics of rural ministry. A considerable body of opinion in recent years has argued the case that the rural church is indeed different, as exampled by Anthony Russell's pioneering work (Russell, 1986, 1993). Once again, however, hard empirical evidence of the kind provided by empirical theology is hard to find. While Davies, Watkins and Winter's (1991) study, *Church and Religion in Rural England*, and Francis' two studies, *Rural Anglicanism* (1985) and *Church Watch* (1996), offer descriptive accounts of aspects of the rural church, they fail to add the comparative dimension of how things are in other areas. While they describe the rural church, they fail to demonstrate that things are actually different from how they are elsewhere.

The challenge of empirical theology to test differences between the rural church and the church in other geographical areas has been pioneered by the Centre for Ministry Studies at the University of Wales, Bangor, through a series of five focussed studies.

The first study, reported in two papers by Francis and Lankshear (1990; 1991), compared the impact of church primary schools on church life in 1,637 rural and 1,316 urban parishes. In rural areas the presence of a church school was reflected in the local church congregation having contact with a higher proportion of 6–9 year olds and adults, compared with churches where there was no church school. This observation is consistent with the view that rural church schools may promote links between their pupils and the local church and that when children attend the local church they encourage their parents to go with them. In urban areas, however, the same pattern did not emerge. It seems less easy to build links between church and school in urban areas than in rural areas.

The second study, reported by Francis and Lankshear (1992), set out to compare the liturgical workload of rural clergy with that of clergy working in other types of parishes. The data included 128 examples of village benefices, 41 single priest towns, and 134 benefices in larger towns, suburban, and urban environments, all within the diocese of Chelmsford. The statistical evidence supported the view that rural environments show more signs of promoting the community model of the church than is the case in suburban and urban environments. A higher proportion of the rural population takes an interest in the parish church, registers on the electoral rolls of the parishes, and attends services at the major festivals. In return for this wider interest, the local vicar is more likely to be expected to service the needs of fringe members, to be available to conduct "private" baptisms on Sunday afternoons and to officiate at the remarriage of divorced parishioners. The Community church is more at home with the language and theology of the *Book of Common Prayer*, while parishioners who work with the community model of the church are less likely to feel responsible for supporting that church financially.

The third study, reported by Francis, Jones, and Lankshear (1996), explored the relationship between baptism policy and church growth in 1,553 rural parishes, 983 urban parishes, and 584 suburban parishes. The data demonstrated that in all three geographical areas, an open baptismal policy is a significant predictor of wider contact with fringe church members through such opportunities as festival communicants. In all three geographical areas, an open baptismal policy leads to more young people and more adults seeking the sacrament of confirmation. Where things are different in the rural church, however, concerns the relationship between baptismal policy and normal Sunday attendance. While baptismal policy is irrelevant to the number of adults who attend service on a normal Sunday in urban and suburban churches, a restrictive baptismal policy is reflected in smaller Sunday congregations in rural areas.

The fourth study, reported by Francis and Lankshear (1997), employed the same database of 1,553 rural churches, 983 urban churches, and 584 suburban churches to explore the different approaches to confirmation according to geographical environment. The data demonstrated four distinctive features of confirmation in rural churches. There is a considerably higher number of confirmands per capita of the population. There is a higher proportion of male confirmands. There is a higher proportion of preteenage and teenage confirmands. The confirmation of younger candidates in the rural church is associated with some positive signs of church growth. By way of contrast emphasis on confirmation under the age of fourteen years in the urban church tends to be associated with signs of church decline. Once again these findings draw attention to the distinctive experience of the rural church and warn against the uncritical generalization of pastoral recommendations modelled on urban experiences.

While the preceding studies focussed on aspects of church life, the fifth study, reported by Francis and Lankshear (1993), focussed more clearly on the experiences of the clergy working in different areas. This study employed path analysis to examine the relationship between clergy age and certain quantitative indices of church life in 1,553 rural parishes and 584 suburban parishes. The data indicated that clergy aged sixty or over working in rural parishes tend to have contact with a smaller number of active church members, as indicated by attendance on a normal Sunday, than younger clergy working within comparable rural parishes, although they maintain contact with the same number of nominal church members, as indicated by the electoral roll and festival communicants. Clergy aged sixty or over working in suburban parishes, on the other hand, have contact with the same number of active church members as younger clergy working within comparable suburban parishes. On the basis of this finding, Francis and Lankshear (1993) concluded that:

> Far from being an ideal context for preretirement ministry, the rural church should now be seen as offering challenges and presenting demands more appropriate to the ministry of younger clergy. Older clergy may now find a more professionally effective and personally satisfying ministry in areas which are able to generate more lay leadership, offer better social and medical facilities, and make gentler demands in terms of serving Sunday liturgy and undertaking pastoral visiting, as may be more frequently the case in suburban areas.

In a subsequent analysis of the deployment of 3,510 Church of England parish clergy, Francis and Lankshear (1994) demonstrated that older clergy are more likely to be serving in rural and multiparish benefices.

In summary, the research evidence clearly lends support to the views that the rural church is different and that the experiences of clergy working in rural areas may be significantly different from the experiences of clergy working in other types of parishes.

Assessing Burnout

The problems of stress and burnout are issues which the clerical profession may share in common with many other professions concerned with caring for people, like doctors, nurses, teachers, social workers, and probation officers. A second strand of research pioneered in the Centre for Ministry Studies at the University of Wales, Bangor, has been the application of theories of burnout developed among other caring professions specifically to the clergy. This strand of research has adapted the model of burnout proposed by Maslach and Jackson (1986) and operationalised through the *Maslach Burnout Inventory*.

Maslach and Jackson conceptualise the "burnout syndrome" as comprising three distinct but interrelated characteristics which can occur among individuals who do "people work" of some kind. One key aspect of the burnout syndrome is increased feelings of emotional exhaustion. As emotional resources are depleted, members of the caring professions feel that they are no longer able to give of themselves at a psychological level. A second key aspect of the burnout syndrome is the development of depersonalization. As their work begins to take its toll, members of the caring professions can begin to adopt negative and cynical attitudes toward, and feelings about, their clients. The process of depersonalization can lead members of the caring professions to view their clients as somehow deserving of their troubles. A third key aspect of the burnout syndrome is the feeling of reduced personal accomplishment. Alongside emotional exhaustion and depersonalization, members of the caring professions may begin to feel unhappy about themselves, and dissatisfied with their accomplishments on the job.

The Maslach Burnout Inventory proposes three scales to assess these three distinct concepts of emotional exhaustion, depersonalization, and lack of personal accomplishment. A number of studies have now reported on the reliability and validity of the Maslach Burnout Inventory in a variety of cultures and among a variety of different professional groups (Schaufeli, Maslach, and Marek 1993). The use of the Maslach Burnout Inventory among clergy in the United States is supported by Rodgerson and Piedmont (1998).

In the original form of the Maslach Burnout Inventory, emotional exhaustion is assessed by a nine item subscale. The items describe feelings of being emotionally overextended and exhausted by one's work. The item with the highest factor loading on this dimension is one referring directly to burnout, "I feel burned out from my work." Depersonalization is assessed by a five item subscale. The items describe an unfeeling and impersonal response towards the individuals in one's care. An example item on this dimension is "I feel I treat some recipients as if they were impersonal objects." Personal accomplishment is assessed by an eight item subscale. The items describe feelings of competence and successful achievement in one's work with people. An example item on this dimension is "I feel I'm positively influencing other people's lives through my work." In contrast to the other two subscales, lower mean scores on the subscale of personal accomplishment correspond to higher degrees of experienced burnout. Maslach and Jackson (1986) score the Maslach Burnout Inventory by inviting respondents to evaluate each of the 22 items on a seven point scale of frequency, from *never*, through *a few times a year or less*, *once a month or less*, *a few times a month*, *once a week*, and *a few times a week*, to *every day*.

Francis obtained permission from the Consulting Psychologists Press to adapt the Maslach Burnout Inventory for use among clergy in England (under license and at a cost). The original adaptation was undertaken in consultation with

Rutledge (1994). This adaptation modified the original instrument in four ways. The American original was Anglicized. The items were shaped to reflect the experience and language of pastoral ministry. Additional items were developed to bring the three subscales to the same length of ten items each. The response scale was changed from a seven point measure of frequency to a five point measure of attitudinal intensity following the convention of Likert (1932), ranging from *agree strongly*, through *agree, not certain,* and *disagree*, to *disagree strongly.*

Currently a set of three interrelated studies is exploring the psychometric properties of the modified burnout inventory among samples of over 1,000 Church of England parochial clergy, over 1,300 Roman Catholic parochial priests and around 900 Pentecostal pastors from the Assemblies of God, Elim, and Apostolic Church.

In summary, the research evidence indicates that it is both appropriate to conceptualise and possible to measure burnout among clergy in terms of the three-dimensional model proposed by Maslach and Jackson and modified by Francis, Rutledge, Louden, Kay and Robbins (2000).

Clergy Personality

Research on burnout among other caring professions points to the important interaction between external or contextual factors and internal characteristics of the individual. In other words, research concerned with identifying the contextual predictors of clergy burnout must also take into account individual differences in the personality characteristics of the clergy involved.

A third strand of research pioneered in the Centre for Ministry Studies at the University of Wales, Bangor, has explored the relevance for research among clergy of the three main models of personality assessment proposed by the Sixteen Personality Factor Questionnaire (Cattell and Stice 1957), the Myers–Briggs Type Indicator (Myers and McCaulley 1985) and the Eysenck Personality Inventory (Eysenck and Eysenck 1964) or the Eysenck Personality Questionnaire (Eysenck and Eysenck 1975). Of these three systems the dimensional model proposed by Hans Eysenck has proved to be the most useful.

In its most recent form Eysenck's model of personality argues that individual differences can be most adequately and economically summarised in terms of three major orthogonal dimensions which he characterises as follows. The two poles of the first dimension are labelled as introversion and extraversion. The two poles of the second dimension are labelled as stability and neuroticism. The two poles of the third dimension are labelled as tenderminded and toughminded (psychoticism). The instruments also contain a lie scale.

Eysenck's extraversion scales measure sociability and impulsivity. The opposite of extraversion is introversion. The high scorer on the extraversion scale is characterised by the test manual as a sociable individual, who likes parties, has many friends, needs to have people to talk to and prefers meeting people to reading or studying alone. The typical extravert craves excitement, takes chances, acts on the spur of the moment, is carefree, easy-going, optimistic, and likes to "laugh and be merry."

Eysenck's neuroticism scales measure emotional lability and overreactivity. The opposite of neuroticism is emotional stability. The high scorer on the neuroticism scale is characterised by the test manual as an anxious, worrying individual, who is moody and frequently depressed, likely to sleep badly and to suffer from various psychosomatic disorders. Eysenck and Eysenck (1975) suggest that if the high scorer on the neuroticism scale "has to be described in one word, one might say that he was a *worrier*; his main characteristic is a constant preoccupation with things that might go wrong, and with a strong emotional reaction of anxiety to these thoughts."

Eysenck's psychoticism scales identify the underlying personality traits which at one extreme define psychotic mental disorders. The opposite of psychoticism is normal personality. The high scorer on the psychoticism scale is characterised by Eysenck and Eysenck (1976), in their study of psychoticism as a dimension of personality, as being "cold, impersonal, hostile, lacking in sympathy, unfriendly, untrustful, odd, unemotional, unhelpful, lacking in insight, strange, with paranoid ideas that people were against him."

Lie scales were originally introduced into personality inventories to detect the tendency of some respondents to "fake good" and so to distort the resultant personality scores (O'Donovan 1969). The notion of the lie scale has not, however, remained as simple as that, and their continued use has resulted in them being interpreted as a personality measure in their own right (McCrae and Costa 1983; Furnham 1986).

Studies employing Eysenck's dimensional model of personality have profiled the personality characteristics of male Anglican parochial clergy (Francis and Rodger 1994a), male Methodist ministers (Jones and Francis 1992), conference-going clergy (Francis and Pearson 1991; Francis and Thomas 1992) and Roman Catholic secular parochial priests (Louden and Francis 1999). They have compared the personality profile of male and female Anglican ordinands (Francis 1991), male and female Anglican clergy (Robbins, Francis, and Rutledge 1997) and male and female Pentecostal ministry candidates (Francis and Kay 1995). They have explored the differences between stipendiary and nonstipendiary clergy (Francis and Robbins 1996), between charismatic and non-charismatic clergy (Francis and Thomas 1997) and between Evangelical and Catholic Anglican clergy (Francis and Thomas 1996). Two studies from this series are, however, of particular importance to assessing the relevance of personality for exploring clergy burnout and comparing the situation of rural clergy with that of clergy serving in other areas.

The first of these two studies was reported by Francis and Rodger (1994b). In this study the short form Revised Eysenck Personality Questionnaire (Eysenck, Eysenck, and Barrett 1985) was completed by 170 male full-time parochial clergy within one Anglican diocese, together with indices of role prioritization, role conflict, and dissatisfaction with ministry. The data demonstrated that Eysenck's three major dimensions of personality (extraversion, neuroticism, and psychoticism) were able to account for significant individual differences in all these key areas of ministry performance and assessment. In particular, it was those clergy who scored high on neuroticism and high on psychoticism who demonstrated most signs of dissatisfaction with ministry and were most likely to entertain thoughts of seeking alternative forms of employment. Such clergy are likely to be ministry burnout candidates.

The second of these two studies was reported by Francis and Lankshear (1998). In this study the short-form Revised Eysenck Personality Questionnaire (Eysenck, Eysenck, and Barrett 1985) was completed by 81 male Anglican clergy in charge of rural benefices and by 72 in charge of urban benefices. Significant differences were found in the personality profiles of the two groups. The rural clergy recorded higher scores on the extraversion scale and on the lie scale. The higher scores of rural clergy on the extraversion scale is consistent with the view that multiparish rural benefices increasingly demand the skills and social energy of the extravert who is able to sustain a wide range of professional relationships across multiple communities. Ironically, the introvert can now more easily escape from the pressures of social interaction in an urban benefice where, in a pluralist and post-Christian society, only a small proportion of the population show interest in the church. The higher scores of rural clergy on the lie scale is consistent with the views that this index measures social conformity and that rural ministry requires a more socially conforming and less radical approach than urban ministry.

In summary, the research evidence indicates that it is both appropriate and necessary to take personality into account in attempts to assess and interpret the social and contextual correlates of burnout among the clergy. Moreover, Eysenck's dimensional model of personality is likely to prove most useful in this context.

METHOD

Sample

The Church Commissioners kindly generated a 15 percent random sample from their database of full-time stipendiary male parochial clergy. From this database 1,476 questionnaires were mailed, and a total of 1,071 thoroughly completed questionnaires were returned, making a response rate of 73 percent.

Of the respondents 3 percent were under the age of thirty, 19 percent were in their thirties, 31 percent in their forties, 31 percent in their fifties, and 16 percent were sixty or over. Of the total sample, 84 percent were married, 30 percent were in rural ministry, and 55 percent had served in their current parishes for less than five years, while a further 25 percent had served in their current parishes for between five and ten years.

Measures

Personality was assessed by the Eysenck Personality Questionnaire (Eysenck and Eysenck 1975) which proposes a 21 item measure of extraversion, a 23 item measure of neuroticism, and a 25 item measure of psychoticism. It also contains a 21 item lie scale. Each item is assessed on a dichotomous scale: *yes* and *no*.

Burnout was assessed by the modified Maslach Burnout Inventory (Francis, Rutledge, Louden, Kay, and Robbins 2000) which proposes a ten item measure of emotional exhaustion, a ten item measure of depersonalization, and a ten item measure of personal accomplishment. Each item is assessed on a five point scale: *agree strongly*, *agree*, *not certain*, *disagree,* and *disagree strongly*.

Multiple choice questions provided information about marital status, years in present parish, number of churches in the benefice, and rurality of parish.

Data Analysis

The data were analysed by multiple regression. Three separate multiple regression equations explored individual differences in emotional exhaustion, depersonalization, and personal accomplishment. The personal accomplishment scores were inverted so that a higher score represented increased burnout in the same way as higher scores on the other two scales.

Each of the three multiple regression equations was set up in the same way. Age was entered into the equation first as a clear biographical variable independent of all other factors. After age had been taken into account, the four personality variables were entered in the order of neuroticism, psychoticism, extraversion, and the lie scale. This order anticipated the comparative predictive strength of the four scales on the basis of previous research. After age and personality had been taken into account, marital status was next entered into the equation. In this case the variable was scored so that a positive correlation would indicate that married clergy recorded a higher score than single clergy, while a negative correlation would indicate that single clergy recorded a higher score than married clergy. After age, personality, and marital status had been taken into account, rurality was next entered into the equation. Rurality was scored so that a positive correlation would indicate that rural clergy recorded a higher score than clergy in nonrural environments, while a negative correlation would indicate that clergy in nonrural environments would record a higher score than rural clergy. Finally, the number of years spent in the parishes and the number of churches in the benefice were entered into the equation. In view of the sample size the probability level for testing statistical significance in these regression equations was set at the one percent.

RESULTS

The first steps of data analysis checked the internal reliability of the four measures of personality and the three measures of burnout using Cronbach's (1951) alpha coefficient. The following alpha coefficients were achieved by the seven scales: emotional exhaustion, 0.89; depersonalization, 0.81; personal accomplishment, 0.78; extraversion, 0.84; neuroticism, 0.86; psychoticism, 0.52; lie scale, 0.78. These statistics demonstrate that the indices of emotional exhaustion, depersonalization, personal accomplishment, extraversion, neuroticism, and the lie scale all function in a satisfactory manner. The lower, but adequate, alpha coefficient recorded by the psychoticism scale is consistent with the known difficulties in operationalising this construct (Francis, Philipchalk, and Brown 1991).

Table 1. Multiple Regression Significance Tests

		Increase					
	R^2	R^2	F	$P<$	Beta	T	$P<$
Emotional Exhaustion							
age	0.0159	0.0159	16.5	.001	−0.1173	−3.7	.001
neuroticism	0.2510	0.2351	319.9	.001	+0.4628	+16.7	.001
psychoticism	0.2628	0.0118	16.3	.001	+0.1381	+5.0	.001
extraversion	0.2839	0.0211	30.0	.001	−0.1500	−5.5	.001
lie scale	0.2870	0.0031	4.4	NS	+0.0557	+2.0	NS
married	0.2905	0.0034	4.9	NS	+0.0605	+2.2	NS
rural	0.2906	0.0001	0.2	NS	+0.0039	+0.1	NS
years in parish	0.2920	0.0014	2.0	NS	+0.0432	+1.4	NS
number of churches	0.2929	0.0009	1.3	NS	+0.0321	+1.1	NS
Depersonalization							
age	0.0337	0.0337	35.6	.001	−0.1365	−4.2	.001
neuroticism	0.1707	0.1370	168.3	.001	+0.3259	+11.4	.001
psychoticism	0.2264	0.0557	73.3	.001	+0.2396	+8.5	.001
extraversion	0.2427	0.0163	21.9	.001	−0.1371	−4.9	.001
lie scale	0.2449	0.0022	2.9	NS	−0.0521	−1.8	NS
married	0.2449	0.0000	0.0	NS	+0.0055	+0.2	NS
rural	0.2455	0.0006	0.8	NS	−0.0222	−0.7	NS
years in parish	0.2479	0.0024	3.2	NS	+0.0555	+1.8	NS
number of churches	0.2479	0.0000	0.0	NS	+0.0008	+0.0	NS
Personal Accomplishment							
age	0.0008	0.0008	0.9	NS	+0.0290	+0.9	NS
neuroticism	0.1000	0.0991	112.2	.001	+0.2101	+7.5	.001
psychoticism	0.1015	0.0015	1.7	NS	+0.0648	+2.3	NS
extraverstion	0.2581	0.1566	214.6	.001	−0.4050	−14.6	.001
lie scale	0.2645	0.0065	8.9	.01	−0.0909	−3.1	.01
married	0.2652	0.0007	1.0	NS	−0.0317	−1.2	NS
rural	0.2739	0.0087	12.2	.001	+0.0957	+3.2	.001
years in parish	0.2744	0.0004	0.6	NS	−0.0225	−0.7	NS
number of churches	0.2741	0.0000	0.0	NS	+0.0032	+0.1	NS

Table one presents the multiple regression significance tests associated with the three equations exploring the predictive power of age, neuroticism, psychoticism, extraversion, lie scale, marital status, rurality, years in parish, and number of churches in benefice on emotional exhaustion, depersonalization, and personal accomplishment.

DISCUSSION

Eight main features of these data deserve discussion. First, age emerged as a significant predictor of emotional exhaustion and depersonalization, but not of personal accomplishment. The significant negative correlation between age and scores both on the emotional exhaustion subscale and on the depersonalization subscale, but not on the personal accomplishment subscale is consistent with findings among other professional groups as reported by Bartz and Maloney (1986), Lee and Ashforth (1991), Jackson, Barnett, Stajich, and Murphy (1993) and Price and Spence (1994). Thus, older clergy are less likely than younger clergy to suffer from either emotional exhaustion or depersonalization. Two theories may account for these differences between younger and older clergy. Younger clergy who suffer from emotional exhaustion or depersonalization may decide to leave parochial ministry either on grounds of ill health or to seek alternative employment. Older clergy may have learnt how better to pace their work so as to avoid such signs of burnout.

Second, neuroticism scores emerged as the strongest and most consistent predictor of individual differences over the three dimensions of burnout. Clergy who scored higher on the neuroticism scale were more likely to suffer from emotional exhaustion, to display signs of depersonalization, and to enjoy fewer feelings of personal accomplishment. This finding is consistent with the finding of Francis and Rodger (1994b) that clergy who score high on Eysenck's neuroticism scale are likely to be more dissatisfied with their ministry. It is also consistent with the finding of Manlove (1993) that scores on Eysenck's neuroticism scale are positively associated with burnout among child care workers and with the finding of Rodgerson and Piedmont (1998) that neuroticism as measured in the five factor model of personality proposed by Costa and McCrae (1992) is the strongest predictor of burnout among clergy.

Third, psychoticism scores emerged as significant predictors of emotional exhaustion and depersonalization, but not of personal accomplishment. Clergy who scored higher on the psychoticism scale were more likely to suffer from emotional exhaustion and to display signs of depersonalization. This is consistent with the wider theory that toughminded individuals are less likely to show empathy to others or to be properly in tune with their own feelings (Eysenck and Eysenck 1976).

Fourth, extraversion scores emerged as significant predictors of emotional exhaustion, depersonalization, and personal accomplishment. Introverted clergy were particularly likely to enjoy fewer feelings of personal accomplishment. Introverted clergy were also more likely to suffer from emotional exhaustion and to display signs of depersonalization. This finding is also consistent with the finding of Rodgerson and Piedmont (1998) who employed the Costa and McCrae (1992) index of extraversion among Baptist clergy in the United States. The relationship between introversion and burnout lends weight to the view that many aspects of the clerical profession presuppose a predisposition toward extraversion. At the same time it has to be recognised that ministry candidates tend to be more introverted than the general population (Francis 1991). Interestingly, no relationship was found between burnout and Eysenck's measure of extraversion among child care workers by Manlove (1993) or among teachers by Capel (1992).

Fifth, lie scale scores emerged as a significant predictor of personal accomplishment, but not of emotional exhaustion, nor of depersonalization. Clergy who scored higher on the lie scale were likely to enjoy higher levels of personal accomplishment. This finding is consistent with the views that low lie scale scores are indicative of a willingness to be nonconformist and that nonconformist clergy are more likely to set their own criteria of personal accomplishment.

Sixth, marital status emerged as irrelevant to scores on all three scales of burnout. The lack of relationship between burnout and marital status is consistent with findings among other professional groups reported by Meadow (1981), Belcastro, Gold, and Grant (1982), Schwab and Iwanicki (1982), Maslach and Jackson (1984; 1985), Dolan (1987), Ackerley, Burnell, Holder, and Kurdek (1988) and Burke and Greenglass (1989). Other studies, however, have produced conflicting results. For example, Maslach and Jackson (1979; 1981) and Vealey, Udry, Zimmerman, and Soliday (1992) found that single and divorced individuals recorded higher scores of emotional exhaustion than those who were married, while Ross, Altmaier, and Russell (1989) found those who were married reported greater emotional exhaustion than those who were single. After taking age and personality into account single clergy appear neither more nor less susceptible to burnout than married clergy.

Seventh, rural ministry emerged as a significant negative predictor of personal accomplishment, but not of emotional exhaustion, nor of depersonalization. Clergy working in rural parishes experienced a lower level of personal accomplishment than clergy working in other kinds of parishes. On the other hand, clergy working in rural parishes were no more likely than clergy working in other kinds of parishes to suffer from emotional exhaustion or to display signs of depersonalization.

Eighth, after taking the preceding factors into account, neither the number of years spent in the parish nor the number of churches in the benefice added further predictive power to any of the three subscales of burnout.

CONCLUSION

This study in empirical theology has tested the theory that rural clergy are under greater stress than clergy working in other kinds of parishes, among a random sample of 1,071 full-time stipendiary male Anglican clergy. Taking the three-dimensional model of burnout proposed by Maslach and Jackson (1986), the data indicate that rural clergy have a lower sense of personal accomplishment than comparable clergy working in other types of parishes, but that they do not suffer from higher levels of emotional exhaustion nor from higher levels of depersonalization. The data also confirm that burnout can be predicted from individual differences in personality. Three main consequences follow from these findings for those with a responsibility for the pastoral care of rural clergy.

First, it is clear that the problems of emotional exhaustion and depersonalization are no more severe among rural clergy than among clergy serving in other forms of parochial ministry. Whatever strategies are developed to help clergy face and overcome these signs of stress and burnout may have equal applicability in rural and non-rural areas.

Second, it is clear that the problems associated with the lack of personal accomplishment may be felt more acutely among clergy serving in rural parishes than among clergy serving in other forms of parochial ministry. It may be appropriate, therefore, for this particular perspective to be emphasised in the pastoral care of rural clergy. Two strategies may be relevant. Where practices like peer-assisted clergy review are supported by rural dioceses, the review process may wish to concentrate on identifying and emphasising those aspects of local ministry from which individual clergy derive a sense of personal accomplishment. Dioceses may be able to identify particular gifts and skills within individual rural clergy which can be exercised more widely than within their own benefice and thereby enable them to draw on a wider sense of personal accomplishment.

Third, it is clear that much of the variation in clergy susceptibility to emotional exhaustion, depersonalization, and lack of personal accomplishment, among those serving in rural ministry as well as among those serving in other forms of parochial ministry, can be predicted from knowledge about individual personality profiles. If the rural church were to take seriously the benefits to parish ministry available from personality psychology, the prime candidates for ministry burnout might be identified well before crises were reached. Such a strategy would make good pastoral sense in terms of protecting parishes from the hurt and decline brought about through clergy burnout. Such a strategy would make good human sense in terms of protecting individual clergy and their families from the torment and frustration brought about through clergy burnout. Such a strategy would make good financial sense in terms of lowering the exit rate from ministry (when clergy are expensive to train) and reducing the strain on parishes (who provide the income in the first place). But it will be no easy matter to convince the church that personality psychology might be a God-given tool in clergy development and deployment.

ACKNOWLEDGMENT

This analysis was sponsored by a Constant H. Jacquet Research Award from the Religious Research Association (RRA). The authors wish to express their thanks for this sponsorship.

REFERENCES

Ackerley, G.D., J. Burnell, D. C. Holder, and L. A. Kurdek. 1988. "Burnout among licensed psychologists." *Professional Psychology: research and practice*, 19, 624–631.

Archbishops' Commission on Rural Areas. 1990. *Faith in the Countryside*. Worthing: Churchman Publishing.

Bartz, C. and J. P. Maloney. 1986. "Burnout among intensive-care nurses." *Research in Nursing and Health*, 9, 147–153.

Belcastro, P. A., R. S. Gold, and J. Grant. 1982. "Stress and burnout: physiologic effects on correctional teachers." *Criminal Justice and Behaviour*, 9, 387–395.

Bowden, A. 1994. *Ministry in the Countryside*. London: Mowbray.

Burke, R. J. and E. R. Greenglass. 1989. "Psychological burnout among men and women in teaching: an examination of the Cherniss model." *Human Relations*, 42, 261–273.

Capel, S. A. 1992. "Stress and burnout in teachers." *European Journal of Teacher Education*, 15, 197–211.

Cattell, R.B. and G. F. Stice. 1957. *Handbook for the Sixteen Personality Factor Questionnaire*, Champaign, IL: Institute for Personality and Ability Testing.

Church in Wales. 1992. *The Church in the Welsh Countryside: a programme for action by the Church in Wales*. Penarth: Church in Wales Board of Mission.

Coate, M. A. 1989. *Clergy Stress: the hidden conflicts in ministry*, London: SPCK.

Costa, P. T., and McCrae, R. R. 1992. *Revised NEO Personality Inventory and NEO Five Factor Inventory: Manual*. Odessa, FL: Psychological Assessment Resources.

Cronbach, L. J. 1951. "Coefficient alpha and the internal structure of tests." *Psychometrika*, 16, 297–334.

Davey, J. 1995. *Burnout: stress in ministry*. Leominster: Gracewing.

Davies, D., C. Watkins, and M. Winter. 1991. *Church and Religion in Rural England*. Edinburgh: T and T Clark.

Dolan, N. 1987. "The relationship between burnout and job–satisfaction in nurses." *Journal of Advanced Nursing*, 12, 3–12.

Eysenck, H. J. and S. B. G. Eysenck. 1964. *Manual of the Eysenck Personality Inventory*. London: University of London Press.

_____. 1975. *Manual of the Eysenck Personality Questionnaire adult and junior*. London: Hodder and Stoughton.

_____. 1976. *Psychoticism as a Dimension of Personality*. London: Hodder and Stoughton.

Eysenck, S. B. G., H. J. Eysenck, and P. Barrett. 1985. "A revised version of the psychoticism scale." *Personality and Individual Differences*, 6, 21–29.

Fletcher, B. 1990. *Clergy Under Stress: a study of homosexual and heterosexual clergy*. London: Mowbray.

Francis, L. J. 1985. *Rural Anglicanism: a future for young Christians?* London: Collins Liturgical Publications.

_____. 1991. "The personality characteristics of Anglican ordinands: feminine men and masculine women?" *Personality and Individual Differences*, 12, 1133–1140.

_____. 1996. *Church Watch: Christianity in the countryside*. London: SPCK.

Francis, L. J., S. H. Jones, and D. W. Lankshear. 1996. "Baptism policy and church growth in Church of England rural, urban, and suburban parishes." *Modern Believing*, 37, 3, 11–24.

Francis, L. J. and W. K. Kay. 1995. "The personality characteristics of Pentecostal ministry candidates." *Personality and Individual Differences*, 18, 581–594.

Francis, L. J. and D. W. Lankshear. 1990. "The impact of church schools on village church life." *Educational Studies*, 16, 117–129.

_____. 1991. "The impact of church schools on urban church life." *School Effectiveness and School Improvement*, 2, 324–335.

_____. 1992. "The rural factor: a comparative survey of village churches and the liturgical work of rural clergy." *Modern Churchman*, 34, 1–9.

_____. 1993. "Ageing Anglican clergy and performance indicators in the rural church, compared with the suburban church." *Ageing and Society*, 13, 339–363.

_____. 1994. "Deployment of ageing clergy within the Church of England." *Psychological Reports*, 75, 366.

_____. 1997. "The rural church is different: the case of Anglican confirmation." *Journal of Empirical Theology*, 10, 5–20.

_____. 1998. "Personality and preference for rural ministry among male Anglican clergy." *Pastoral Psychology*, 46, 163–166.

Francis, L. J. and P. R. Pearson. 1991. "Personality characteristics of midcareer Anglican clergy." *Social Behaviour and Personality*, 19, 81–84.

Francis, L. J., R. Philipchalk, and L. B. Brown. 1991. "The comparability of the short form EPQ–R with the EPQ among students in England, the USA, Canada and Australia." *Personality and Individual Differences*, 12, 1129–1132.

Francis, L. J. and M. Robbins. 1996. "Differences in the personality profile of stipendiary and nonstipendiary female Anglican parochial clergy in Britain and Ireland." *Contact*, 119, 26–32.

Francis, L. J. and R. Rodger. 1994a. "The personality profile of Anglican clergymen." *Contact*, 113, 27–32.

_____. 1994b. The influence of personality on clergy role prioritization, role influences, conflict and dissatisfaction with ministry." *Personality and Individual Differences*, 16, 947–957.

Francis, L. J., C. Rutledge, S. Louden, W. K. Kay, and M. Robbins. 2000. "Assessing clergy burnout: a study among Anglican clergy, Roman Catholic priests and Pentecostal pastors." Manuscript in preparation.

Francis, L. J. and T. H. Thomas. 1992. "Personality profile of conference–going clergy in England." *Psychological Reports*, 70, 682.

_____. 1996. "Are Anglo Catholic priests more feminine? a study among male Anglican clergy." *Pastoral Sciences*, 15, 15–22.

_____. 1997. "Are charismatic ministers less stable? a study among male Anglican clergy." *Review of Religious Research*, 39, 61–69.

Furnham, A. 1986. "Response bias, social desirability and dissimulation." *Personality and Individual Differences*, 7, 385–400.

Galton, F. 1872. Statistical inquiries into the efficacy of prayer." *Fortnightly Review*, 12, 125–135.

Jackson, R. A., C. W. Barnett, G. V. Stajich, and J. E. Murphy. 1993. "An analysis of burnout among school of pharmacy faculty." *American Journal of Pharmaceutical Education*, 57, 9–17.

Jones, D. L. and L. J. Francis. 1992. "Personality profile of Methodist ministers in England." *Psychological Reports*, 70, 538.

Kirk, M. and T. Leary. 1994. *Holy matrimony? an exploration of marriage and ministry*. Oxford: Lynx.

Lee, R. T. and B. E. Ashforth 1991. "Work-unit structure and processes and job-related stresses as predictors of managerial burnout." *Journal of Applied Social Psychology*, 21, 1831–1847.

Likert, R. 1932. "A technique for the measurement of attitudes." *Archives of Psychology*, 140, 1–55.

Louden, S. H. and Francis, L. J. 1999. "The personality profile of Roman Catholic parochial secular priests in England and Wales." *Review of Religious Research*, 41, 65–79.

McCrae, R. R. and P. T. Costa. 1983. "Social desirability scales: more substance than style." *Journal of Consulting and Clinical Psychology*, 51, 882–888.

Manlove, E. E. 1993. "Multiple correlates of burnout in child care workers." *Early Childhood Research Quarterly*, 8, 499–518.

Maslach, C. and S. E. Jackson. 1979. "Burned-out cops and their families." *Psychology Today*, 12, 59–62.

_____. 1981. "The measurement of experienced burnout." *Journal of Occupational Behaviour*, 22, 99–113.

_____. 1984. "Patterns of burnout among a national sample of public contact workers." *Journal of Health and Human Resources Administration*, 7, 189–212.

_____. 1985. "The role of sex and family variables in burnout." *Sex Roles*, 12, 837–851.

Maslach, C. and S. Jackson. 1986. *The Maslach Burnout Inventory*, 2nd edition. Palo Alto, CA: Consulting Psychologists Press.

Meadow, K. P. 1981. "Burnout in professionals working with deaf children." *American Annals of the Deaf*, 126, 13–22.

Myers, I. B. and M. H. McCaulley. 1985. *Manual: a guide to the development and use of the Myers–Briggs Type Indicator*, Palo Alto, CA: Consulting Psychologists Press.

O'Donovan, D. 1969. "An historical review of the lie scale: with particular reference to the Maudsley Personality Inventory." *Papers in Psychology*, 3, 13–19.

Price, L. and S. H. Spence. 1994. "Burnout symptoms among drug and alcohol service employees: gender differences in the interaction between work and home stresses." *Anxiety Stress and Coping*, 7, 67–84.

Robbins, M., L. J. Francis, and C. Rutledge. 1997. "The personality characteristics of Anglican stipendiary parochial clergy in England: gender differences revisited." *Personality and Individual Differences*, 23, 199–204.

Rodgerson, T. E. and R. L. Piedmont. 1998. Assessing the incremental validity of the Religious Problem-Solving Scale in the prediction of clergy burnout." *Journal for the Scientific Study of Religion*, 37, 517–527.

Ross, R. R., E. M. Altmaier, and D. W. Russell. 1989. "Job stress, social support, and burnout among counselling centre staff." *Journal of Counselling Psychology*, 36, 464–470.

Russell, A. 1986. *The Country Parish*, London: SPCK.

_____. 1993. *The Country Parson*. London: SPCK.

Rutledge, C. J. F. 1994. "Parochial clergy today: a study of role, personality and burnout among clergy in the Church of England." Lampeter: unpublished M.Phil. dissertation, University of Wales, Lampeter.

Sanford, J. A. 1982. *Ministry Burnout*. London: Arthur James.

Schaufeli, W. B., C. Maslach, and T. Marek (eds.). 1993. *Professional Burnout: recent developments in theory and research*. London: Taylor and Francis.

Schwab, R. L. and E. F. Iwanicki. 1982. "Who are burned out teachers?" *Educational Research Quarterly*, 7, 5–16.

Vealey, R. S., E. M. Udry, V. Zimmerman, and J. Soliday. 1992. "Intrapersonal and situational predictors of coaching burnout." *Journal of Sport and Exercise Psychology*, 14, 40–58.

CONTEMPORARY IRISH PRIESTS IN AMERICA

William L. Smith

ABSTRACT

This paper describes the experiences of Irish-born and Irish-seminary educated Roman Catholic priests who live and work in dioceses in the United States. They reside primarily in the West, South, and Southwest. A variety of questions contained in a mail survey questionnaire were completed by 402 Irish priests who are alumni of five Irish seminaries. The priests were asked about their seminary preparation, the influence of American culture on their lives, how they view their ethnicity, whether they are treated differently because they are from Ireland, how satisfied they are with priesthood, what problems they face as priests, their ecclesiological and theological concerns, and their views of the impact of the Second Vatican Council on the Church. They will likely be the last of a long continuous line of Irish priests to serve in the United States.

Research in the Social Scientific Study of Religion, Volume 11, pages 193-207.
Copyright © 2000 by JAI Press Inc.
All rights of reproduction in any form reserved.
ISBN: 0-7623-0656-4

Immigration to America fueled Catholic growth during the early 1800s–1900s and groups of Irish, German, Italian, Polish, French Canadian, Mexican, and others contributed to the ethnic diversity of the Church. Some authors feel the Irish and the Germans had the most influence on American Catholicism (Dolan, 1985, pp. 127–128). Morris (1997 pp. vii–viii) is of the opinion that the roots of American Catholicism rest in nineteenth century Ireland. This is due not only to the role played by Irish priests, but also to the millions of Irish immigrants who were part of the Irish diaspora in America fueled by the great potato famine (Miller 1985). The militant, bureaucratic, and strict style of nineteenth centuryAmerican Catholicism can be attributed to the Irish. American Catholicism is still characterized, to some extent, by these traits, but it is much more autonomous and pluralistic than monolithic (D'Antonio 1994). Autonomy and pluralism, partly a result of modernism, the American ethos, and the reforms of the Second Vatican Council, are at the center of a much heated debate regarding the future of the Roman Catholic Church (Burns 1996).

While Irish-born and Irish-seminary educated priests have played a significant role in the staffing of American churches since the 1800s, large numbers of Irish priests are no longer available for service in the United States. Ireland, like the United States, is experiencing a decline in priestly vocations. The Catholic Church in the United States, since the convening of Vatican II, has experienced a decline in the number of priestly vocations and ordained priests. However, the Catholic population has continued to experience expansive growth. As of 1998, there were 31,657 diocesan priests, 320 fewer than in 1997. In 1988, there was one diocesan priest for every 1,538 Catholics, versus one per 1,945 Catholics in 1998 (*The Official Catholic Directory* 1998). By 2015, Young (1998, p. 7) estimates that the number of priests in the United States will have diminished by approximately 45 percent since 1966.

Most Irish priests reside in California, Texas, and Florida, but they can be found throughout the United States with most located in the West, South, and Southwest. Approximately 4,000 Irish priests have served in the United States and presently there are somewhere between 1,150–1,250 (Smith 1998).

This paper describes the experiences of contemporary Irish-born and Irish-seminary educated priests in the United States. This group does not include those Irish-born priests who were educated in American seminaries, nor does it include American-born priests of Irish descent. I will present a summary of their responses to a variety of questions I asked them in a survey. These answers reveal some of their experiences and beliefs about their seminary preparation in Ireland, the influence of American culture on their lives, how they view their ethnicity, how satisfied they are with priesthood, what problems they face as priests, their ecclesiological and theological concerns, and the impact of the Second Vatican Council on the Church. Probably more revealing than the summary tables I have included in this essay are the spontaneous quotes I have taken directly from the surveys. The priests' comments are very powerful and meaningful and it is in these passages that they describe their lives in America.

METHOD

I became interested in this topic several years ago while I was attending Mass in Florida. The priest, who was saying the Mass, was Irish-born and Irish-seminary educated. He spoke about priestly vocations and how he came to live in the United States. A short time later, I began checking the literature for information on Irish priests and I found that it was sparse. This led me to this project and my attempt to answer the following questions: How many Irish priests have served in the United States? Where did they serve? Why did they come here? What have they experienced in the United States?

After reviewing several studies of American priests, Fichter (1968), Hoge, Shields, and Griffin (1995), Greeley (1972), and Hemrick and Hoge (1991), I designed a survey to measure some similar concerns and issues that were discussed in these studies. Since the present study is exploratory and descriptive in nature, I did not have formalized hypotheses.

After consulting several local Irish priests, I was informed that there were six seminaries in Ireland that had educated the vast majority of Irish priests in the United States. The six seminaries are: St. John's College, Waterford; St. Peter's College, Wexford; St. Patrick's College, Thurles; St. Patrick's College, Carlow; St. Kieran's College, Kilkenny; and All Hallows College, Dublin. St. Patrick's College, Maynooth, is the National Seminary and 88 Irish priests who have served in the United States were educated there. I contacted the six seminaries and five of them provided the names and addresses of their alumni in the United States. St. John's, St. Peter's, St. Patrick's, Thurles, and St. Patrick's, Carlow, are diocesan seminaries, and All Hallows is a missionary seminary founded by John Hand. When the Irish bishops rebuked efforts to start an American missionary seminary in Ireland in 1837–1838, Hand received papal approval and founded All Hallows College. Priests have been educated there not only for the American missions, but for countries around the world where the Irish have immigrated (Morris 1997, p. 48).

The five seminaries provided me with 998 names and addresses of which 889 were usable. Some did not have complete addresses and some of the priests had died since the lists were compiled. I mailed the surveys (five pages long and consisting of 15 questions, 10 of which were open-ended) and the follow-up letters in the fall of 1996 and the winter of 1997 to the following number of alumni: (275) All Hallows; (242) St. Patrick's, Carlow; (146) St. John's; (143) St. Patrick's, Thurles; and (83) St. Peter's. The response rates were: All Hallows, 43 percent (124); St. Patrick's, Carlow, 45 percent (110); St. John's, 33 percent (49); St. Patrick's, Thurles 48 percent (69); and St. Peter's, 60 percent (50). Of the 889 priests surveyed, 402 or 45 percent responded.

FINDINGS

Overall Results

As a cohort, Irish priests in the United States are older than their American diocesan counterparts. The mean age for Irish priests in this study is 62.0, while it is 54.9 for American diocesan priests (Hoge, Shields, and Griffin 1995, p. 198). The difference in age between the Irish priests and their American counterparts is explained by the fact that fewer priests have been recruited from Ireland in the last twenty years, thus inflating the average age. The age distribution of the respondents is: 20's (2), 30's (11), 40's (22), 50's (128), 60's (142), 70's (76), 80's (19), and 90's (2). The number of years they have resided in the United States is: 2–10 (17), 11–20 (11), 21–30 (97), 31–40 (144), 41–50 (95), 51–60 (30), and 61–69 (7).

There are 181 Catholic dioceses in the United States and 77 of them are home to the respondents. Forty-seven of these dioceses had fewer than 5 respondents, while 25 of these dioceses had only 1 respondent. The following dioceses had 10 or more respondents: Atlanta (10), Camden, NJ (11), Miami (11), Mobile (11), Phoenix (11), San Diego (11), Great Falls–Billings, MT (12), Jackson, MS (14), San Antonio (14), Biloxi, MS (19), Sacramento (26), and Los Angeles (38). Fourteen dioceses were each home to between 6–9 of the respondents: Albany (6), Monterey (6), Paterson, NJ (6), Wichita (6), Corpus Christi (7), Jefferson City, MO (7), St. Augustine (7), Palm Beach (8), Seattle (8), Yakima, WA (8), Duluth (9), Orange, CA (9), Orlando (9), and Savannah (9).

The following categories reflect the majority of their current duties: Pastor 67.5 percent (270), Associate Pastor 6.5 percent (26), Bishop .8 percent (3), and Retired 13.5 percent (54). A small number of priests were Teachers 2.0 percent (8), Counselors 1.3 percent (5), Chaplains 6.0 percent (24), and some held Chancery positions 4.3 percent (17). Even those who were retired tended to help out in parishes on a part-time basis or whenever needed, especially on weekends.

American bishops or their representatives had recruited 43 percent (173) of the priests, while 57 percent (227) had volunteered for service in a diocese. In either case, Ireland, up until recently, had a surplus of priests and religious. Most of these men had not been selected by their local bishops to serve in Ireland and they needed sponsorship of a bishop to attend the seminary. So whether they were individually recruited or volunteered does not make any difference.

Of those surveyed, 76.1 percent (306) did not prefer to stay in Ireland, while 9.2 percent (37) would have liked to stay in Ireland, and 13.2 percent (53) had mixed views. Most of those wanting to leave saw more opportunity for themselves in the United States and they believed they were needed much more there. If they would have stayed in Ireland, most of them would have been sent to England, Scotland, or Wales for 5 to 10 years before they were needed in their home dioceses. In addition, promotion to Pastor would take much longer in Ireland than in the

United States. Ireland, even today, is the most priest-rich country in the world. See Table 1 for a partial summary of the survey results.

The following quotes highlight the comments made by the priests regarding whether they would have preferred to stay in Ireland:

> No. Even as a seminarian I felt that the Irish clergy were too rigid and restrictive. Besides, there was then (and to some extent, still) in Ireland a sort of clergy 'caste' with which I could not identify.

> Being a priest in Ireland did not interest me. I preferred the challenge of working as a priest in the United States, and I was attracted by the progressiveness of the American Church in comparison to the Irish Church.

> No and for two main reasons. Firstly, I felt there was an overabundance of priests in Ireland. Secondly, and perhaps more importantly, I thought that the Church in the U.S. was more of a challenge for healthy faith development.

Table 1. Partial Summary of Survey Results

Preferred to Stay in Ireland		Adequate Seminary Preparation	
yes	9.2 (37)	yes	55.0 (221)
no	76.1 (306)	no	20.4 (82)
mixed	13.2 (53)	mixed	23.4 (94)
Influenced by American Culture		**Irish or Irish American**	
yes	69.2 (278)	Irish	46.8 (188)
no	20.1 (81)	Irish	
mixed	9.5 (38)	American	39.1 (157)
		both	12.9 (52)
		neither	.5 (2)
Treated Differently		**Satisfied with Priesthood**	
yes	51.0 (205)	versy satisfied	66.7 (268)
no	42.3 (170)	satisfied	23.9 (96)
mixed	6.0 (24)	somewhat sat.	7.2 (29)
		not satisfied	1.5 (6)
Problems		**Ecclesiological and Theological Issues**	
overwork	17.4 (70)	ord. of women	19.7 (79)
loneliness	15.7 (63)	ord. of m. men	15.2 (61)
no problems	12.4 (50)	option for priests	
celibacy	10.7 (43)	to marry	12.9 (52)
shortage of clergy	9.7 (39)	former priests to	
		be reactivated	12.7 (51)
		lack of vocations	10.9 (44)
		shortage of priests	10.7 (43)
		celibacy	9.7 (39)
		no concerns	4.5 (18)
Impact of Vatican II			
far enough	51.5 (207)		
too far	8.7 (35)		
not far enough	38.8 (156)		
(N = 402)			

For the most part, these priests were positive about the education they received at the Irish seminaries. If there was one major flaw in their preparation for priesthood it was in their ignorance of American culture. The majority of them did not blame the seminaries for this oversight; they stated that one can never really be prepared for such a change. Even those who received some education in American history and culture experienced culture shock and a period of adjustment. Most were pleased with the theological and philosophical background they received, but they lamented the lack of cultural preparation. For many, the first several years in the United States were a painful period of adjustment. As a specific example, an elderly priest stated that they were uninformed about the American custom of bathing daily. During his seminary years, as was customary throughout Europe at that time, they bathed once a week. As one can imagine, this lack of information created some uncomfortable situations for this priest in his first months in the United States. Fifty-five percent (221) believed they were adequately prepared by their seminary for service in the United States, while 20.4 percent (82) stated they were not adequately prepared, and 23.4 percent (94) had mixed feelings.

The following quotes depict the comments made by the priests regarding their level of preparation by their seminaries for service in the United States:

> Good question. Were given the very basics and of course the Seminary staff did not know a thing about ministry in the States. Their only experience was in Ireland and I think none of them had done any pastoral work. They came from Maynooth and right into Carlow. There was no emphasis whatever on pastoral work—just intellectual and staying the course.

> Yes, spiritually and intellectually. No, culturally. A bit of a shock. In Ireland I had never met a Black Person or a Mexican or an Asian. I'm not sure that I knew more than one Protestant family.

> Yes. I feel we got an excellent education. We were encouraged to learn everything possible about the U.S. We even had a course in U.S. history. The only negative I have felt is that they didn't teach us to be assertive. When I first arrived I remember feeling how self-assured the American-trained priests were. They talked a lot but said very little—yet they did so with great confidence and aplomb. We were trained to be 'person' oriented whereas the U.S. trained seem to be more "program" orientated. Our tendency is to spend time with individuals whenever possible—greeting them outside church, the sick, the school, funerals, etc., etc. They are into goals, objectives, evaluations, etc.—an external paper trail. Obviously the above is an exaggeration there is some 'cross-over.' However the tendencies are still valid.

> Spiritually–Yes; Theologically–Yes; Emotionally–It took many years for me to accustom myself to Miami Beach, where I was assigned as a Chaplain in Mount Sinai Hospital—Jewish. I had never met a Jew.

Another question asked whether American culture had influenced their theology and philosophy of life. Not surprisingly, 69.2 percent (278) said yes, while 20.1 percent (81) replied it had not, and 9.5 percent (38) were undecided.

These comments exemplify the thoughts of the priests on this issue:

> Yes. The clash of American/Christian values has forced me to reexamine the theology I was taught. The pluralism of American society makes me rely more on Scripture than on theology or the Magisterium. Very little is black and white, cut and dried, in pastoral ministry.

> Yes. Divorced/Blended Families, etc. I've had to struggle with a lot of things. I am grateful for the values I received in my home. The consumerism and materialism can be overwhelming at times. The dollar is power but not the key to happiness. Helping people to see God as a source of happiness has become a main theme of my theology.

> I am sure it has! But how can you tell? I suppose the only way is to compare myself with contemporaries who have spent their priesthood in Ireland. They seem to be locked in a time zone similar to the church in America in the late sixties. They have the Liturgy in English but they barely let go of the old. You get the sense that they may play golf in clerical dress. I have been a pastor for 25 years—they for less than 10 years.

I wanted to see to what degree the priests had assimilated into American society, so I asked whether they considered themselves more Irish than Irish American. In response, 46.8 percent (188) said they were Irish, 39.1 percent (157) Irish American, 12.9 percent (52) both, and 0.5 percent (2) neither. A common reply was that in Ireland they were considered to be Irish American and in the United States they were considered Irish.

The following comments summarize their thoughts on ethnicity:

> Yes, I am much much much much more Irish than Irish American. In fact I don't consider myself at all Irish American...It does, however disturb me and at times it makes me angry and upset, when Americans greet me with a fake brogue...Sometimes, I wish I could initiate litigation against them for ethnic harassment! No, I'm not joking!...Even though I have never lost my Irish accent and visit my home two or three times a year, I am still considered a 'Yank' in Ireland. They'll tell me that I say Mass—'a wee bit differently—you'd know you were "out foreign" for a long time—no you don't have a Yankee accent but you say some words that sound different—it's marvelous that you haven't lost your Irish language and still speak it fluently, but when you speak English one would know you hadn't always lived in Ireland—not that you're full of Americanese or that you're "damn yankee" sort of...but, you're not Irish like us'!!! That's very hurtful to me...and it's hard having to live with it. However, it's true!!!!

> I would say more Irish American. I go to the theater on Broadway and that has opened me up to contemporary issues...I also read a lot, go to movies, and have tried to update myself on American history...The decision to become a citizen was not easy but once made I had no regrets. I still have my Irish passport. I am a dual citizen. I still visit Ireland just about once a year...I am Irish but believe I have a cosmopolitan outlook on life. I still love Irish music and try to stay abreast of the Irish political scene and its culture.

Following up on the previous question, I asked them if they are treated differently by American Catholics because they are from Ireland. About half, 51.0 percent (205) indicated they are treated differently, 42.35 percent (170) said no, and 6.0 percent (24) had mixed feelings.

The following comments highlight their perceptions of being treated differently because they are from Ireland:

Very definitely. My opinion is that most parishioners in American parishes, at least in the Southeastern dioceses, would prefer an Irish priest to an American priest. If this is so, I suspect the reason for it is that the Irish are more pastoral, less bureaucratic, more personal, less rational/academic. Of course it's quite chic in academe and among American women religious to be anti-Irish, but not so among ordinary parishioners. Being thus favored has its disadvantages however. Some Irish priests play the 'the Irish ticket' to a shameful degree, substituting charm for substance. And some Americans are absolutely fixated in a Barry Fitzgerald/Bing Crosby 'Going My Way' notion of the Irish and nothing one says or does seems to get through to them. I did not come to the U.S. to set up 'little Irelands' in my parish!

Yes I think so. American Catholics seem to take a great liking to Irish priests. But I do not think that this is simply because of the brogue or being Irish. My experience is that most Irish priests seem to have a stability about them and an ability to relate with people and to listen to their concerns. Most Irish priests I know put people before 'business' and 'organizations.'

Perhaps a little anecdote will best answer this question. A quote from the Bishop in his conversation to a fellow Bishop, 'I can send a Mexican priest and even an Anglo priest, and often the people won't take to them, but I'll send them an Irish priest and they think they are getting Jesus Christ.' I think there is a distinct advantage being from Ireland, of course I wouldn't say I'm exactly Jesus Christ.

No. The people in parishes have been wonderful. Our biggest difficulty in the beginning was with the native clergy. They seemed to resent us, particularly if we got a promotion.

A common perception held by Catholics and the American public is that priests are not happy with their priesthood and they are experiencing a crisis in morale. But Hoge, Shields, and Griffin's survey (1995) reported that priests are not experiencing a crisis in morale and levels of morale and happiness were higher in 1985 and 1993 than in 1970. The same can be said of the Irish priests in the present study: 66.7 percent (268) were very satisfied with their priesthood, 23.9 percent (96) satisfied, 7.2 percent (29) somewhat satisfied, and 1.5 percent (6) not satisfied.

These quotations summarize the priests' thoughts on how satisfied they are with their priesthood:

It is the greatest gift God gave me, but I have not done nearly enough for Him. I have made too many mistakes.

Very dissatisfied. I like my priesthood but the system 'Stinks.' I think if Jesus Christ were to return today he would be excommunicated in a month by the Cardinal Ratzinger's of the Church. The system also tries to control a man's mind, wallet, and testicles. There isn't much left after that.

All in all I am quite happy. But would I ask my nephews to think of the priesthood today. Well that is another story. After they finished College, maybe. In fact I have put that question to different groups of Irish priests and they felt the same way. Many feel we are not welcome here now. Besides, the U.S. should produce its own priests or do without. There are some things which cannot be bought. I would not discourage a man from coming but I feel the support systems are no longer there. I feel in our society any one in public ministry is treated like a utility.

Very satisfied. I was drawn into the Priesthood by my love of the Mass and the Eucharist. No matter how difficult the going has been over the years, I have been rejuvenated by celebrating daily Mass. I have often remarked to my colleagues 'Where could we find more beautiful work?'

While they are satisfied with their priesthood, they also have their fair share of problems. I asked them what problems they had as a priest. The following categories were the most enumerated: Overwork 17.4 percent (70), Loneliness 15.7 percent (63), No Problems 12.4 percent (50), Celibacy 10.7 percent (43), and Shortage of Clergy 9.7 percent (39). While these five categories had the most responses, there were 47 response codes created for this question. The following categories also contained large numbers of responses: Administrative Duties 8.5 percent (34), Lack of Sharing/Relationships 7.5 percent (30), Living up to the Expectations Others Have of You 7.3 percent (29), Retirement 6.8 percent (27), Not Enough Time to Get Work Done 6.3 percent (25), Keeping up With a Changing Church 5.8 percent (23), Leadership in the Church 5.8 percent (23), and Illness/Health 5.0 percent (20).

Hoge, Shields, and Griffin (1995) found that between 1970 and 1993 the types and seriousness of the problems experienced by priests had changed very little, although they did report increases in two categories, too much work and unrealistic demands and expectations made by lay people. The two greatest problems these priests were dealing with was coping with authority and satisfying the rising demands of lay people. These problems are also of concern to Irish priests.

The following quote is reflective of what was expressed by these priests:

> Celibacy has been an issue for me. I see both the practical and spiritual value in celibacy. Yet I find it very difficult. If they allowed us to marry I would do so. Particularly so the last few years I'd like someone to share life with. Only since the last 5–10 years has this been an issue for me personally. Yet I have many wonderful friends, married couples, single people, priests, men, women.

I wanted to know what ecclesiological and theological issues they were concerned with. Fifty-one issues were identified, with the following receiving the greatest number of responses: Ordination of Women 19.7 percent (79), Ordination of Married Men 15.2 percent (61), Option for Priests to Marry/Optional Celibacy 12.9 percent (52), Allow Priests who Married to Become Reactivated 12.7 percent (51), Lack of Vocations 10.9 percent (44), Shortage of Priests 10.7 percent (43), Celibacy 9.7 percent (39), and No Concerns 4.5 percent (18). Other issues receiving large numbers of responses include: Marriage Annulments 8.0 percent (31), Lack of Leadership in the Church 8.0 percent (31), Moral Issues 7.0 percent (27), Birth Control 6.7 percent (26), and the Role of Women 5.7 percent (22).

The following comments reflect the priests' thoughts about ecclesiological and theological issues:

> The issue of women and their rightful place in the Church, especially ministry. The Pope's iron hand; His unwillingness to bend, or to realize the Church is really falling apart. He needs to retire and rest.
>
> Priest shortage is going to be devastating if it continues unabated; equating priesthood with celibacy. I am very grateful for the many wonderful women who serve the Church. We would not

exist without them. I do not know how long we can keep them while shutting them out from
the priesthood. On the other hand, most of the really dedicated lay women do not seem to be
interested in being a priest. That being said, I am concerned with the 'feminization' of the Church.

The issues are a continuation of the problems above (previous question on problems they face).
Priests are aging and tired. One contemporary said it best, 'When I look over my shoulder there
is no one following.'

The influence of the Second Vatican Council on the lives of Catholics is an
important topic for any researcher studying contemporary Catholicism (Seidler
and Meyer 1989). I asked the priests if the changes attributed to Vatican II went
too far, far enough, or not far enough in modernizing Catholicism. The largest
group of priests 51.5 percent (207) stated that Vatican II had gone far enough,
while 38.8 percent (156) replied it had not gone far enough, and 8.7 percent (35)
indicated it had gone too far.

The following comments summarize the thoughts of the priests regarding
Vatican II:

It seems to me the changes have only begun—and are moving along nicely; these changes have
a divine momentum and cannot be forced. I believe we are at the end of 500-plus years of hierarchical–clerically led and controlled church. We do not yet see clearly what form/model/
shape the church of the future will take—but the elements of that future model have been set
in motion by the principles and changes begun with Vatican II:—the vernacular in worship; a
return to the Scriptures; a rereading of the Church's history; a participatory liturgy; a reempha-
sis on the local churches; the role of the laity in virtue of their baptism; the recognition of the
goodness of the world and of history as revelatory—and a more humble notion of the role of
the Church; the truth only subsists in the church, which is now seen as being in service of the
larger, more enduring reality, the Kingdom. These will be the creative dynamics and the con-
stitutive elements of the Church of the future—all set in motion by that divinely inspired,
watershed experience, the Vatican II Council. Despite curial efforts to the contrary, I believe
we are on the front edge of a new epoch in the life of the Church.

The changes were not gradual enough and were not adequately explained to the people. Otherwise—the Council was not intended to modernize the Church. But to reform it.

The changes brought about by Vatican II were fine. They opened up the areas of equality,
evangelization, subsidiarity, and ecumenism. They got people taking the mission of the church
seriously. The retrenchment that is taking place is antimission and puts the emphasis back on
the institution as an end in itself rather than as an instrument of grace.

Vatican II went far enough but most Bishops were poor leaders and did not guide an orderly
implementation of the changes approved by Vatican II. For that reason we priests were given
no or little support by our Bishops in our efforts to implement these changes. We struggled
with the people during these years of change. Maybe we are healthier spiritually because of
this. Result: people rely on their personal conscience more today.

In addition to my structured inquiries, on the last page of the survey, I provided
space for the priests to write additional comments. They responded with 38 different types of remarks. The category receiving the greatest number of responses
was Supportive of Project/Good Luck, 16.9 percent (68); Personal Note, 16.2 percent (65); Their Addresses, 5.2 percent (21); Very Fulfilled and Satisfied as a

Priest/Love Priesthood, 5.0 percent (20); and Proud of Role Irish Priests Have Played in the United States, 4.7 percent (19).

The following are indicative of their closing spontaneous comments:

There is no substitute for scholarship and this factor seemed to be ignored in the selection of Bishops. The old boys club has ruled the roost for too long and left us with an anemic hierarchy. Throwing a D.D. at a fool does not change the character of a fool, but makes him a dangerously loose cannon.

For all of the Roman 'stuff,' I feel that the Spirit is moving still, unseen, unheard...It's the little things that keep me energized (not always happy, but nearly always challenged): the goodness of people, the lovely innocence of children, the profound faith of many sick and elderly people and their simple, humble trust in the priest. These and many similar experiences keep me going.

We have been fortunate in this country to have had the influence of Irish priests. I believe our vocation as F.B.I.'s is different in style and character than those who are native sons. The missionary spirit, the leaving of family, the spirituality of the Irish Church have been imported to the U.S. Church. The benefits of this has been evident. We have been loyal and faithful servants. The Irish priest has been very often dismissed by the native born clergy and hierarchy. The hierarchy has not accepted us and today being an Irish-born priest excludes you from that body. We do have some representatives but they are few. The American Church has squandered the talents of its Irish clergy. The Irish clergy have built many great parishes in America. They built a church that has moved Catholics into the mainstream of American life.

The Bishops hang onto the old model. How many of them will confront Mother Angelica's ecclesiology?

Irish priests have served well in Atlanta. For the most part, they have been great leaders of the parishes. People really like them because they work hard and are always available 24 hours a day and they work well with people. Some have become power hungry and have had an impact on the general morale of the clergy.

I can't understand why the newly ordained (say the last 15 years) are so conservative. It's strange for the Pastor to be the liberal at a table with priests who come close to fingering their rosaries during dinner. But most of all my ideas and Philosophy are destroyed by their pre-Vatican views and by their insensitivity to people who don't live up to their Philosophy of God and religion (very very demanding).

Many of us were convinced we had 'arrived' at ordination. We were not encouraged to seek higher education. We were led to believe the 'system' would take care of us and we were treated like morons by Bishops impressed with their own importance. One became labeled a maverick if you made an effort to take some responsibility for your own personal growth and development. We became rivals with one another and learned to compete for promotion to better parishes and 'brotherhood' of the priesthood was nonexistent. The fact that the Church still thrives can only be attributed to the existence and presence of the Holy Spirit. By the way, I love the Church and priesthood and consider myself a damn good priest.

There are potentially so many possibilities in the career-oriented world in which we find ourselves, that priesthood and the sacrifices demanded of it is way down the list. In one sense, this is not a bad thing, because priesthood should not be considered in the realm of it being really a career move. No 'career' on this planet is worth the price of celibacy, yet the priestly calling, the true vocation to express one's faith with one's whole life, can be worth the sacrifices made to achieve its ultimate goal: that is, true intimate union with Christ and all that flows from it. The priest must therefore be a spiritual man above and beyond all other considerations.

Table 2.   Survey Results by Seminary

	St. Patrick's, Carlow N = 110	St. John's N = 49	All Hallows N = 124	St. Peter's N = 50	St. Patrick's, Thurles N = 69
Would Have Preferred to Stay in Ireland					
yes	10.2 (11)	8.5 (4)	3.3 (4)	18.0 (9)	13.0 (9)
no	72.2 (78)	76.6 (36)	86.8 (105)	78.0 (39)	68.1 (47)
mixed	17.6 (19)	14.9 (7)	9.9 (2)	4.0 (2)	18.8 (13)
Adequate Seminary Preparation for U.S. Ministry					
yes	63.3 (69)	53.2 (25)	58.7 (71)	52.0 (26)	42.0 (29)
no	14.7 (16)	31.9 (15)	15.7 (19)	18.0 (9)	33.3 (23)
mixed	22.0 (24)	14.9 (7)	25.6 (31)	30.0 (15)	24.6 (17)
Influenced by American Culture					
yes	77.1 (84)	78.7 (37)	66.9 (81)	46.0 (23)	76.8 (53)
no	22.0 (24)	21.3 (10)	14.0 (17)	36.0 (18)	15.9 (11)
mixed	.9 (1)	none	19.0 (23)	18.0 (9)	7.2 (5)
Irish/Irish American Identity					
Irish	49.1 (54)	42.9 (210)	45.5 (55)	48.0 (24)	48.5 (33)
Irish American	36.4 (40)	46.9 (23)	42.1 (51)	34.0 (17)	38.2 (26)
both	14.5 (16)	10.2 (5)	12.4 (15)	16.0 (8)	11.8 (8)
neither	none	none	none	2.0 (1)	1.5 (1)
Treated Differently by Parishioners					
yes	53.6 (59)	55.1 (27)	51.2 (62)	52.0 (26)	45.6 (31)
no	41.8 (46)	44.9 (22)	37.2 (45)	44.0 (22)	51.5 (35)
mixed	4.5 (5)	none	11.6 (14)	4.0 (2)	.9 (2)
Satisfaction with Priesthood					
very satisfied	65.5 (72)	73.5 (36)	59.5 (72)	78.0 (39)	70.6 (48)
satisfied	25.5 (28)	18.4 (9)	27.3 (33)	22.0 (11)	22.1 (15)
somewhat satisfied	8.2 (9)	6.1 (3)	11.6 (14)	none	4.4 (3)
not satisfied	.9 (1)	2.0 (1)	1.7 (2)	none	2.9 (2)
Problems					
loneliness	13.0 (14)	12.2 (6)	17.2 (21)	16.0 (8)	20.6 (14)
overwork	18.5 (20)	16.3 (8)	18.0 (22)	14.0 (7)	19.1 (13)
celibacy	11.1 (12)	6.1 (3)	13.9 (17)	6.0 (3)	11.8 (8)
priest shortage	14.8 (16)	12.2 (6)	8.2 (10)	6.0 (3)	5.9 (4)
no problems	11.1 (12)	10.2 (5)	13.9 (17)	20.0 (10)	8.8 (6)
Eccesiological and Theological Concerns					
ordination of women	19.6 (21)	16.7 (8)	24.4 (29)	20.0 (9)	17.9 (12)
ordination of married	15.0 (16)	18.8 (9)	18.5 (22)	13.3 (6)	11.9 (8)
new vocations	16.8 (18)	6.3 (3)	9.2 (11)	4.4 (2)	14.9 (10)
priest shortage	10.9 (12)	14.3 (7)	10.6 (13)	10.0 (5)	8.7 (6)
option to marry	13.1 (14)	16.7 (8)	12.6 (15)	13.3 (6)	13.4 (9)
celibacy	11.2 (12)	10.4 (5)	12.6 (15)	6.7 (3)	6.0 (4)
Impact of Vatican II Reforms					
far enough	48.1 (52)	51.0 (25)	51.6 (63)	66.0 (33)	48.5 (33)
too far	6.5 (7)	12.2 (6)	8.2 (10)	8.0 (4)	11.8 (8)
not far enough	45.4 (49)	36.7(18)	40.2 (49)	26.0 (13)	39.7 (27)

Seminary Comparisons

When I was contacting the seminaries to seek their cooperation and participation in this project, I told them I would summarize the findings by seminary and compare and contrast them. I thought this would be a natural thing to do since I asked the respondents what they thought about their seminary preparation. There is little variation between the seminary cohorts in their responses to the survey questions (see Table 2). A lower percent of alumni of All Hallows preferred to stay in Ireland than those from the other seminaries. St. Patrick's, Thurles, had the fewest alumni indicating they were adequately prepared by their seminary. St. Peter's alumni appear to be the most resistant to American culture. There is surprisingly little variation across seminaries in the percent of priests who perceive themselves as being Irish versus Irish American. The same can be said for their answers to whether they have been treated differently because they are from Ireland. A lower percent of All Hallows and St. Patrick's, Carlow, graduates report being very satisfied in their priesthood and All Hallows alumni are more likely to report that they are somewhat satisfied with their priesthood. St. Patrick's, Thurles, graduates report a slightly higher incidence of loneliness. Celibacy, as a problem, is reported by a lower percent of alumni of from St. John's and St. Peter's. A higher percentage of St. Peter's alumni report they have no problems. Regarding eccelsiological and theological issues, vocations was less of an issue for St. Peter's and St. John's alumni. St. Peter's graduates had the highest percentage responding that Vatican II had gone far enough and the lowest percentage in responding thatVatican II had not gone far enough.

CONCLUSION

Irish priests in the United States are a dying breed and it is important to recognize them and learn what we can about their experiences before time runs its course. They have played a significant role in the staffing of parishes in the West, South, and Southwest and they have left their mark throughout the country. It is unlikely that we will see large numbers of Irish priests recruited for service in the United States this century. Ireland and western Europe are experiencing a decline in vocations to the priesthood.

There appears to be very little variation in the responses given by the alumni of the five seminaries regarding their experiences and beliefs. The aging or graying of this population poses real problems for dioceses like Los Angeles, Sacramento, and San Diego. Dioceses in California, Texas, Florida, and even Montana, especially the Diocese of Great Falls–Billings, will be hard-hit by staffing shortages if they do not increase native-born vocations or find another foreign source for priests.

Most Irish priests in the United States either were recruited or volunteered to serve in the United States. They are slightly older than their American counterparts and most of them have been in the United States for between 30–50 years. More than three-quarters of them did not prefer to stay in Ireland and for the most part they believe they were adequately prepared by their seminaries for service in the United States. Although they have come under the influence of American culture, almost half of them consider themselves more Irish than Irish American. About half of them believe they are treated differently because they are Irish and more than half of them are very satisfied with their priesthood. While they are satisfied with their priesthood, they acknowledge that they are frequently overworked and lonely. They believe some of the more pressing ecclesiological and theological issues include the ordination of women, the ordination of married men, celibacy, lack of vocations, and the shortage of priests. About one half of the priests stated that Vatican II reforms had gone far enough, yet almost 40 percent replied the reforms had not gone far enough.

This paper has been one small step toward understanding the experiences and beliefs of an immigrant group of Irish priests in the United States. It would be useful to know what impact these men have had on the Catholic Church, especially its beliefs and practices, and the local communities they have resided in. We need, therefore, to ask their parishioners, fellow clergy and religious, non-Catholics, and the priests themselves about their role. Besides their spiritual impact, it would be interesting to see what impact these priests have had regarding the more physical concerns of the Church, such as the building of parishes, or what has become known in Catholic culture as "brick-and-mortar issues."

Other immigrant groups of American priests also need to be studied. A growing number of Polish, African, Indian, and Asian (e.g., Vietnamese and Philippino) priests are filling the parish staff positions once occupied by Irish-born or native-born priests. This is a topic ripe for further study and analysis.

ACKNOWLEDGMENT

This project was supported by a Hibernian Research Award from the Cushwa Center for the Study of American Catholicism at the University of Notre Dame and an unsolicited donation from an anonymous Irish-born priest. The author is grateful for the assistance provided by Rev. William O. O'Neill, Rector of the Cathedral of St. John the Baptist, Savannah, Georgia, and graduate assistants, Rebecca Holt and Jennifer Futch.

REFERENCES

Burns, G. 1996. "Studying the Political Culture of American Catholicism." *Sociology of Religion*, 57, 37–53.
D'Antonio, W. V. 1994. "Autonomy and Democracy in an Autocratic Organization: The Case of the Roman Catholic Church." *Sociology of Religion*, 55, 379–396.

Dolan, J. P. 1985. *The American Catholic Experience: A History From Colonial Times to the Present.* Garden City, NY: Doubleday.

Fichter, J. H. 1968. *America's Forgotten Priests-What They are Saying.* NY: Harper and Row.

Greeley, A. M. 1972. *The Catholic Priest in the United States: Sociological Investigations.* Washington, DC: United States Catholic Conference.

Hemrick, E. F. and D. R. Hoge. 1991. *A Survey of Priests Ordained Five to Nine Years.* Washington, DC: Seminary Department of the National Catholic Education Association.

Hoge, D. R., J. J. Shields, and D. L. Griffin. 1995. "Changes in Satisfaction and Institutional Attitudes of Catholic Priests, 1970–1993." *Sociology of Religion,* 56, 195–213.

Miller, Kerby A. 1985. *Emigrants and Exiles: Ireland and the Irish Exodus to North America.* NY: Oxford University Press.

Morris, C. 1997. *American Catholic: The Saints and Sinners Who Built America's Most Powerful Church.* NY: Times Books.

The Official Catholic Directory. 1998. New Providence, NJ: Kenedy and Sons.

Seidler, J. and K. Meyer. 1989. *Conflict and Change in the Catholic Church.* New Brunswick, NJ: Rutgers University Press.

Smith, W. L. 1998. "Irish Priests and American Catholicism: A Match Made in Heaven." Pp. 49–73 in J. M. Greer and D. O. Moberg, eds., *Research in the Social Scientific Study of Religion.* Stamford, CT: JAI Press.

Young, L. A. 1998. "Assessing and Updating the Schoenherr–Young Projections of Clergy Decline in the United States Roman Catholic Church." *Sociology of Religion,* 59, 7–23.

PROMISE KEEPERS IN PERSPECTIVE
ORGANIZATIONAL CHARACTERISTICS OF
A MEN'S MOVEMENT

Amy Schindler and Jennifer Carroll Lena

ABSTRACT

The Promise Keepers offers an interesting site for an exploration of the characteristics of an atypical religious bureaucracy. Applying Eugene Litwak's (1985) task specific theory to the Promise Keepers' formal organization and small groups provides us with a framework for understanding how these two contradictory group structures function smoothly in tandem. In this exploratory study, we find that in lieu of a centralized ministry, the Seven Promises of the Promise Keepers serve both to integrate members of the small groups and to maintain an ideal distance between the small groups and the formal organization.

In 1995, Nation of Islam leader Louis Farrakhan made history by organizing the Million Man March. Farrakhan called for African-American men to participate in a national Day of Atonement, and 870,000 of these men marched on Washington, D.C. The Stand in the Gap rally, organized by the Promise Keepers (PK) in Octo-

Research in the Social Scientific Study of Religion, Volume 11, pages 209-224.
Copyright © 2000 by JAI Press Inc.
All rights of reproduction in any form reserved.
ISBN: 0-7623-0656-4

ber of 1997, saw hundreds of thousands of men of all races and all Christian denominations gathered on the National Mall in a similar outburst of spirituality and contrition. Though these all-male marches exemplify the public face of contemporary religious men's movements, there is more to the everyday workings of these organizations than the sweating, enthusiastic men, "chanting "Je-sus" over and over again like the "de-fense" cheer at football games" (Goodstein 1997, p. A1). The Promise Keepers, an all male Christian Evangelical organization which incorporates the small accountability group as an important component of their overall goals, provides an interesting site for an investigation of the organizational structure of a men's movement.

One of the major theoretical challenges to formulating a theory of how primary groups and formal organizations coexist and complement each other is that the two types of group structures often have incompatible functions. Eugene Litwak's task specific theory hypothesizes that, "in a modern society one must have both large-scale formal organizations and small primary groups (i.e., family, neighbors, friends) to manage most tasks" (Litwak 1985, p. 1). Though primary groups are in conflict with formal organizations, they also need formal organizations in order to function at peak efficiency, and vice versa. We will suggest that the two types of organizational structure: the face-to-face small group, and the bureaucracy characterized by a detailed division of labor and large size, coexist in harmony in the Promise Keepers for several reasons. The Seven Promises, which every Promise Keeper must abide by, provide a mechanism for quick integration, similar to the role of the Twelve Steps in Alcoholics Anonymous (AA). Second, the Promises play a slightly different role in the bureaucracy as compared to the small group, thus allowing the two structures to maintain an ideal distance.

Formal organizations in industrialized societies require merit-based assessments of criteria, and differential occupational and geographic mobility based on ability (Litwak 1985, p. 254). These structural characteristics have been considered antithetical to traditional primary group structures by Max Weber and Talcott Parsons. In the late 1800s and early 1900s, European sociologists were concerned that industrialization was leading to a decline of community, family, folk society—in short, that modern industrial society would result in a diminution of primary groups. Weber felt that the form of the monocratic bureaucracy was so contradictory to the structure of the conjugal family that both types of group structures could not exist simultaneously in strong form (Parsons and Henderson 1957). Parsons questioned Weber's assumption that primary groups fulfilled no functions that were essential to the survival of society. Parsons felt that only primary groups could socialize children and provide for the everyday tension management of individuals. Yet, the question remained as to how primary groups could survive within a society that values organization, technology, and science. Parsons' answer was to conceptually isolate formal organizations and primary groups—to create a gulf between these contradictory group structures so as to minimize conflict. Such a separation enables the avoidance of obligations that go beyond work, a rational division of labor, and occupational and geographical mobility to coexist with primary groups in modern society (Parsons and Bales 1955).

However, actual data has shown that formal organizations and primary groups don't operate in completely separate spheres in modern society. For example, the formal organizational structure of the school relies heavily on the involvement of parents for success in educating children, and hospitals rely on patients' families to absorb part of the care-giver role (Fischer and Eustis, 1994; Litwak, Meyer, and Hollister, 1977; Noelker and Bass, 1989). Nor is the isolation of formal organizations and informal groups by any means the ideal situation for managing tasks related to health care, business, socialization, or any of the other myriad aspects of everyday life. Eugene Litwak, in formulating the "task specific theory," hypothesized that both primary groups and formal organizations have continued to thrive because these groups are dependent on each other. The task specific theory suggests that both primary groups and formal organizations can survive in modern industrial society despite these groups having conflicting structures; the two different types of groups manage different and complementary aspects of the same goals, or different goals entirely (Litwak 1985, p. 253). Groups and tasks can be classified according to a common set of structural dimensions in order to determine which tasks can best be performed by which groups. Both primary groups and formal organizations can best deliver those services which match the group's structural characteristics (Litwak 1985, p. 255). Primary groups and formal organizations alike can modify their structures to minimize conflict.

In this paper, we will examine the primary group and formal organizational structure of the Promise Keepers in order to assess the linkage mechanisms which bind the groups together and enable operation at peak efficiency.

METHODOLOGY

In the fall of 1997, the authors of this paper found themselves taking a seminar on organizations with Professor Eugene Litwak. In the process of generating a paper for the course, we became intrigued with the Promise Keepers as an organizational research site which incorporated both small groups and formal organizations. Eugene Litwak's "task specific theory" proceeds from his fascination with the coordination of these two organizational structures (Litwak 1985). We offer this paper as an exploration of how such coordination can occur. Our focus, therefore, is on the characteristics of both types of structures, and on the ideology which facilitates balance between small primary groups and formal organizations. Our investigation of the Promise Keepers' organizational structure centered on an exegesis of Litwak's theory, and on the complementary literature on mutual aid groups and men's organizations. Our study of their ideology derives from the Promise Keepers' official publications and web site, an interview with the New York PK regional representative, and newspaper and magazine articles. Our methods do not include an analysis of the pervasiveness of the official Promise Keepers ideology. We cannot in good faith offer any generalization about the spread of the actual practice of the tenets of PK among the group's adherents. In future studies this question should be addressed and is the complement of the findings in this paper.[1]

INSPIRATION FOR THE ESTABLISHMENT OF THE PROMISE KEEPERS

Promise Keepers founder Coach Bill McCartney, formerly coach of the Colorado Buffaloes, established both the formal organization and the small groups for men who shared with him a common history of work and family problems. An interview with McCartney's wife, Lyndi, revealed that McCartney suffered from addictive behavior, as he "could not drink alcohol without drinking to excess." This addiction led to behavior disorders, and ultimately, to adultery (Goodstein 10/29/97, p. A24). In what he has called "career idolatry," McCartney worked 16–hour days, seven days a week, simultaneously coaching football and basketball teams. His children remarked that even when he was physically with them, he wasn't really there. Evidence of how dangerously out of touch McCartney was with his family came when he never noticed that his wife had developed a severe eating disorder, and when his daughter twice became pregnant out-of-wedlock by two different players on his Colorado football team (Goodstein 10/29/97, p. A24).

McCartney now describes himself as, "a sinner saved by grace" (Goodstein 10/29/97, p. A24). After being "born again," McCartney gave up alcohol; also, his faith brought his family together for prayer services and Bible study. At the same time as he founded the Promise Keepers, the McCartneys began to attend sessions with a Christian counselor to save their marriage, and the coach quit coaching in order to spend more time with his family (Goodstein 10/29/97, p. A24). In a prototype of the PK accountability groups, Coach McCartney committed himself to meeting regularly for prayer and study with four other men (Abraham 1997, p. 53). In his transformation from fallen man to family man, McCartney realized that he was not alone. He felt that, "too many men were getting their priorities out of alignment," and that because of the way he had failed to reach balance in his own life he could see their mistakes (Dart 1997, p. B4). McCartney was inspired to use his experiences to start the Promise Keepers because he "did not see a lot of groups out there helping men deal with these issues" (Dart 1997, p. B4).

In 1996, McCartney founded the Promise Keepers and became the CEO of the organization. He located the Promise Keepers headquarters in Denver, Colorado, where his offices are shared with President Randy Phillips and chief operating officer Thomas Fortson. Also located in Denver are the organization's legal offices, their publications staff, and their stadium event staff, which amounts to

452 paid employees located in the Denver offices. In addition, the Promise Keepers have eight Regional Offices, which are run by a paid staff of 5–10 people, in addition to a somewhat sizable volunteer staff. These offices are responsible for handling local press inquiries, orientation of new members, and providing resources to local churches and members.

On April 1, 1998, 345 members of the Promise Keepers' paid staff were laid off following the decision to shift from a reliance on the fees collected at stadium events to a donation-based income structure, and the ensuing declaration of bankruptcy by the organization. However, the staff continued to work on a volunteer basis during the layoff, and by April 16, 1998, enough donations had poured in to enable the rehiring of the entire staff. In regards to this incredible recovery, Coach Bill McCartney noted that, "Promise Keepers can recall its staff around the United States because the Body of Christ is responding...people who love Jesus have told us they want us to continue. They are saying, 'The ministry of Promise Keepers must go on. There's too much good being done here'" ("Promise Keepers Ends Layoff," http://www.promisekeepers.org/media/, 9/17/98).

On an even more local level, the Promise Keepers maintain thirty-six Field Representative Offices, which are staffed by 2–5 paid employees, as well as some volunteers. These offices cover all fifty states, and their main responsibility is to distribute information about the Promise Keepers on a local level (Benjamin, November 6, 1997). Finally, the Promise Keepers have set as a goal representation in every one of the 400,000 churches in the United States. This will presumably be accomplished through "key men," or "ambassadors," who give personal voice to the Promise Keepers in their own church, or religious congregation (Abraham 1997). Although this is not stated by the organization, there is some indication that these key men are also leaders of small Promise Keeper bible-study groups. This will be addressed in the section entitled "Linkage Mechanisms."

One Promise Keepers New York representative said to us in an interview, "the goal of our organization is to go out of business" (Benjamin, November 6, 1997). The stated grounds for this opinion is that the Promise Keepers' purpose is to act as a temporary mediator to help men rejuvenate social relationships between themselves and the people and organizations in their lives. It is hoped that eventually spirituality and the ability to form meaningful relationships will increase to such a level that Promise Keepers will no longer be needed. To this end, the Promise Keepers maintains no membership list; attendees at the stadium conferences may fill out a "Committed Promise Keepers Card," which enters their information into a database, used only to identify men who may live in geographic areas with little or no Promise Keepers presence. There are also no dues for members, and while stadium conferences used to require a $60 registration fee, now there is no mandatory fee (PK Net, http:///www.promisekeepers.org, October 8, 1997 and September 17, 1998). The organization had an anticipated 1997 budget of $117 million, but ran into serious financial difficulties in the process of switching to donation-based funding. Around 72 percent of the Promise Keepers' income had come from the fees collected at stadium events before the decision to collect only donations. Additional money is generated by the sale of hats, tee-shirts, and other merchandising. In 1995, $14 million was generated through such sales, and another $800,000 came in through the sales of books, CDs, and magazines (PK Net). The Promise Keepers have joined the Evangelical Churches for Financial Accountability, which commits them to a yearly audit from an independent auditing service.

PROMISE KEEPERS' FORMAL ORGANIZATION

A *New York Times* article which appeared on October 27, 1997, entitled, "At Mass Events, Americans Looking to One Another," proclaims that the recent Million Man March, Million Women March, and the Promise Keeper's own Stand In the Gap March on Washington, D.C., "propose solutions based on changing the individual rather than changing government policy, which was generally the strategy decades ago." This is most certainly an astute observation as these rallies were organized to raise consciousness, in the government and in the private sector, but were also trumped as mobilization strategies to push their participants toward action at home. The article goes on to quote Randall Balmer, a professor of religion at Barnard as saying, "People are beginning to move outside of institutions, drawing sustenance from other groups that appear to be more spontaneous and, in many ways, anti-institution" (Janofsky 1997, p. A21). We will argue that nothing could be farther from the truth in regard to the organizational structure of the Promise Keepers; while the Promise Keepers do encourage the existence of small groups, which may be viewed as spontaneous and anti-institutional, they also support a massive infrastructure organized, for the most part, around the model of a bureaucracy. In this section of our paper, we will investigate the nature of the institutional structure of the Promise Keepers in light of Litwak's task specific theory, in order to better understand the exact nature of this structure.

Litwak's argument begins with an understanding of the contention by Parsons (1955), Weber (1957), and others that formal organizations and primary groups have contradictory structures. This implies that the two structures are better suited to fulfilling different tasks. Formal organizations motivate people through economic incentives, and emphasize ties free of affectivity, dominated by impersonal, objective evaluations, and thus formal organizations, according to Litwak, are best suited to handle tasks requiring technical knowledge. Litwak writes that the division of labor that creates technical knowledge, "requires that the experts only deal with people in segmental, specialized circumstances, and not have continual face-to-face interaction" (Litwak 1985, p. 11).

We have been proceeding from the assumption that primary groups and organizations each have structures more compatible with particular types of tasks. However, Litwak asserts that multiple tasks and structures are possible, and that while tasks and structures may differ, goal orientations may be shared. In regard to the former, Litwak writes that, "there is a continuum of organizational structures as well as one of tasks. Primary groups can handle the most extreme nonuniform tasks, human relations structures can manage moderately nonuniform tasks, and rationalistic structures can manage nonuniform tasks least of all" (Litwak 1985, p. 14). It is clear that we must first look at the attributes of the formal organizational structure of the Promise Keepers in order to match this structure to tasks, and then to understand its compatibility with the primary group model it supports.

The question still remains as to how we would classify the organizational model represented by the Promise Keepers using Litwak's parameters. He often classifies organizations along the dimensions of: continuous proximity, long-term commitment, size, internalized commitment of individual to organization, the presence of a detailed division of labor, recruitment on technical knowledge, and presence of a common lifestyle. For comparison's sake, we will classify Weber's typical monocratic bureaucracy along these dimensions. Such an organization would be classified by lack of continuous proximity, lack of long-term commitment, large size, no internalized commitment by the individual, a detailed division of labor, recruitment on technical knowledge, and lack of a common lifestyle.

There is evidence that demonstrates that the organization of the Promise Keepers makes interesting departures from the classical Weberian monocratic bureaucracy. The Promise Keepers match this model on the first three guidelines: lack of continuous proximity, lack of long-term commitment, and large size all describe this organization. However, members of the Promise Keepers staff often describe or demonstrate internalized personal commitment to the organization. This is due to the organization's recruitment, not on the basis of technical knowledge, but rather on the basis of this very commitment. The organization's New York regional representative explained to us that technical training is provided for those who do not already possess it during the hiring process (Benjamin, November 6, 1997). Recruitment is therefore not based on an evaluation of technical skills, though training does result in a detailed division of labor. One additional departure from the monocratic bureaucratic model would be the emphasis within the organization on a common lifestyle. This selection bias may be a product of internal recruitment, or it may be a by-product of the nature of the tasks that the Promise Keepers purports as goals.

SIMILARITIES WITH RELIGIOUS BUREAUCRACIES

There are very few traditional organizational structures which have such internalized commitment and such reliance on a common lifestyle. The only groups which are similarly situated on the continuum of structures are other religious bureaucracies. Jim Jones' Peoples Temple was one such organization. Here too, we see evidence of an organization with a highly detailed division of labor, large size, and lacking continuous proximity between its members. We also see evidence in the Peoples Temple of recruitment, not on the basis of technical knowledge, but on the basis of one's internalized commitment to the goals of the organization. John Hall, in "Collective Welfare as Resource Mobilization in the Peoples Temple: A Case Study of a Poor People's Religious Movement," noted that, "in the past century, secular culture itself has undergone a transition from predominately folk styles to an overwhelmingly mass culture, and some of the churches have succumbed to 'fighting fire with fire' by adopting the technology and sensibilities of mass culture to promote their own message. The upshot of 'modernization' is that religions today are businesses, often big businesses" (Hall 1988, p. 66S). Much like the Peoples Temple, the Promise Keepers are big business and utilize the latest technology, from audio-visual packages to the Internet to disseminate their message. What differentiates the Peoples Temple and the Promise Keepers is the latter's incorporation of small groups as necessary alternative structural places in which members can experience the formal organization. Promise Keepers not only have much in common with other religious bureaucracies, but also share many characteristics with self-help groups such as Alcoholics Anonymous, which is altogether in keeping with the foundation of Alcoholics Anonymous as an offshoot of a zealous religious sect, the Oxford Group.

SIMILARITIES WITH SELF-HELP GROUPS

In the process leading to realization and recovery, self-help and mutual aid groups often have officially articulated steps which their members must follow. In Alcoholics Anonymous, these steps are widely known as the Twelve Steps. McCartney similarly outlines Seven Promises to which a Promise Keeper must ascribe. Promise Keepers are men who:

1. Honor Jesus Christ through worship, prayer, and obedience to His Word in the power of the Holy Spirit.
2. Pursue vital relationships with a few other men, understanding that they need brothers to help them keep their promises.
3. Practice spiritual, moral, ethical, and sexual purity.
4. Build strong marriages and families through love, protection, and biblical values.
5. Support the mission of their church by honoring and praying for their pastors and by actively giving their time and resources.
6. Reach beyond any racial and denominational barriers to demonstrate the power of biblical unity.
7. Influence their world, being obedient to the Great Commandment (love— Mark 12:30–31) and the Great Commission (evangelism—Matthew 28:19–20) (Gorsuch 1994, p. 25).

The Promise Keepers formal organization presents these Seven Promises as "clear-cut purposes," which provide, "a fairly simple foundation upon which to build a men's group" (Gorsuch 1994, p. 25).

The second Promise that the Promise Keepers must hold to is being, "committed to pursuing vital relationships with a few other men, understanding that he needs brothers to help him keep his promises" (Horner, Ralston, and Sunde 1995, p. 11). The Promise Keepers organization feels that this promise can best be fulfilled through men forming small "accountability groups." Promise Keepers suggests that "accountability" means the willingness of a man to submit his life to a group to whom he grants, "the right to inspect key personal and professional matters" (Abraham 1997, p. 49). The small self-help or accountability groups formed by men who are part of the Promise Keepers are primary groups that function in tandem with the larger Promise Keeper formal organization. The accountability groups share the structural characteristics of the self-help groups, in that they do not require continuous proximity, a detailed division of labor, or recruitment on the basis of technical knowledge. The accountability groups typically meet once or twice a week, the division of labor is only that between the rotating leader and the members, and the recruitment is on the basis of a common interest in studying the Bible and becoming better husbands and fathers (Gorsuch 1994, p. 26). The accountability groups are also similar to mutual aid groups in that they are moderate in size, usually eight to ten men. They require an internalized commitment to the worldview of the Promise Keepers and a long term commitment to belong to the group and to further spiritual growth through continued Bible study and interaction with other men in the group setting. A common lifestyle in aspects that pertain to the goals of the group, such as a shared belief in Christianity and the value of monogamous marriage is also necessary. Thus, the primary groups that Promise Keeper accountability groups most match in structure are self-help or mutual aid groups, as we will see below.

The goals of the Promise Keepers small groups are to help men learn to modify destructive behaviors and to break out of cycles of isolation through developing trust and intimacy with other men and through learning to, "live with Jesus Christ as the center of your life, one day at a time" (Gorsuch 1994, p. 69). According to the literature published by Promise Keepers, the feminism of the 1960s and 1970s raised a debate in American consciousness about the nature of sexuality that has left the American male caught in a series of "double-binds" with respect to his masculinity (Gorsuch 1994, p. 102). The double-bind pulls men between the extremes of emotionality and stoicism; hard work toward promotions and being a meaningful presence at home; and other paradoxes involved in the modern "sensitive" norm of masculinity (Gorsuch 1994, p. 102). Uncertainty over the male role in the modern family, community, and workplace, leads to three patterns of destructive behavior: 1) addictive behaviors having to do with sex, chemicals, alcohol, work, and so forth; 2) the development of the "loner" or "friendless" nature; and, 3) cycles of isolation that are characterized by burnout, depression, and wounding (feeling betrayed by self and others) (Gorsuch 1994).

The Promise Keepers small group format of Bible study and mutual aid is designed to combat these destructive activities and behaviors by replacing them with more positive interpersonal interactions. The growth of personal relationships, according to this worldview, is key to coming to a belief in God through Jesus Christ, developing faith, and learning to love other men in a "manly way" (Gorsuch 1994, p. 12). The steps involved in fostering these relationships in a small group setting are very clearly identified in available guides for establishing PK accountability groups, *Brothers!: Calling Men Into Vital Relationships* (1994) and *Promise Keepers Study Series* (1995). The progressive steps of the group relational goals are likened to a baseball diamond, as the Promise Keepers in keeping with earlier forms of "muscular Christianity" often rely on sports metaphors to talk about spiritual growth (Gorsuch 1994, p. 16). First base is "Acquaintances," and is the stage when men learn to accept one another without judgment. Second base is "Friends," and it is at this stage that the men learn to encourage one another by taking an active role in a brother's life (Gorsuch 1994, p. 14). Third base is "Brothers," when the men are expected to lovingly exhort one another to new spiritual and emotional heights. And, home plate is "Christlike," and the stage at which the men are prepared to be men of integrity and "become more like Christ" (Gorsuch 1994, p. 19). Each of these bases involves building trust and commitment between men by breaking down relations of self-protection and encouraging cooperation and sharing; by developing teamwork and listening skills; and by developing intimacy skills, interdependence, and mutual respect (Gorsuch 1994, pp. 19, 38). When followed through in a full course of Bible study and rap sessions, these steps are meant to lead to an end in destructive or harmful behaviors and continued reliance on constructive patterns of caring, accountability, and leadership that will extend beyond the confines of the group and into work, home, and the community.

The structural characteristics of the goals of PK small groups, discussed above, match the structural characteristics of the self-help style group. Forming caring relationships does not require continuous proximity, nor is it reliant on a detailed division of labor or recruitment on the basis of technical knowledge. Indeed, for the type of self-help groups that resemble the PK accountability groups, group leaders are often most effective when they are men who merely have experience with the same types of issues the men in the group are dealing with—in this case, abuse, addiction, infidelity, crises of masculinity, and questions of faith, all of which can be addressed in a nontechnical way. According to Marc Galanter, "the admission of helplessness before one's problems and the bonding together with those similarly afflicted appears to work well as a self-help formula for many compulsive behaviors" (Galanter 1989, p. 188). The only division of labor at all in the group is that between leader and group members, but even this division is minimized by terming the leader a "player-coach" (Gorsuch 1994, p. 38).

However, forming a circle of companionship and trust is not a task which could be routinized, or which would benefit from a high division of labor. Building trust and brotherhood are also tasks which require a small sized group, generally, though Litwak has referred to ethnic subsocialization groups as larger units of acquaintances, most friendship groups are small or moderate in size (Litwak 1985, p. 231). Following the steps prescribed to overcome destructive behaviors, and keeping to the Seven Promises requires an internalized commitment to the worldview of the Promise Keepers, and also requires a long term commitment to attend sessions with other men. Finally, the tasks of eliminating destructive behaviors and building intimate relationships necessarily call for a degree of common lifestyle among the men involved.

Self-help groups, such as those formed to deal with addictions, dependencies, and bereavement, are similar in format and aims to the PK accountability groups. Structurally, such groups resemble voluntary associations (Lieberman and Borman 1979, p. 17). There are six characteristics commonly attributed to self-help groups:

1. The group is voluntary, often small, and may exist with or without a parent organization. The group may be firmly organized or in the process of organizing. Members seek both assistance for themselves and to be of assistance to other members of the group.
2. Group members share a common problem or interest; for example, an unmet need, a handicap, or a life-disrupting problem.
3. Group members share a common purpose.
4. Group members share common experiences. Along with sharing a common problem, they have usually experienced rejections or unsatisfactory relations with agencies and/or society in general.
5. Groups use common approaches to solving problems; for example, face-to-face social interaction, activity, and advocacy.
6. The group is likely to be committed to a cause or ideology. (Weber and Cohen 1982, p. 15)

Additionally, self-help groups are usually understood to be noninstitutional, citizen-organized groups, that are founded to address needs that are not met by established institutions (Weber and Cohen 1982, p. 334). An empirical study of self-help and support groups conducted in 1978 by Nancy Gourash, in the *American Journal of Community Psychology*, found that help-seeking declines with age, and that it is more common for whites than blacks to join self-help groups. Also, self-help users tend to be young, white, educated, middle-class, and female. Newer studies have shown a shift in the profile of self-help group members, as with an increase in the range and diversity of problems addressed by such groups. Class is no longer a differentiating factor in membership (Lieberman and Borman 1979, p. 120).

Self-help focuses the responsibility for change on the individual within a support system of other individuals sharing the same problem (Weber and Cohen 1982, p. 304). This approach assumes the locus of the problem lies with the individual. However, for an analysis of the self-help groups to begin and end with an individual/psychological explanation would draw attention away from the principles of organization that govern this type of association (Weber and Cohen 1982, p. 10).

LINKAGE MECHANISMS

One of the major challenges to formulating a theory of groups is that primary structures and formal organizations often have incompatible functions. Primary groups are in conflict with formal organizations, but they also need formal organizations in order to function at peak efficiency. If these two types of groups become too tightly bound, there is a danger of one structure destroying the other; yet, if the groups are too distant, they do not perform effectively. Litwak suggests that the answer to this theoretical dilemma lies in a "balance" theory of coordination (Litwak, Meyer, and Hollister 1977). Balance entails the operation of organizational linkages that bring primary groups and formal organizations to a midpoint in distance, which is the key to coordinating complementary needs for common goals. The assumptions behind a balance theory and the operation of linkages is that: 1) there is an asymmetry of linkages—primary groups have different problems reaching into formal organizations; 2) primary groups and formal organizations have some overlapping goals; and, 3) primary groups and formal organizations are not always separated geographically. Linkages keep the two structures at an optimal distance.

We have been progressively heading toward an understanding of how small groups and a large organizational structure can work within the same corporation. We have suggested that comprehending this arrangement requires that we understand the structure of the small group and the structure of the formal organization, as well as the tasks or goals they seek to fulfill. Seeking the ideal balance which allows the two structures to work in concert has raised some concerns earlier in this paper. First, we mentioned in the section on the Promise Keepers' formal organization the role played by "key men" or "ambassadors," who are often also playing the role of leader in an accountability group. This suggests that some role sharing is accomplished by individuals who have important, but different positions in the formal organization and the small group. Though representatives of the formal organization publicly disavow having any direct control over the functioning of the small groups, the dual role of the key man as representative of the formal organization and leader of the small group implies that the opposite is the case. There is a literal overlay of staff between the two structures. This role sharing of individuals in the organization is a link between the formal organization and the small group; however, we also must understand how rank-and-file members of the Promise Keepers build their relationships with each other on the basis of common beliefs despite their divergence along the lines of race, class, and even denomination.

The Seven Promises which bind members to each other, both within the formal organization and within the small groups, suggest that an explanation of their function in both might be warranted. The Seven Promises serve as the official belief system of the Promise Keepers formal organization and of the Promise Keepers accountability groups. Members of the self-help group collective necessarily adopt an ideology or belief system which needs to be understood not just as a conversion of belief on the individual level, but as a mechanism of rapid integration used to bind group members together, as these "fixed codes of behavior" are applicable across class and racial boundaries (Galanter 1989, p. 182). The underlying ideology of a self-help group like Alcoholics Anonymous is that there is a specific set of beliefs for members to adopt which promises improvement in psychological and physical well-being. Alcoholics Anonymous was inspired by the transcendental religious experience of its charismatic leader, Bill W., and the Promise Keepers found a similar inspiration in the religious awakening of its leader, Bill McCartney. It should be no surprise to the reader that ten of the twelve steps of Alcoholics Anonymous were derived from Bill W.'s experiences with the Oxford Group, a turn of the century zealous religious sect (Galanter 1989, pp. 177–178). From the start, "AA displayed characteristics of a charismatic sect: strongly felt shared belief, intense cohesiveness, experiences of altered consciousness, and a potent influence on member's behavior" (Galanter 1989, p. 178). These promises also represent a strategy for joining together to end disruptive behaviors so that normal occupational, marital, and community roles can be resumed (Wasserman and Danforth 1988, p. 63).

Mellen Kennedy and Keith Humphreys, in "Understanding Worldview Transformation in Members of Mutual Help Groups" (1994), argue that across contexts and cultures, psychological healing requires changes in the "worldview" or "assumptive world" of the sufferer (Kennedy and Humphreys 1994, p. 182). The assumptive world is "a highly structured, complex, interacting set of values, expectations, and images of oneself and others, which guide and are in turn guided by a person's perceptions and behavior and which are closely related to his emotional states and his feelings of well-being" (Kennedy and Humphreys 1994, p. 182). Mutual help groups are one setting where a change in worldview can take place. Worldview changes may include transformations in beliefs about the self, relationships with others, universal order, and the problem area (Kennedy and Humphreys 1994, p. 187).

Using the worldview transformation approach to understand the dynamics of self-help groups, it becomes clear that the self-help group is not just a program for treatment, recovery, or coping, but is a community of belief (Kennedy and Humphreys 1994, p. 182). A worldview is at the core of the mutual help group, and this set of beliefs which constitutes the approach to life advocated by the group leadership is passed on to members through a specialized system of teachings (Kennedy and Humphreys 1994, p. 183). Well established self-help groups, such as Alcoholics Anonymous, have developed extensive literature to explain their "program." AA has the "Twelve Steps," which outline the nature of the problem addressed by the group, goals to strive for in overcoming this problem, and courses of action necessary to obtain those goals (Kennedy and Humphreys 1994, p. 184). Also, AA runs an independent press, Alcoholics Anonymous World Services, which publishes the approved literature that outlines the road to spiritual and physical recovery for alcoholics—books like *The Big Book*, *As Bill Sees It*, and *Came to Believe* (Schaler 1996, p. 10). *Twelve Traditions* was published by AA in an effort to guide group management, and this along with the other publications outlines a concrete belief system and strategy to be adopted by individuals who make up AA groups, and for the leadership of such groups (Lieberman and Borman 1979, p. 34).

Self-help groups, in placing the responsibility for healing and growth on the individual within the context of group membership, demand that group members quickly come to trust and rely on one another. This trust is expected to quickly take root between individuals who have no prior acquaintance outside of the group. Litwak (1985) suggests that short-term friendships, often developed in situations of high mobility like urban neighborhoods and college dorms, must have "mechanisms of quick integration" to enable new friends to form trusting and affectionate bonds in a very short time period (Litwak 1985, p. 209). Within the context of self-help groups, we would like to suggest that common beliefs and worldviews, as outlined by the group leadership or parent organization, serve as a mechanism of rapid integration between group members.

Linkages also keep formal organizations and primary groups at an optimal closeness. The "Seven Promises of a Promise Keeper" function as the written statement of business ethics for the organization, as well as functioning as the impetus for joining an accountability group (promise two), and dictating the norms of conduct within it. It was the third promise, "Practice spiritual, moral, ethical, and sexual purity," which prompted Bill McCartney and his staff to join the Evangelical Council for Financial Accountability. The sixth promise, "Reach beyond any racial and denominational barriers to demonstrate the power of biblical unity," has resulted in the preferential hiring of many Black, Hispanic and Asian men within the formal organization. In these examples we can see how The Seven Promises function as an influence on the formal organization.

The Seven Promises have a somewhat different impact on the accountability groups. The second promise, "Pursue vital relationships with a few other men..." is the very reason behind the establishment of such groups under the rubric of the parent organization. Often the perspective of the small group member on the purpose of the Seven Promises is the voice that we hear from representatives of the formal organization. To that end, President Randy Phillips states, "The promises are not designed as a new list of commandments...rather they are meant to guide us...to transform us within so that we might see transformation in our homes, among our friends, in our churches, and ultimately, in our nation." (Abraham, 1997, p. 34) The Seven Promises seem to have a deep meaning to the members of the small group: they are their raison d'être, they provide a model for appropriate behavior, and even a model for individual action toward social change.

Litwak's task-specific model has provided some very useful guidelines for analyzing the structural dimensions of different groups. Among these parameters are size, geographic proximity, length of commitment, detailed division of labor, recruitment on technical knowledge, presence of a common lifestyle, and internalized commitment. Our results suggest that the centrality of the Seven Promises in functioning as a method of quick integration, and a linkage mechanism that maintains optimal distance between the formal organization and the small group, suggest additional dimensions by which to classify groups. While Litwak defines internalized commitment in terms of commitment to an individual or a family, we suggest that internalized commitment to an ideal, or a set of ideals, should also be considered as a structural characteristic. Internalized commitment to the Seven Promises not only binds individual members to the formal organization, and members of small groups to each other, but serves as a mechanism by which members might move to different groups with minimal disruption. In a normal friendship structure the commitment is to an individual personality. Within AA, or other self-help structures, commitment might be to a mentor, or a survivor of the affliction. Here, however, all members are equal and instant "brothers" because the structure of the integration mechanisms assumes gradual assimilation, and accomplishes this with the help of explicit guidelines, and a clearly stated belief system. The facade of a familial bond is a strong one and could not be possible without such a formalized system of belief and integration.

The Promise Keepers offers an interesting site both for an exploration of the structural characteristics of an atypical religious bureaucracy and as a contemporary men's movement. In our exploratory study, we find that in lieu of a centralized ministry, the Seven Promises of a Promise Keeper serve to integrate members of the small groups and to maintain an ideal distance between the small groups and the formal organization. We conclude the mechanisms of rapid integration which promote a feeling of brotherhood on the basis of a shared commitment to the Seven Promises, allow the Promise Keepers to maintain a balance between the small groups and the large bureaucracy.

NOTE

1. In contrast to Litwak, Arlie Hochschild, in her recent book, *The Time Bind*, finds that expressive values once manifested in the family have currently been transposed into the workplace.

REFERENCES

Abraham, K. 1997. *Who Are the Promise Keepers?: Understanding the Christian Men's Movement.* New York: Doubleday.

Benjamin, R. November 6, 1997. Interviewed by Jennifer Lena, telephone. New York.

Dart, B. 1997, September 28. "From Gridiron Glory to Bully Pulpit, Founder has Critics." *The Providence Sunday Journal,* B1.

Farrakhan, L. 1997. "Holy Day of Atonement." speech, 10/16/97. online. http//www.dayofatonement.org/.

Fischer, L. R. and N. N.Eustis. 1994. "Care at Home: Family Caregivers and Home Caregivers." In E. Kahana, D.E. Biegel, and M.L. Wykle (eds.) *Family Caregiving Across the Lifespan.* Thousand Oaks, CA: Sage Publications.

Galanter, Marc. 1989. *Cults: Faith, Healing and Coercion.* NY: Oxford University Press.

Goodstein, L. 1997, October 29. "A Marriage Gone Bad Struggles for Redemption." *The New York Times,* A24.

_____. 1997, September 29. "For Christian Men's Group, Racial Harmony Starts at the Local Level." *The New York Times,* p. A12.

_____. 1997, October 5. "Hundreds of Thousands Gather On the Mall in a Day of Prayers." *The New York Times,* p. A1.

Gorsuch, G. 1994. *Brothers!: Calling Men Into Vital Relationships.* Colorado Springs: Navpress.

Hall, J. R. 1988. "Collective Mobilization as Resource Mobilization in Peoples Temple: A Case Study of a Poor People's Religious Social Movement." *Sociological Analysis,* 49, 64–77.

Horner, B., R. Ralston, and D. Sunde. 1995. *Promise Builders Study Series.* Boulder: Promise Keepers.

Janofsky, M. 1997, October 27. "At Mass Events, Americans Looking To One Another." *The New York Times,* A21.

Kennedy, M., and K. Humphreys. 1994. "Understanding Worldview Transformation in Members of Mutual Help Groups." In F. Lavoie, T. Borkman, and B. Gidron (eds.), *Self-Help and Mutual Aid Groups: International and Multicultural Perspectives.* NY: Haworth.

Lieberman, M. and L. D. Borman. 1979. *Self-Help Groups for Coping With Crisis.* Washington: Jossey-Bass.

Litwak, E. 1985. *Helping the Elderly.* NY: The Guilford Press.

Litwak, E., H. J. Meyer, and C. D. Hollister. 1977. "The Role of Linkage Mechanisms Between Bureaucracies and Families: Education and Health as Empirical Cases in Point." In R.J. Liebert and A. W. Imershein (eds.), *Power, Paradigm, and Community Research.* Beverly Hills, CA: Sage.

Noelker, L. S. and D. M. Bass. 1989. "Home Care for Elderly Persons: Linkages Between Formal Organizations and Informal Caregivers. *The Journals of Gerontology,* 44, S63–S70.

Parsons, T. and R. F. Bales. 1955. *Family, Socialization, and Interaction Process.* Glencoe, IL: Free Press.

Parsons, T. and A. M. Henderson. 1957. *Max Weber: The Theory of Social and Economic Organizations.* NY: Free Press.

PK Net, http://www.PromiseKeepers.org, October 8, 1997.

Schaler, J. A. 1996. "Spiritual Thinking in Addiction-Treatment Providers: The Spiritual Belief Scale (SBS)." *Alcohol Treatment Quarterly,* 14 (3), 7–33.

Wasserman, H. and H. E. Danforth. 1988. *The Human Bond: Support Groups and Mutual Aid.* NY: Springer.

Weber, G. H. and L. M. Cohen. 1982. *Beliefs and Self-Help: Cross-Cultural Perspectives and Approaches.* NY: Human Sciences Press.

DEMOGRAPHIC CHANGE AND SECULARIZATION IN AN ASIAN NEW RELIGIOUS MOVEMENT
THE BRAHMA KUMARIS IN THE WESTERN WORLD, PART II

Julia Day Howell and Peter L. Nelson

ABSTRACT

This paper examines the interaction between demographic change, social structural change, and ideological change in a New Religious Movement, the Brahma Kumaris, which in the last three decades has spread from its home in India to the West and other parts of the world. Focusing on the Australian branches that have supplied much of the impetus for the spread of the movement beyond India, the paper documents the gradual normalization of the age profile from a prototypically youthful base and the increasing incorporation of career people into its membership. Mobilization of Western members' professional skills to design culturally-appropriate outreach activities has lessened the tendency of certain institutional adaptations to isolate the organization from potential new recruits. The growing proportion of

Research in the Social Scientific Study of Religion, Volume 11, pages 225-239.

mature and professionally engaged members has also facilitated a softening of the organization's "world rejecting" (Wallis 1979; 1984) stance in Western branches. A sliding of the movement toward secularization is arrested, however, by differentiation of the core spiritual activities of fully committed members from their activities concerned with service to the wider society.

INTRODUCTION

The Brahma Kumaris (BKs), founded in 1937 in what is now Pakistan, have become an international movement. They now claim 450,000 "students" (full members and others) in 3200 centers spread across 70 countries and territories (www.bkwsu.com). Until recently, however, understanding of the movement's organizational structure and membership profile has been based substantially on studies of the organization in India (e.g., Babb 1986; cf. Howell 1998; Whaling 1995). Our previous report in this serial (Howell and Nelson, 1997), contributed to understanding of the BKs' internationalization by detailing structural adaptations made by Western branches in response to local social conditions and analyzing how those adaptations reflect on Stark's (1987) model of New Religious Movement (NRM) survival. Here we extend our analysis of BK accommodation to new environments by examining the way internal demographic changes have affected the Western branches' relationships with the wider society.

Our analysis is based primarily on interviews, participant observation, and survey material gathered in Australia. Australian BKs have played an especially prominent role in founding "overseas" branches, not just in Australia but in other Western as well as Asian countries. Our supplementary interviews and observations in the principal BK centers in London, England, and Mt. Abu, India, as well as those done in regional centers in New Delhi, India, Nuneham, Courtney and Oxford England, and in New York and Los Angeles in the United States, suggest that the Australian BK experience is broadly similar to that of other Western branches. (The partial exceptions are branches in England made up predominantly of Indian migrants and their children. Whereas in other Western countries people of Indian descent make up a small percentage of the membership, for example just 8 percent in Australia, about two thirds of BKs in the United Kingdom have an Indian background [Howell and Nelson 1997, p. 9]).

As described in our 1997 article (pp. 6–7), the core beliefs of the Brahma Kumaris (colloquially known as "Raja Yoga" for its meditation technique) are a millenarian variant of Hindu traditions. Their theology is monotheistic, and the goal of enlightenment is replaced by one of rebirth in a heavenly Golden Age. They believe that the cataclysmic destruction of the world is rapidly approaching and is but another closing of the endlessly repeating Hindu cycle of four ages; its Golden Age is followed by progressively deteriorating Silver, Bronze and Iron Ages. Now the world is in the final days of decay and ruin, what the BKs call the

"Confluence Age." It is a dire moment just at the close of the Iron Age, but nonetheless a time of special opportunity. Those who modify their lifestyle to purify body and mind and use BK meditation practices can look forward to new life in the Golden Age after the rapidly impending destruction of the present world. All others must wait to be reborn in one of the later and inferior ages suitable to their lesser spiritual capacities.

These beliefs have been understood to imply that "work in the world" is useless, whether it consists of efforts to achieve salvation through acts of charity or contributions to positive social change. Accordingly, conventional BK outreach activities have been limited to the objective of making Brahma Baba's "Godly knowledge" available to those souls fated to accept it so that they may begin the purification that will qualify them for their destined place in the Golden Age. Other souls, in the conventional BK view, can only be taught to calm their minds in order to alleviate the distress of the troubles into which the world is descending. The movement thus has been strongly inward-looking, focused on drawing in "Baba's children," with each child who already is found working strenuously to qualify for the on-rushing Golden Age.

In our 1997 article we analyzed the way in which certain residential and structural modifications that were necessitated by the extension of the movement to Western countries reinforced the inward-looking and world rejecting orientation of the BKs and created clear boundaries between insiders and outsiders. The sharpening of insider-outsider boundaries of the movement in the West helped the BKs there to sustain a culturally alien belief system and highly demanding spiritual regime, thereby mitigating one of the factors, cultural incongruity, that Stark (1987, pp. 13–23) identifies as detractors from the viability of NRMs. However sharpened movement boundaries also compounded the problem of recruitment already constricted by celibacy rules. We showed that in the West (unlike India) this potential cost of isolation was counterbalanced by the requirement for full members (*brahmins*) to maintain outside employment (Howell and Nelson 1997).

Here we examine the way changes in the demographic profile of the Australian membership and the increasing recruitment of people with highly developed career commitments have combined with the requirement that *brahmins* do outside paid work to minimize structural tendencies towards isolation. Further, we show that these centrifugal tendencies have been associated over time with a softening of the "world rejecting" stance of the movement. This ideational accommodation has benefits for movement "success" (Stark 1987), but it also carries potential costs in that it raises the possibility of a slide toward secularization and thereby loss of the movement's distinctive "spiritual" appeal. Nonetheless, the BKs in the West have been able to preserve their attractiveness to people seeking "other-worldly" salvation by retaining, out of public view, a core of restricted and highly charged spiritual activities for fully committed members.

DEMOGRAPHIC CHANGE

The involvement of nearly all Western BKs in outside work creates social contacts that have the potential to overcome the isolation that their purity rules and
high levels of coresidence tend to create (Howell and Nelson 1997), but the significance of work contacts can vary with the level of people's commitments to
that work. Also an individual's maturity, of which age is one indicator, is likely to
moderate the extent to which competing commitments and views developed
through them are likely to be asserted. These demographic factors have changed
over the history of the organization in Australia, as revealed in our interviews with
long-time members and in the survey we carried out in 1992.

Our questionnaire, including questions on social background, types and frequency of involvement with the organization, and attitudes to spiritual and social
issues, was distributed in all of the Australian BK centers to people considered by
the center officials to be following all the rules and practices incumbent upon
fully committed members. Questionnaires were received from 194 of the estimated 250 full members. (As BK officials in the United States and the United
Kingdom did not wish to have the questionnaire distributed there, the Australian
survey is the sole source of the statistical material presented here.)

Changing Age Distributions

Long-term *brahmins* have reported that very young adults predominated in the
first cohort of Australian BKs. But as this cohort came into their thirties during the
1980s a wider range of age groups started to join the movement, in a process of
"like attracting like" that Wilson (1987, p. 39) has observed in other maturing
NRMs. The aging of the membership is reflected in the age profile evidenced in
the 1992 survey that was distributed to all *brahmins* considered old enough (pre-
teen and above) to have made a personal commitment to the requisite practices.
Thus, discounting young children who could not figure in the survey, there is a
fairly normal age distribution among the 194 respondents, ranging from 10 to 84
years with a median age of 35 and a mean of 36.5. This compares to a median age
of 31.9 for the whole Australian population at the time, according to the
Australian Bureau of Statistics (1998).

Occupational Backgrounds

Along with the influx of people across a wider range of ages has come a greater
diversity of occupations among the membership. Many of the young adults who
entered the movement in the 1970s had not yet committed themselves to a trade
or profession and were encouraged to find work that would not redirect too much
of their time and attention outside the organization. However long-time members
who had been active in the mid-1980s reported that from that time new recruits

Table 1. Employment Categories: Australian Brahma Kumaris (ages 10-84) in 1992 and the Australian Population (aged 14+) in 1991

Group	Count	BK Survey Percent	Population Percent
Business	5	2.58	NI
Clerk	31	16.00	9
Entertainment	8	4.12	NI
Home duties	11	5.67	17
Management & administration	22	11.30	7
Machine & plant operators	1	0.52	NI
Pensioner	5	2.58	16
Professional	33	17.00	9
Sales & personal service	24	12.40	10
Self-employed	2	1.03	NI
Student	18	9.28	8
Trades	20	10.30	15
Unemployed	2	1.03	5
Unskilled	7	3.61	5
Not stated	5	2.58	NI

Notes: NI = category not included in the NCADA survey. "Pensioner" = all in receipt of monetary benefits from the state; "Student" includes secondary and tertiary.

Sources: 1992 survey of Australian BKs by the authors and Australian National Campaign Against Drug Abuse (NCADA) Social Issues Survey (Social Science Data Archives 1991).

included many who had already established themselves in an occupation and did not accept the necessity of leaving that type of work. We see from the 1992 survey that the *brahmins* by then numbered amongst themselves a high proportion of professional people (17 percent) and persons with other areas of high skill and training. Also, only a very small percentage of BKs were unskilled (3.6 percent) and unemployed (1.0 percent in a country where the national rate of unemployment was around 10.5 percent).[1] Table 1 provides the survey breakdown for employment together with national employment figures for persons aged fourteen and older from the National Campaign Against Drug Abuse Social Issues Survey (Social Science Data Archives, 1991).

Educational Backgrounds

The levels of education reported reflect the predominance among BKs of people in jobs requiring high levels of skill and education. More than half (53.6 percent) reported some tertiary education in a country where by 1993 only 19 percent of adults aged 15 to 64 had at least some tertiary study (Australian Bureau of Statistics 1998, p. 74). The middle class educational and occupational profile of the BKs in Australia thus resembles that of NRMs in other Western countries where such groups have higher than average educational and occupational backgrounds (Wilson 1981, p. v).

Gender Profile

The change in the age and occupational profiles of the BKs in Australia has been associated with marked changes in another demographic feature: gender. Despite the fact that the BKs in India are a heavily female organization, both in membership and leadership, and the top administrative and teaching posts in India and London have always been held by women, the movement was brought to Australia by European brothers and in the 1970s the Australian membership was predominantly male (Howell 1998, pp. 455–456). By 1992, however, females, making up just over 54 percent of the Australian membership, outnumber males, but not by a wide margin (p. 456). The proportion of females in the BKs had just exceeded that in the population at large, where in 1991 50.16 percent were female (Australian Bureau of Statistics 1998, p. 2).

ATTITUDES TOWARD THE WIDER COMMUNITY

With the changed social profile of the organization has come a more open attitude to the wider community. This is evident in a range of areas, from greater acceptance of *brahmins'* involvement in and borrowing from other spiritual and cultural domains to further erosion of the insider–outsider "boundary" of the organization. The impact of the changed social profile of Australian *brahmins* has been substantial because the older, professionally skilled, work force-involved *brahmins* are not confined to lower membership statuses in the organization; they include sisters as well as brothers, center-dwellers as well as those living in *bhavans* (BK share houses), and private homes.

Changed attitudes to the spiritual and cultural life of the wider community can be seen in a new readiness on the part of *brahmins* to make use of programs other than their own for physical and personal betterment. Until recently the Brahma Kumari teachings and way of life were considered wholly sufficient. Continued affiliation with the many other religious or spiritual groups in which BKs had participated before becoming *brahmins* was frowned upon. New exploration in these areas, or in alternative fitness regimes and healing programs, such as hatha yoga, Tai Chi, therapeutic massage, or even swimming, was seen as an unnecessary and probably deleterious competing interest.

Gradually, Australian *brahmins* have gained acceptance for some modifications to their BK regimes (like cutting down on sugar, a much beloved and symbolically significant treat for Indian sisters and brothers), as well as for modest use of some alternative health practices. There is, for example, moderate involvement by all *brahmins* (38.7 percent of all respondents) in other spiritual or personal betterment practices. However, people who have at some time resided in centers (that is, *brahmins* who have been role models and leaders in the family) reported less than half that level of involvement (16.7 percent). Also, in spite of some participation in other spiritual and personal growth practices outside of the BK methodology, there remains little connection to other religions among *brahmins* in general (5.2 percent had such outside affiliations at the survey date) and no reported connections for those *brahmins* who have ever lived in centers.

Looking at insider–outsider boundaries, some long term and highly respected Australian BKs whose professions oblige them to engage in business lunches have relaxed the prohibition against eating food cooked by people who are not fellow *brahmins*. When work requires it, they join colleagues in restaurant meals but look for vegetarian items on the menu. In this way the *brahmin/ non-brahmin* boundary does not become an issue, and the *brahmins* in question see themselves as thereby having a greater opportunity to be viewed sympathetically because they model more fundamental spiritual values in their work.

Insider–outsider boundaries have also been softened in other ways. Long-term *brahmins* in Australia reflected on the lessening intensity of expectation during the 1990s for people exposed to the BK teachings to either take the whole *brahmin* "package" or to acknowledge that they are not meant to be one of the family and go elsewhere. Thus some centers today have occasional special activities of interest to people who have done "the course" (that is, the standard course where they would have learned the BK way of meditating and the basics of BK spiritual understandings) but who do not follow all of the purity rules nor come to a center regularly for morning meditations. These activities include meditations for world peace, as well as sessions where people learn skills for self-reflection, enhancing interpersonal communication, and the like. They provide a means to keep in touch with sympathetic but not fully committed people in the wider community and to promote a positive image of the organization. How far this spirit of openness has developed was demonstrated in 1998 when the Sydney BK leadership actually hosted a "reunion" for former *brahmins* (whose rejection of the full purity regime had resulted in their estrangement from the organization). They were even encouraged to bring along their partners and children to re-enliven their spiritual connection with the BK family.

Australian and other Western centers have also developed a wide range of programs other than their standard course for people who have never taken that course and may never do so. Like the activities for non-*brahmins* who have done the course (and to an extent overlapping with them), these programs teach cognitive skills, such as meditation and creative visualization, removed from the doctrinal context of the standard BK course. In Australia these skills courses have been adapted and taken to special needs groups as diverse as stressed professionals and business managers, the unemployed, physical abuse victims, and substance abusers. Similarly, Barker (1992, p. 169) reports that in the UK the Brahma Kumaris have offered their positive thinking and meditation skills programs to police cadets and Members of Parliament as well as to schools and prisons where there is little or no expectation, at least in the short term, that people might make a total commitment to "the Knowledge" and become *brahmins*. While there remains the idea that these courses in general can be a means to draw to BK teachings people who would have been put off by a first encounter with its more foreign elements, the teaching is combined with a concern to help people in the variety of ways they might want to be helped, rather than strictly in the terms that BKs feel would be best.

Long-term BKs see the origins of these community service activities in the professional involvements of the older *brahmins* who started entering the organization in the 1980s. This group of people had to resist pressure to see their professional lives as being without spiritual significance and they worked to gain acceptance for using their diverse creative talents to wed their new spiritual understandings with their skills from the secular domain. Designing programs that could explain meditation in relation to contemporary psychotherapies or cast the BK world view as a completion or enhancement of scientific cosmologies helped the innovating *brahmins* integrate their spiritual and professional lives while domesticating some of the foreignness of the BK teachings for Western consumption.

Although there has been an element of resistance to detheologized and Westernized programs produced outside India, an impetus to reach out to the non-*brahmin* world also came from the highest levels of the international organization itself. Thus the international leadership at Mt. Abu cultivated an association with the United Nations, and eventually won affiliation with its Department of Public Information, consultative status with UNICEF and general consultative status with the United Nations Economic and Social Council (ECOSOC).

Links with the United Nations developed in part through a series of highly demanding international projects proposed by Westerners but carried out with the full support of the Mt. Abu leadership. These began in 1985 and were aimed at promoting conditions that would bring peace of mind and better quality of life to all people of the world. The first of these was the "Million Minutes of Peace" project that operated in eighty countries in conjunction with the United Nations 1986 International Year of Peace. It was followed by the "Global Cooperation for a Better World" project run in 122 countries by the Brahma Kumaris in association with the United Nations as one of the UN's designated "Peace Messenger" organizations. These cooperative efforts laid the basis for the upgrading of ties between the Brahma Kumaris and UN bodies in the 1990s and culminated in the participation of a top BK administrator in the Earth Summit in Rio in 1992, in the Barbados UN Conference on the Sustainable Development of Small Island and Developing States in 1994, and in the Fourth World Conference on Women in Beijing in 1995.

EXPANDING SCOPE OF THEOLOGICAL INTERPRETATION

Along with the BKs' greater willingness to make use of spiritual and cultural elements from the wider society and the blurring of lines between insiders and outsiders has come a growing range of interpretations concerning the significance of service for salvation. Alongside *brahmins* propounding the classical BK position that world history takes its course regardless of the efforts of individuals and renders futile all attempts to "reshape the world directly" (Babb 1986, p. 151), we hear BKs on the contemporary Australian scene describing the need to *create* the new world as the old world crumbles around us. There is even evidence now of a belief that non-*brahmins* have a significant role to play in this reconstruction and hence BKs should have a broader concern for them.

Long-term BKs sympathetic with these new interpretations thus note that inspiration for a change in attitude toward service to the world came from the highest possible source: the *murlis* (daily lessons) that bring divine guidance to the family through the voice of the organization's official medium. In the mid-1980s, they observe, the *murlis* began to stress that all humankind are Baba's children, even if some are special in the degree of commitment they offer him. As such they are deserving of "regard" and concern.

The literature that accompanied the United Nations' projects also showed an evolution in attitude toward service to Baba's "other children." The Million Minutes of Peace fostered the conventional goal of encouraging all people to practice some technique for calming the mind as an aid to facing the perils of the times and mobilized a high level of expertise to pursue this goal without coloring the project with BK theology. The Global Cooperation project then went further, asking people of all sorts to formulate their personal "vision for a better world." The summation of this project, a glossy illustrated book, describes itself as "a manual for personal involvement in building a better world" (Brahma Kumaris Spiritual University 1992, p. 8). It presents proposals concerned with such diverse areas as "living in balance with nature," "respect, understanding and tolerance," "science and quality of life," and "democratic government and people participation" from non-*brahmins*. The novel significance attributed to the efforts of non-*brahmins*, which *brahmins* can support and help refine, is highlighted in its preface in which one of the organization's two chief administrators, Dadi Prakashmani, says, "The testimony of people from around the world...makes clear that the process of transformation from evil to good is under way. It is our hope that this book will help intensify and broaden it" (p. xi).

This new kind of service effort and the new language accompanying it have encouraged Australian BKs' interest in a wider range of speculation concerning the millennium and the role their service to the world might have in it. Thus there is reflection on the suddenness of the total catastrophe: perhaps it will be somewhat drawn out? In any case, there will still be a period of building—perhaps even fifty years or so—when the skills and talents of individuals will be needed to remake the society that will be the home for the reborn daughters and sons of Brahma in the Golden Age. This now makes "work in the world" *in order to make the world a better place* significant. It also allows the work of non-*brahmins*, as well as that of *brahmins*, to be deemed significant in the reconstruction. In this emergent view, spiritual meaning is attached not just to acts of kindness toward Baba's lesser children (whose pain can be eased as they face the destruction of the world through learning to calm their minds), but also to acts of reforming and restructuring institutions by infusing them with new attitudes and values.

IMPEDIMENTS TO SECULARIZATION

In discussing the conditions that promote the success of religious movement organizations Stark (1987, p. 23) argues that they "must not make [their] peace with this world too rapidly or too fully." If they do, the "secularized" movements lose their "market edge," offering too little that cannot be found more easily in fully secular contexts. In the case of the Brahma Kumaris, attempts to offer others ways to spiritualize their lives without necessarily becoming *brahmins* carries the risk of an unintended reciprocal action: secularization of the movement itself. As boundaries between insiders and outsiders blur and as more effort is put into service activities that offer demythologized BK understandings combined with mainline psychotherapeutic and management techniques, the movement is faced with greater need to deal with outside influences. As these influences are largely Western in origin, and Westerners are at the forefront of introducing them, the international organization also has to concern itself with tensions between culturally conservative Indian members and non-Indian BKs.

There are, however, impediments in the way of an accelerating slide toward secularization. These consist in the differentiation of activities that are open to participants who have made different levels of commitment and the reservation of a core set of highly significant spiritual activities for only the most committed members. Thus the new service activities using partially secularized teaching materials are counter-balanced by other, more restricted activities. The door to these is the standard "course" that teaches BK meditation techniques, purity rules, and theology. The course is the entry point into the organization for those sufficiently interested, although to be sure many are not. For those who are, completion of the standard course opens the way for participation in the regular BK meditations, *murli* readings and talks at local and national centers and retreats. While these activities are more open to non-*brahmins* now than in the past, they are still primarily for the *brahmin* family. Particularly at the early morning sessions, there is a strong sense of intimacy and an explicit focus on elements of the tradition that are most challenging to non-*brahmins*. There the tradition is lived without apology, translation, or dilution; one is there not in the first instance to relieve stress or to equip oneself to provide better business leadership but to be with God as taught and manifested through a particular Indian teacher.

Yet the most highly spiritually charged and most intimate of all BK activities is the pilgrimage to Mt. Abu and the actual meeting with Brahma Baba at the Madhuban retreat center through the agency of the senior sister Dadi Gulzar. A talented medium, Dadi Gulzar has served as a vehicle for Brahma Baba to speak to his *brahmin* family since the time of his physical passing. Although many others report meeting Baba in their meditations, only Dadi Gulzar is allowed to publicly manifest his presence through her physical body, speaking with his voice and gesturing to his children. These meetings are, moreover, multiply significant because the "child," standing before Dadi Gulzar when she is acting as a medium for Brahma Baba, also understands herself to be standing before and talking to God, for whom Brahma Baba himself acts as a medium.

Brahma Baba's appearances through the medium Dadi Gulzar occur only on certain scheduled occasions, and these cannot be attended by just anyone, not even any *brahmin*. It is true that the Madhuban facility has been opened to non-*brahmin* visitors in recent years as part of the effort to forge links with the wider society. Thus on what was once known as "VIP retreats," selected visitors are given the opportunity once a year to participate in a special program on spiritual themes and learn something of the BK philosophy. But no visitors are allowed in Madhuban when Dadi Gulzar is scheduled to manifest the presence of Baba. Then only *brahmins* who have been following the purity rules for at least six months and have been vetted by their home centers are allowed to attend.

The pilgrimage then becomes an affirmation of a commitment not only made but maintained. In recognition of this sustained commitment, each *brahmin* pilgrim to Madhuban is given a silver ring inscribed with the BK symbol of "the Supreme Soul." The rings are normally worn all the time on the wedding ring finger. The pilgrimage is also an entrance into private mysteries: one can physically go, as it were, to the center of the universe (cf. Turner and Turner 1978, pp.30–34) to the very place where the soon to be destroyed world will be reborn in the Golden Age as a joyful kingdom of God, and there one can actually meet and talk to God. Even given some reinterpretation of how the millennium is to come and what its significance is for "work in the world," all this is very far from secularization.

SUMMARY

This paper has documented changes in the demographic profile of the Australian branches of the Brahma Kumaris and the increasing openness of the organization to the wider society. With growing numbers of older and more career-committed members in this Western branch, the organization has developed outreach programs to nonmembers and innovated ways of involving people who are not prepared to commit themselves fully to BK practices. It has even made gestures of reconciliation with former brothers and sisters, encouraging their participation on the periphery of the organization. Moreover, fully practicing BKs themselves are now more willing to make use of outside programs for their own physical and even mental betterment. They also have found ways of interpreting their purity rules to make social interaction with business associates and colleagues easier.

Along with greater openness to the wider society has come a concern on the part of some members to reassess the salvific value of work in the world. Thus the view that it is futile to try to moderate the course of world destruction now is sometimes amended to suggest that the seeds of the new world must be planted in the old. Thus some hold that the shaping of more positive institutions in this time of impending destruction is actually needed to provide the basis for the happy society of the coming Golden Age.

CONCLUSION

The theological and structural adaptations made by the Brahma Kumaris in Australia and other Western countries, as described here and in Howell and Nelson (1997), are suggestive of what Richardson (1988, pp. 9–10) has identified as a possible movement of more totalistic or communal religious movement organizations toward more congregational forms in institutionally differentiated and culturally open societies. Barker's (1988, pp.178–179) observations on the softening of membership categories in the maturing Unification Church may also suggest a similar trend.

If such shifts from a totalistic movement organization and a strongly world rejecting stance toward greater accommodation are not uncommon, neither are they risk free. As Stark (1987, p. 23) observed, too much accommodation with the world can erode a religious movement's "market edge" over fully secular institutions. We have argued that the Brahma Kumaris have some protection against this. A serious threat to the viability of the Brahma Kumaris through secularization is not likely to develop because secularizing elements of Western culture are incorporated mainly through BK service programs intended for nonmembers. Members can use their professional skills in creating detheologized renderings of their spiritual path for outsiders, yet in different, more intimate settings they can continue to engage in an intensely religious practice.

It is nonetheless important to note that the BK practices that presently protect the organization from weakening through secularization are themselves not entirely secure. One issue here is the possible loss of unity and vitality the Brahma Kumaris might suffer in the absence of the medium, Dadi Gulzar, who brings the divine into the physical presence of committed members. Like the other senior sisters who were companions of the founder, Dadi Gulzar is now well on in years and has significant health problems. Her loss would be felt as the loss of a uniquely vivid form of personal contact with God, and the movement would lose an extraordinarily intense ritual focus.

Should age or death deprive the organization of Dadi Gulzar's vital services, there would also be immediate implications for decision-making, since divine guidance for the organization has come through her. It is not that the divine would be silent: all *brahmins* seek to encounter God through their founder in meditation, and many feel they are successful in this. In the past the organization has actually had to deal with apparently authoritative pronouncements of Baba's wishes from too many sources and for that reason in recent years has prohibited anyone but the one medium from delivering messages from him. Her passing would thus raise again the question as to who, if anyone, could provide authoritative guidance from God. Too many sources of messages would threaten unity; yet no acceptable successor could lend momentum to secularization.

Another core religious practice under some pressure is sexual abstinence. Of all the purity rules this is arguably the one most closely bound up with the Brahma Kumaris' identity and the one that most strikingly sets the BKs apart from secular movements. Its adoption by the Indian women who pioneered the movement made the Brahma Kumaris radically different from other Hindu paths to God, and many of those women paid dearly to maintain their commitment to it. Yet in the West, as we have shown, a precedent for exercising personal judgment has been set in the case of the noncommensality rule, and *brahmins* are using more individual discretion in the areas of dress and use of non-BK aids to personal development.

In this environment it is inevitable that other purity rules will also come into question. Although BKs are strongly socialized not to challenge the views of seniors, either in private conversations or in group lessons, in Australia some genuine discussion groups are now emerging on an informal basis and are bringing into the open opinions on sexual relations that in the past could not have been explored publicly. Whether changed views on such a crucial value as chastity will be tolerated and, if so, whether they can be incorporated into BK practice without destroying the *brahmin* family remain to be seen.

The impetus to accommodation which has come into the Brahma Kumaris through the Western branches has been cautiously appreciated by the senior Indian leadership, who have utilized it in developing supportive relationships with government officials and international bodies like the United Nations. Outreach activities have been particularly important in raising the BKs' public profile, and care has been taken to make the most positive use of the desire of talented Western *brahmins* to contribute to the organization through their skills, knowledge, and connections. Yet even as the numbers of long term, experienced, and dedicated Western *brahmins* increase and they continue to play important roles in international service projects, Westerners still have not had their talents utilized at the most senior levels of the organization. The question of ethnic bias thus arises and adds to the potential for dissension as the senior Indian sisters advance in years and succession issues grow more acute.

In sum, the recent evolution of the BKs in the West illustrates that "world rejection" and "accommodation" are not necessarily "either/or" choices for religious organizations. While it is reasonable to conceive of these stances toward everyday life in society as representing poles on a continuum along which an organization may shift over time, we need not assume that the stances are adopted consistently or uniformly across a single organization at any one point in time. This is not to say simply that there will always be attitudinal differences among individuals, but rather that different arenas of activities and structures within an organization may be sites at which different stances may be simultaneously acted out. Interesting sociological questions then arise as to the value and viability of combining potentially contradictory attitudes in particular ways and in particular institutional locations within a single organization. The BKs' current strategy of insulating its core "world rejecting" activities from peripheral activities that make much greater accommodation to the wider society for now appears to be highly successful. The organization has survived into the late 1990s, not only in India, but in the West and elsewhere in the world, and its student body has continued to grow, although there are signs of tension. How long the BKs' binary strategy enables the organization to support seekers with such a wide variety of needs remains to be seen.

ACKNOWLEDGMENT

The research reported herein was supported by grants from the Australian Research Council and Griffith University. The authors gratefully acknowledge the helpful comments of the anonymous reviewers and RSSSR editor David O. Moberg.

NOTE

1.   The higher proportion of professional and highly skilled people in the movement in the 1990s may also be due in part to the effect of Australian immigration policies. Since 1947 when the nation turned to immigration to boost its population, it has favored applicants (including prospective Indian migrants) with good job skills. While Australians of Indian descent were not in the first cohort of *brahmins* in the 1970s, by the 1990s they accounted for about 8 percent of the membership.

Note also, as regards percentage unemployed, that the NCADA figure in Table 1 is the percentage in the sample for that survey, not the percentage registered as unemployed of the job eligible population as reported by governments (and referred to in the text).

REFERENCES

Australian Bureau of Statistics. 1998. *Australian Social Trends 1998*. Canberra: Australian Bureau of Statistics.
Babb, L. 1986. *Redemptive Encounters: Three Modern Styles in the Hindu Tradition*. Berkeley: University of California Press.

Barker, E. 1988. "Defection from the Unification Church: Some Statistics and Distinctions." Pp. 166–84 in *Falling from the Faith, Causes and Consequences of Religious Apostasy* edited by D.G. Bromley. London: Sage Publications.

Barker, E. 1992. *New Religious Movements, A Practical Introduction*. London: Her Majesty's Stationery Office.

Brahma Kumaris World Spiritual University. 1992. *Visions of a Better World*. London: The University.

Howell, J. D. 1997. "ASC Induction Techniques, Religious Experiences and Commitment to New Religious Movements." *Sociology of Religion* 58, 141–164.

_____. 1998. "Gender Role Experimentation in New Religious Movements: Clarification of the Brahma Kumari Case." *Journal for the Scientific Study of Religion* 37, 453–461.

Howell, J. D. and P.L. Nelson. 1997. "Structural Adaptation and 'Success' in the Transplantation of an Asian New Religious Movement: The Brahma Kumaris in the Western World, Part I." *Research in the Social Scientific Study of Religion,* 8,1–34.

Hummel, R. and B. Hardin. 1983. "Asiatic Religions in Europe." *Concilium* [Paris] 181, 23–28.

Richardson, J. T. 1988. "Money and Power in New Religions, An Introduction." Pp. 1–22 in *Money and Power in the New Religions* edited by J. T. Richardson. Lewiston, NY: Edwin Mellen Press.

Social Science Data Archives. 1991. *National Campaign Against Drug Abuse Social Issues Survey*. Canberra: Australian National University [computer file].

Stark, R. 1987. "How New Religions Succeed: A Theoretical Model." Pp. 11–29 in *The Future of New Religious Movements* edited by D. Bromley & P. Hammond. Macon, GA: Mercer University Press.

Turner, V. & E. Turner. 1978. *Image and Pilgrimage in Christian Culture: Anthropological Perspectives*. NY: Columbia University Press.

Wallis, R. 1979. "The Elementary Forms of the New Religious Life." Pp. 191–211 in *Annual Review of the Social Sciences of Religion,* Vol. 3. Berlin: Mouton.

_____. 1984. *The Elementary Forms of the New Religious Life*. London: Routledge & Kegan Paul.

Whaling, F. 1995. "The Brahma Kumaris." *Journal of Contemporary Religion,* 1, 3–28.

Wilson, B. 1981. *The Social Impact of New Religious Movements*. NY: Rose of Sharon Press.

_____. 1987. "Factors in the Failure of New Religious Movements." Pp. 30–45 in *The Future of New Religious Movements* edited by D. Bromley and P. Hammond. Macon, GA: Mercer University Press.

www.bkwsu.com/about/admin.ht. Brahma Kumaris World Spiritual Organisation. 1995. Brahma Kumaris –Administration. Accessed May 1999.

ABOUT THE CONTRIBUTORS

Alexander Agadjanian is an Associate Professor at Arizona State University. He received his M. A. at Moscow State University with majors in History and Social Sciences in 1981. He completed his "Candidate of Sciences" dissertation at the Institute of Oriental Studies, Russian Academy of Sciences in 1986, and completed his doctoral degree in 1992 at the same institution. Since 1993 his research interest has been contemporary Russian religion.

Sharon E. Cheston is Professor of Pastoral Counseling and Director of Academic Operations for the Graduate Programs in Pastoral Counseling at Loyola College in Maryland. She is a member of American Counseling Association, and past president of its division for Counseling and Values. Her research interests include abortion trauma, the Medjugorje phenomenon, and psychotherapy of child victims of cults or incest. She has recently published *Making Effective Referrals*.

Richard J. Csarny recently received his Ph.D. in Pastoral Counseling from Loyola College in Maryland. He is a pastoral counselor and the Director of Quality Improvement at Duke University Medical Center Occupational Mental Health Programs, and Visiting Lecturer at Duke Divinity School. His interests involve the effect of spirituality on workplace mental health.

Cornel du Toit received his doctorate in 1984 in Dogmatics and Christian Ethics. He is head of the Research Institute for Theology and Religion at the University of South Africa. He has published 23 articles, edited 14 books and contributed to 21 books. He has read 44 papers at academic conferences.

Leslie J. Francis is Professor of Practical Theology in the University of Wales, Bangor, UK. His recent books include *Personality Type and Scripture: Exploring Mark's Gospel* (1997), *Gone but not Forgotten: Church Leaving and Returning*

(1998), and *The Long Diaconate: Women Deacons and the Delayed Journey to Priesthood* (1999).

Joanne Marie Greer is Professor of Pastoral Counseling and Director of Doctoral Research, Graduate Programs in Pastoral Counseling, Loyola College in Maryland. She is a member of Society for the Scientific Study of Religion, American Psychological Association and a certified member of American Psychoanalytic Association and International Psychoanalytic Association. She is coeditor of *Research in the Social Scientific Study of Religion*, and Editor of *Abstracts of Research in Pastoral Care and Counseling*. Her research interests are empirical validations of psychoanalytic theory, computerized text analysis, and cross-cultural psychology of religion.

Andreas Häger holds a Master's degree in sociology from the Åbo Akademi University, in Turku, Finland. His Ph.D. thesis on Christian views of popular music will be completed during the year 2000 at Uppsala University, Uppsala, Sweden. His fields of interest include the relation between religion and popular culture as well as issues of religion and education.

Julia Day Howell is an anthropologist with over twenty years experience in research on Asian religions, New Religious Movements (both in Asia and Western countries), and social change in complex societies. With a Ph.D. from Stanford University, she now lectures in Asian Studies at Griffith University in Brisbane, Australia.

Judith V. Kehe is a pastoral counselor in Baltimore, Maryland, and on the adjunct faculty of Loyola College in Maryland. She also acts as a clinical supervisor and mentor for Master's clinical students.

Pui-Yan Lam is a Ph.D. candidate in Sociology at Washington State University. She is currently working on her dissertation which examines cross-national patterns of voluntary association participation. Her areas of interests also include sociology of religion, social organization, and quantitative methodology.

Jennifer Carroll Lena is currently working toward the completion of her Ph.D. in Sociology at Columbia University. Her research involves studies on various aspects of culture, primarily religion and music.

Stephen H. Louden, Ph.D., is a Research Fellow at the Centre for Ministry Studies, University of Wales, Bangor, UK. His current research is concerned with Catholic clergy.

David O. Moberg is Professor Emeritus at Marquette University. He is widely published in the empirical study of religion, is on the editorial boards of several scholarly journals, and is a founding editor of *Research in the Social Scientific Study of Religion.* His most recent book is *Aging and Spirituality: Spiritual Dimensions of Aging Theory, Research, Practice, and Policy,* for which he is editor and coauthor, in press for publication by The Haworth Pastoral Press.

Peter L. Nelson is on the faculty of the Department of Psychology, West Georgia College, Carrollton, Georgia. He is a psychologist holding a PhD in Studies in Religion from the University of Queensland. He works as a consultant in psychology and social science research methods.

Ralph Piedmont is the Director of the Institute for Religious and Psychological Research, and is Associate Professor of Pastoral counseling at Loyola College in Maryland. A member of the American Psychological Association and American Counseling Association, he is also on the editorial board of *Measurement and Evaluation in Counseling and Development.* His research interests center on the Five-Factor Model of personality and its relationship to spiritual phenomena, and the impact of Spiritual Transcendence on mental and physical health outcomes.

Carlo Prandi is Professor of Sociology of Religion at University of Parma, Italy. He is a member of the Society for the Scientific Study of Religion and of the Sociology of Religion Study Group. His research deals with the relationship between sociology and history of religion, popular religion, the monotheisms, and the sociological history of sanctity. His most recent book is *La Tradizione Religiosa*, released in February 2000.

Thomas Rotolo is Assistant Professor of Sociology at Washington State University. His current research focuses on various individual and structural-level features of voluntary associations. He also enjoys statistical programming.

Christopher J.F. Rutledge, Ph.D., is Vicar of St. Mark's Church, Talbot Village, and Research Associate in the Centre for Ministry Studies, University of Wales, Bangor, UK. His current research is concerned with clergy stress and burnout.

Amy Schindler is a doctoral student in Sociology at Columbia University. Her research interests are law, social movements, and religion. She thanks the Columbia Graduate Department of Sociology for the Lazersfeld Fellowship that made possible the research published in this volume.

William L. Smith is Associate Professor of Sociology in the Department of Sociology and Anthropology at Georgia Southern University. He received his

Ph.D. from the University of Notre Dame. His research and teaching interests include family, community, race and ethnicity, and religion. He has written a variety of articles and book chapters on such topics as pedagogy, new religious movements, communal life, racial and ethnic relations, family studies, and Irish priests. He is the author of *Families and Communes: An Examination of Nontraditional Lifestyles* (Sage Publications, 1999).

William J. Sneck, S. J., is Professor of Pastoral Counseling at Loyola College in Maryland. He is also a Jesuit priest, a Jungian psychologist, and a member of the American Psychological Association, Society for Scientific Study of Religion, and American Association of Pastoral Counselors. His research interests are the "hard" emotions of hurt, anger, guilt, shame, and fear. He has recently published *Charismatic Spiritual Gifts: A Phenomenological Analysis.*

INDEX OF NAMES

SUBJECT INDEX